SOLDIERS OF THE CROSS

Soldiers of the Cross

Confederate Soldier-Christians and the Impact of War on Their Faith

Kent T. Dollar

Mercer University Press
Macon, Georgia
25th Anniversary

ISBN 0-86554-926-5
MUP/H662

© September 2005 Mercer University Press
1400 Coleman Avenue
Macon, Georgia 31207

First Edition.

Library of Congress Cataloging-in-Publication Data

Dollar, Kent T.
Soldiers of the cross : Confederate soldier-Christians and the impact of
war on their faith / Kent T. Dollar.
p. cm.
Includes bibliographical references and index.
ISBN 0-86554-926-5 (hardback : alk. paper)
1. United States—History—Civil War, 1861-1865—Religious aspects—Christianity. 2.
United States—History—Civil War, 1861-1865—Social aspects.
3. Soldiers—Confederate States of America—Social conditions.
4. Soldiers—Religious life—Confederate States of America.
5. Christians—Confederate States of America—Social conditions.
I. Title.
E635.D65 2005
277.5'081—dc22
2005002831

CONTENTS

Illustrations

For Elvin Sharp, my loving grandfather

1909–2003

ACKNOWLEDGMENTS

This book would not have been possible without the assistance of many people to whom I am deeply indebted. Although space will not permit me to name them individually, I wish to thank the archivists and librarians at: Mississippi Department of Archives and History; Southern Historical Collection of the University of North Carolina; Watson Memorial Library of Northwestern State University; Draughon Library of Auburn University; Presbyterian Historical Society; Special Collections department of the University of Tennessee; Tennessee State Library and Archives; Capps Archives and Museum of Delta State University; Wilson Library of Millsaps College; Leyburn Library of Washington and Lee University; Virginia Historical Society; Virginia Military Institute; Virginia State Library; King Library of the University of Kentucky; Louisiana Division of Historic Preservation; Eleanor S. Brockenbrough Library of the Museum of the Confederacy; William Alexander Percy Memorial Library of Greenville, Mississippi; McIver's Grant Public Library of Dyersburg, Tennessee; and, the National Archives. Without their generous assistance, this book could not have been written.

Several individuals went out of their way to assist me and deserve special mention. Renée Richard, an archivist at the Catholic Diocese of Baton Rouge, provided much needed insight (on more than one occasion) into the beliefs and activities of Catholics in nineteenth-century Louisiana. I am very grateful to Anne Webster of the Mississippi Department of Archives and History, who was never too busy to track down information on William Nugent and Galloway Methodist Church in Jackson, Mississippi. Nell Thomas, a long-time member of the First United Methodist Church in Greenville, Mississippi, helped me with the murky details of Nugent's religious past. Also, I am indebted to Reverends John Stone and Ladson Mills of Knoxville, Tennessee, Reverend Robert Hartenfeld of Long Beach, Mississippi, and Dr. Thomas Leach of Union, Mississippi, for their insight into the Christian faith and their respective denominations. I owe a debt of gratitude to Roy L. Mott of Fulton, Alabama, who generously provided information on and photographs of Clarke County, Alabama, the home of Talbert Holt. He furthermore located the church to which the Holts belonged (including the probable site of Talbert's grave), a difficult task indeed. I wish also to thank the ministers and staffs of Robert E. Lee Memorial Church and the Presbyterian Church of Lexington, Virginia, and St. Stephen's Episcopal Church of Petersburg, Virginia. They allowed me unfettered access to their records and presented me with written histories of their respective churches. Ms. Janie Putman, Ms. Mary Alice Badget, and Ms. Betty Hammond of the Methodist Church in Friendship, Tennessee, were especially hospitable. They allowed me access to documents in their possession on Alfred Fielder and took me on a tour of Friendship, including the site of Fielder's farm and grave. And, I would like to thank Scott LeRay, a relative of Judge Felix Poché, for generously providing me with a postwar photograph of Poché.

In addition, I would like to acknowledge my debt to several individuals at the University of Tennessee, Knoxville: Professors Paul Bergeron, Lorri Glover, George Harris, Kurt Piehler, Frank Van Aalst, Bruce Wheeler, and Charles "Chuck" Johnson (who passed away recently but is thought of often); and my graduate school buddies, J. D. Fowler and Mark Williams. Their encouragement, support and guidance meant more than they will ever know. I would also like to thank my fellow historians at Tennessee Technological University for their interest in and support of this book. Words cannot express my gratitude to Steve Ash, my mentor and friend. I know of no other way to express it than to admit humbly that I am the historian I am today because of him. And, it is a debt I can never repay.

My greatest debt I owe to my wife, Lisa, who always believed in me. During my many years of graduate school, she continually demonstrated her love for me and encouraged me to pursue my dream. She was, and continues to be, an unending source of support. And I want to offer a special thank you to my children, Rachel and Hannah, whose mere existence reminded me daily what is really important in life. Other family members and friends offered support as well, for which I am eternally grateful. Truly, I am blessed.

1. Alfred T. Fielder in 1870
*Courtesy of the Tennessee
Historical Society.*

2. William L. Nugent, ca.
1890 *Courtesy of Mississippi
Department of Archives &
History.*

3. Gen. William N. Pendleton
*Courtesy of Special Collections,
Leyburn Library, Washington and
Lee University.*

as it did during Pendleton's time. Parson Pendleton used the top
floor as a school. *Photograph by author.*

5. Rev. Edward O. Guerrant, ca. 1880 *Courtesy of the Presbyterian Historical Society, Presbyterian Church (USA), Montreat, North Carolina.*

6. Felix P. Poché, ca. 1880 *Courtesy of Scott LeRay, Norco, Louisiana.*

7. St. Michael's Catholic Church in Convent, Louisiana, where Felix Poché was a faithful member until his death. The steeple was added in 1875. *Courtesy of the Louisiana Department of Culture, Recreation, and Tourism, Office of Cultural Development, Division of Historic Preservation.*

8. New Hope Baptist Church, an African-American church, now stands at the site of Talbert Holt's home church in old Choctaw Corner. *Courtesy of Roy L. Mott, Fulton, Alabama.*

9. Maj. Giles B. Cooke *Courtesy of the Virginia Historical Society, Richmond, Virginia.*

10. Lt. Alexander T. Barclay *Courtesy of Special Collections, Leyburn Library, Washington and Lee University.*

xvi

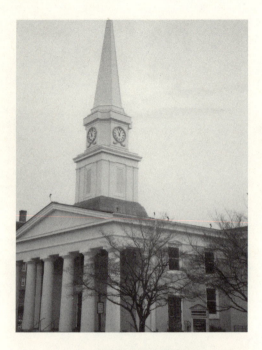

11. Lexington Presbyterian Church, where Ted Barclay served as both deacon and ruling elder. Thomas J. "Stonewall" Jackson was also a member of the church while he lived in Lexington. *Photograph by author.*

12. Robert A. Moore *Courtesy of Broadfoot Publishing Company.*

13. Cooke's diary entry for 14 June 1862 shows his daily routine of prayer and Bible study, which he began soon after his profession of faith. *Courtesy of the Virginia Historical Society, Richmond, Virginia.*

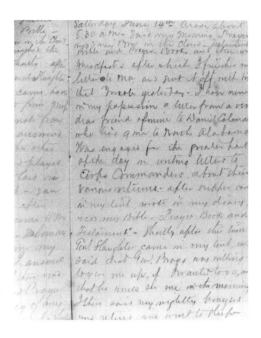

14. R. E. Lee Memorial Church (formerly Grace Episcopal Church), as it looks today. Pendleton never saw the completed edifice. *Photograph by author.*

15. Felix Poché's postwar plantation (now a bed & breakfast) as it looks today. *Courtesy of the Poché Plantation, Convent, Louisiana.*

16. The cemetery behind New Hope Baptist Church where Talbert Holt is thought to be buried in an unmarked grave. *Courtesy of Roy L. Mott, Fulton, Alabama.*

17. St. Stephen's Episcopal Church
Courtesy of St. Stephen's Episcopal
Church, Petersburg, Virginia.

18. Washington and Lee University (formerly Washington College),
Ted Barclay's alma mater. Barclay served on the board of trustees
after the war. *Photograph by author.*

Introduction

On 3 March 1865 Captain Alfred T. Fielder of the 12th Tennessee Infantry recorded these words in his diary: "I have come up through many difficulties and dangers but God's unseen hand has protected and shielded me thus far for which I am thankful and feel in my heart willing to trust him in the future believing his grace will be sufficient for me." Fielder's reflection, written on his fifty-first birthday, evinces war's maturing effect on his religious faith. Since his enlistment in the Friendship Volunteers in the summer of 1861, the Tennessean had endured nearly four years of adversity unlike any he had known. He traversed "the valley of the shadow of death" on many occasions during fierce battles in which thousands were killed or maimed, including many of his comrades. Fielder himself survived close calls and suffered two wounds. Moreover, while serving, he left his family behind in Tennessee. They continually crowded his mind, and as the war moved farther south he grew more concerned for their safety. More importantly, it seemed to Fielder that he exercised very little control, if any, over his fate or that of his family. So Fielder, a long-time Methodist and devout Christian, laid his petitions for protection at his "fathers throne." The Confederate captain placed his trust in an "Almighty God," learned to rely more on God, and as his own words tell us, God was faithful.[1]

The tribulations engendered by the American Civil War prompted many soldiers of the South to contemplate spiritual matters. Confederate soldiers frequently commented about religion in their letters, diaries and journals. They noted, for example, the

---

[1] Ann York Franklin, ed., *The Civil War Diaries of Capt. Alfred Tyler Fielder, 12th Tennessee Regiment Infantry, Company B, 1861–1865* (Louisville KY: self published, 1996) 1, 82, 161, 219; Ps 23:4.

irreligiousness of many fellow soldiers, the immorality in the camps, the church services they attended, and, in particular, their belief in Providence. Indeed, many soldiers appear to have become more religious as the war progressed. In the fall of 1862, revivals broke out in the Army of Northern Virginia, followed by others in the Army of Tennessee, initiating a wave of Confederate revivalism that peaked during the winter of 1863–1864. Chaplains, missionaries and local ministers preached to eager audiences and thousands of battle-hardened fighting men professed faith in Christ, thus becoming "soldiers of the cross." Did these soldiers seek immediate solace in the Lord only to revert to their old, sinful ways when the prospect of death abated? Did their war-inspired faith endure? What about those Rebel soldiers, like Fielder, who at the time of their enlistment were already Christians? How did the war affect their faith?[2]

---

[2] The increasing religious interest among the Confederate troops led Giles Buckner Cooke, an army staff officer, to characterize Confederate troops as "soldiers of the cross." See Giles Buckner Cooke diary, 16 May 1862, Giles Buckner Cooke Papers, Virginia Historical Society, Richmond. The reports of widespread religious sentiments, massive revivals, and thousands of professions of faith in Christ in the Confederate armies have long garnered the attention of Civil War historians. One of the pioneers in examining "Rebel religion" was Bell I. Wiley. In his classic *Life of Johnny Reb: the Common Soldier of the Confederacy*, Wiley devotes considerable attention to religion in the camps. He concludes that soldiers grew more interested in religion as the war progressed. According to Wiley, Southerners' religious backgrounds, defeats in 1863 and the efforts of chaplains and ministers triggered the massive revivals in the Confederate armies. Although Wiley's book is dated, his conclusions are for the most part sound; more importantly, however, Wiley's study stimulated further research on religion in the Confederate ranks. Herman Norton advances the study of Confederate religion in *Rebel Religion: The Story of Confederate Chaplains*. Although Norton rather uncritically lauds the chaplains, he contributes considerably to the understanding of their activities and the conditions under which they functioned. Norton argues that the chaplains were hampered by the Confederate government as well as by the travails of war, yet they succeeded in meeting many of the spiritual needs of the front-line troops, often going far beyond the call of duty. In addition to preaching, chaplains rallied their troops, counseled the sick and wounded, and in some cases even maintained libraries. Their biggest contribution, however, was fostering the revivals that resulted in thousands of conversions.

Other historians have looked more closely at Confederate revivalism. Drew Gilpin Faust addresses this issue in her influential 1987 essay, "Christian Soldiers:

The Meaning of Revivalism in the Confederate Army." Faust concludes that the war's hardships prompted many soldiers to settle spiritual matters and that religious enthusiasm especially increased after battles. She also maintains that revivalism was more common in the Confederate armies than in the Union armies because Southerners were more religiously homogenous than were the Northerners. Other historians such as Larry J. Daniel and James I. Robertson agree with Faust. Daniel, who discusses the revivals in *Soldiering in the Army of Tennessee*, says that hardship and deprivation in the Rebel army prompted many to search for solace, and they found it in religion. Robertson, a student of Bell I. Wiley, agrees that hardships and the fear of death led many to God, but he doubts the sincerity of many of the converts.

Areas of religion examined by historians include its impact on the Southern home front. Two studies in particular address this issue: *Confederate Morale and Church Propaganda* by James W. Silver; and Richard E. Beringer et al., *Why the South Lost the Civil War*. These two books come to somewhat different conclusions regarding the relationship between religion and Confederate morale. Silver, who concentrates primarily on the churches and clergy, contends that the Southern ministers were unwavering in their support of the South's cause and played a significant role in sustaining morale within their congregations. From another perspective, Beringer maintains that religion undermined Southern morale as soldiers interpreted decisive losses—particularly those during 1863—as evidence that the Lord did not favor the South. That conclusion has been seconded by Gardiner H. Shattuck in *A Shield and Hiding Place: The Religious Life of the Civil War Armies*.

The impact of religion on soldiers' courage and combat motivation has been addressed in several recent studies. Samuel J. Watson's 1994 article "Religion and Combat Motivation in the Confederate Armies," points out three ways in which religious faith strengthened motivation: it fostered feelings of community among the troops; it provided comfort, which countered the effects of fear; and it provided a justification for killing fellow men and having to watch comrades die. Earl J. Hess in *The Union Soldier in Battle: Enduring the Ordeal of Combat* and James McPherson in *For Cause and Comrades: Why Men Fought in the Civil War* also consider the role of religion in helping soldiers cope with their war experiences. Both conclude that religion comforted Christian soldiers and encouraged them to persevere. According to Hess, religion "steadied [the soldier's] emotions at a critical time and provided a rock on which he based his courage."

For additional discussion, see Bell I Wiley, *The Life of Johnny Reb: The Common Soldier of the Confederacy* (Baton Rouge: Louisiana State University Press, 1943) 174–75, 180–84; Herman Norton, *Rebel Religion: The Story of Confederate Chaplains* (St. Louis: Bethany Press, 1961) 23–32, 57–58, 81–93; Drew Gilpin Faust, "Christian Soldiers: The Meaning of Revivalism in the Confederate Army," *Journal of Southern History* 53 (February 1987): 64, 67–68, 71–72; Larry J. Daniel, *Soldiering in the Army of Tennessee* (Chapel Hill: University of North Carolina Press, 1991) 116–17, 123; James I. Robertson, *Soldiers Blue and Gray* (Columbia: University of South Carolina Press, 1988) 173, 186–88; James W. Silver, *Confederate Morale and Church Propaganda* (New York: W. W. Norton and Company, 1967) 55–63, 82–93; Richard E. Beringer

A neglected area in Civil War scholarship is the impact of the war on the religious faith of Confederate Christian soldiers. Tens of thousands of Southern Christians enlisted in the Rebel armies at the war's outset. Some became chaplains; most served in the ranks. On the whole, these soldiers became more religious as the war progressed, but what was the long-term effect of four years of war and defeat on the faith of individual soldier-Christians? Historians agree that war does indeed shape its participants, but how did it shape in particular the religious faith of soldier-Christians? How were their beliefs and practices transformed by the trials of war? The impact of the Civil War on the faith of Christian Confederate soldiers is the topic of this book.[3]

This topic is significant in three ways. First, any event that transformed thousands of individuals is important, particularly when the transformation concerns something as consequential as a person's

---

et al., *Why the South Lost the Civil War* (Athens: University of Georgia Press, 1986) 268, 278; Gardiner H. Shattuck, *A Shield and Hiding Place: The Religious Life of the Civil War Armies* (Macon GA: Mercer University Press, 1987) 9–11; Samuel J. Watson, "Religion and Combat Motivation in the Confederate Armies," *Journal of Military History* 58 (January 1994): 34–36; James McPherson, *For Cause and Comrades: Why Men Fought in the Civil War* (New York/Oxford: Oxford University Press, 1997) 63–71; Earl J. Hess, *The Union Soldier in Battle: Enduring the Ordeal of Combat* (Lawrence: University Press of Kansas, 1997) 104.

[3] James McPherson points out that Christian soldiers became more religious as the war progressed, but he offers little more than generalizations. In his excellent book, *A Consuming Fire: The Fall of the Confederacy in the Mind of the White Christian South*, Eugene Genovese discusses briefly the impact of defeat on Confederate Christian soldiers. He contends that while losing the war broke the spirits of many Christian veterans, others experienced a renewal of faith. Genovese, however, fails to follow up on this general assertion; and as he continues to discuss the Christians in the postwar South, he does not distinguish between veterans and civilians. In his effort to cover the vast "religious world" of Civil War soldiers in *While God Is Marching On: The Religious World of Civil War Soldiers*, Steven E. Woodworth devotes little attention to war's impact on the faith of individual soldiers. In short, he provides us a good description of the "forest," but tells us little about the "trees." See McPherson, *For Cause and Comrades*, 63–67; Eugene D. Genovese, *A Consuming Fire: The Fall of the Confederacy in the Mind of the White Christian South* (Athens: University of Georgia Press, 1998) 64; Steven E. Woodworth, *While God Is Marching On: The Religious World of Civil War Soldiers* (Lawrence: University Press of Kansas, 2001) passim.

religious faith. While a number of historians have studied how faith affected the war, none has studied how the war affected faith. Second, this study sheds new light on a subject previously examined by historians—the irreligiosity of the troops early in the war. Historians have asserted that early on soldiers frequently succumbed to the temptations prevalent in camp and that only as the war dragged on did they return to their religious roots. This study suggests that, for devout Christian soldiers, such was not the case. From the beginnings of their military enlistment these men attempted to maintain some degree of their religious faith in even the most difficult of circumstances. They attended services, read their Bibles, prayed frequently and associated with others who shared their views. Finally, this research is significant because it will bring to light the role these Christian soldiers played in their postwar churches and communities. Many of these soldier-Christians, some of whom were too young to have played an important part in antebellum churches, returned home after the war as men with strong religious convictions. How did this deepened faith affect their lives after the war? The postwar story of the soldier-Christians has not been told, but must be.[4]

In his recent book, *A Year in the South: Four Lives in 1865*, Stephen V. Ash points out the significance of historical studies that focus on individuals: "Storytellers confront the same dilemma as painters and photographers: the broader their perspective, the more comprehensive their scene, but the less distinct their subjects' features. A narrative that tries to embrace all the Southern people…risks reducing them to a faceless crowd." The assertion is right on the mark. In order to determine most fully war's impact on faith, the historian must closely examine the lives of select individuals.[5]

The stories of nine Confederate Christian soldiers examined in this book vividly illustrate the impact of the Civil War on faith. This

---

[4] Wiley, *Life of Johnny Reb*, 174–75; Shattuck, *Shield and Hiding Place*, 96.
[5] Stephen V. Ash, *A Year in the South: Four Lives in 1865* (New York: Palgrave Macmillan, 2002) xiii.

study includes an examination of the antebellum, wartime, and in most cases, postwar lives of nine Confederate Christian soldiers who represent a cross-section of Southern society, Southern religion, and the Confederate military. (Two of the men died during the war.) This is not to say that the conclusions drawn here are applicable to all Christian soldiers who participated in the war, or that this should be the final word on the subject. Indeed, this work is a starting point only and further research on this important subject is warranted.

The nine men whose lives and faith are herein examined were selected based on several factors. First and foremost, they left detailed records of their wartime activities and thoughts, especially those of a religious nature. These records consist primarily of diaries and letters written to loved ones. Of course, neither of these types of sources are a complete record of the soldiers' experiences, or more importantly, of their thoughts. Daily diaries often became toilsome to maintain during wartime. For example, Captain Edward O. Guerrant, an officer who served on the staff of General Humphrey Marshall, was frequently in arrears when it came to recording his experiences. Once while traveling through southwestern Virginia in April 1863, Guerrant noted that he had brought his diary up to date but admitted that he had "forgotten much." Writers of personal letters, likewise, failed to record every detail of the events in which they took part or of which they were witnesses. Although a writer may reflect more pensively in a letter than in hurriedly-written diary entries, more often than not soldiers' letters were dispersed over several days. Writers, therefore, often neglected to mention all their activities or thoughts since their last letter. The letters of Private Hiram Talbert Holt of the 38th Alabama Infantry provide a good example. In letters to his wife, Carrie, the Alabamian included references to religion and his growing faith, even instructing Carrie in religious matters. Nevertheless, he seldom mentioned attending religious services in camp. After Holt's death in February 1864, his chaplain, A. D. McCoy, wrote to Carrie and noted that in addition to exemplifying the character of a devout Christian, Talbert had regularly attended worship services.[6]

James McPherson, in *What They Fought For, 1861–1865*, points out that in the extant Confederate diaries and personal letters the upper echelon of Southern society is overrepresented, particularly by attorneys and planters. More often than not these lawyers and planters held an officer's rank, thus diminishing the scope of representation across the far greater numbers of non-well-to-do Southerners among the enlisted personnel. Despite the accuracy of McPherson's assertion, the nine men studied herein are a good representation of important components of Southern society. Of the nine, five either resided on plantations in 1860 or were affiliated with planter families. One of the five was a farmer during 1860, and owned a handful of slaves. Two of the five were young men who resided on their families' plantations, and one of these attended a local college. Two had been raised on plantations, but by 1860 were both struggling to succeed as newly-licensed attorneys.[7]

The remaining four men in this book held a variety of occupations. One taught school and had prepared to enter the ministry; another taught school and operated a small farm. The third studied law, while the fourth served as an Episcopal minister and operated a small farm. All of the men included in this study were closely tied to the institution of slavery. If they themselves did not own slaves, members of their families did.

The ages of the nine soldiers ranged from seventeen to fifty. Five of the nine were married, three having been married less than two years prior to the outbreak of the war. The soldiers' family situations are particularly relevant in this study. It is evident from their writings that those who left spouses and families behind were

---

[6] Edward O. Guerrant diary, 26 April, 21 May, 15 June 1863, Edward O. Guerrant Papers, Southern Historical Collection, University of North Carolina, Chapel Hill; A. D. McCoy to Carrie Holt, no date (typescript), Robert Partin Papers, Draughon Library, Auburn University, Alabama.

[7] James M. McPherson, *What They Fought For, 1861–1865* (Baton Rouge: Louisiana State University Press, 1994) 14–16.

anxious about their loved ones. The single men did not carry nearly so great a burden.

The nine Confederate soldiers represented several Southern states. Three hailed from the upper-South state of Virginia, while one claimed Tennessee as his home. The deep-South contingent includes two Mississippians, one Alabamian, and one Louisianan. The border state of Kentucky accounts for the final soldier.

The group also represents a cross-section of the Confederate military. Five men enlisted as privates, four in the infantry and one in cavalry; although four of them later attained officer's rank, they served as privates or non-commissioned officers for a significant portion of the war. Three signed on as staff officers and all, save one, served in that capacity for the duration of the war. And, one, beginning his service as an artillery officer, eventually reached the rank of brigadier-general.

These men also belonged to different Confederate armies. Three served in commands attached to the Army of Northern Virginia, while three others soldiered in the Army of Tennessee. Soldiers who served on the periphery are also included. One spent the first two years of the war at Fort Morgan, Alabama, near Mobile, until his regiment was reassigned to the Army of Tennessee. The soldier from Louisiana fought in the Trans-Mississippi Department, while the Kentuckian served in southwestern Virginia.

This study considers *Christian* soldiers exclusively; but of course, the antebellum South was comprised of many different Christian denominations. Most, but not all, of these denominations were evangelical and Protestant. As Charles Reagan Wilson affirms in *Religion in the South*, these made up "the dominant religious impulse of the South." Three of the nine men belonged to the Methodist Church, two were Presbyterians, and one a Baptist. Although evangelical Protestant churches dominated the antebellum Southern landscape, other, more liturgical faiths also existed and merit inclusion. This book also includes two men of the Episcopal faith and a Roman Catholic from southern Louisiana. It should be noted, however, that the two Episcopalians closely resemble what Donald Mathews describes in *Religion in the Old South* as "Evangelical

Episcopalians." While adhering to many of the articles of the Episcopal faith, these evangelical Episcopalians embraced some of the principles of their evangelical brethren, in particular the necessity of a personal conversion experience. The Catholic soldier, on the other hand, adhered strictly to traditional Roman Catholic beliefs.[8]

With so many different Christian soldiers represented, the term *Christian* begs to be defined. The term was, and continues to be, interpreted differently within Christianity itself. In this study, the term is used only as it was defined at the time by the respective denominations to which our subjects belonged. For the evangelical Protestant denominations, including evangelical Episcopalians, defining what was meant by the term Christian is relatively straightforward. A Christian was one who underwent a personal conversion experience; made a profession of faith in Jesus Christ for spiritual salvation; and whose regenerated life reflected his Christianity in thought and deed. For the Roman Catholics, the specific criteria defining what it was to be a Christian were different. Catholic Christianity was defined more by obedient participation in the community and sacramental life of the Church than by personal religious experience. A close examination of the antebellum religious life of this book's Catholic subject reveals that he was indeed a devoted member of the Church. Having been raised within a longstanding family tradition of pious Catholicism, he devoutly attended Confession and Mass, even when circumstances made it difficult. He held firmly to the abiding articles of faith of the Roman Catholic Church.

In addition to different expressions of Christian faith, these men also represented different levels of spiritual maturity. Three of the soldier-Christians could be characterized as older, more mature Christians. They had experienced conversion much earlier than the others, and two of them attained leadership positions in their

---

[8] Charles Reagan Wilson, ed., *Religion in the South* (Jackson: University Press of Mississippi, 1985) 3; Donald G. Mathews, *Religion in the Old South* (Chicago: University of Chicago Press, 1977) 130–31; E. Clowes Chorley, *Men and Movements in the American Episcopal Church* (New York: Charles Scribner's Sons, 1946) 44, 65–66.

churches and communities long before the Civil War. Three were new converts or Christian neophytes. Younger in age, two of these men professed faith in Christ within four years prior to the outbreak of the war. The Catholic soldier is placed in this category because, although, his spiritual maturity cannot be traced by a conversion experience, his age and spiritual condition are comparable to those of the others in this category. The remaining three attended church services during the antebellum period, but did not experience conversions until the war. Indeed, these men embodied most dramatically war's impact on faith. Before the war, their faith consisted of little more than attending church services with their families; however, four years of war transformed these men into devout believers.

The methodology used to determine the impact of war on these soldiers' faith is simple. An attempt was made to identify the characteristics of each man's faith by examining his life before the war. For the younger men this proved more difficult, since little record of their earlier lives exists. In these instances, however, census and church records, particularly those of their family church, proved useful. The older men either kept diaries or corresponded regularly enough that the characteristics of their antebellum faith were identifiable.

As for their wartime faith, all nine soldiers tell the story with their own words. Each man either kept a diary or penned numerous letters in which he spoke openly about religion and his religious activities. Therefore, the methodology for this study centered around identifying and interpreting these meaningful religious references and tracing the soldiers' spiritual progress as the war dragged on. A methodology like that of Michael Barton in *Goodmen: The Character of Civil War Soldiers*, also proved useful. Determining the number of religious expressions and when they occurred was essential in explaining what prompted them. Anxieties and concerns, particularly the prospect of death, appear to have prompted most religious references. Naturally it would seem, soldiers seemed the most reflective when battle appeared imminent, or after they had survived a fierce engagement. But battles were not the only cause for concern.

Thoughts of home and loved ones often generated anxiety, particularly for those who had left behind spouses and children. Away from home and unable to protect their families, these men relied on God to do so.[9]

A methodology based on identifying and interpreting references to religion leads to a question: were all religious references meaningful? The answer is "No." Closing salutations in many letters are a good example of superficial religious expressions. While these might include a phrase like "May God bless you," such a phrase hardly expressed deep feelings. Furthermore, some non-Christian soldiers closed their letters in the same manner. To a large degree, whether a reference was meaningful depends on the context in which it was written. Meaningful expressions were generally more reflective and, more often than not, triggered by a specific event or concern.[10]

Finally, this study includes an examination of the surviving Christian veterans during the postwar period to about 1885, concentrating again on the manifestations of their faith. Sources such as diaries, journals and correspondence that continue into the postwar period proved useful, as did church records, association and conference minutes, and census records. The mid-1880s is a good stopping point for a couple of reasons: First, the impact of war on one's faith is something realized sooner rather than later after the war. As time distanced veterans from the war, it is more difficult to link their postwar activities and faith to their wartime experiences. Second, in the mid-1880s several of these veterans experienced major changes in their professions or lives.

---

[9] Barton's study is a quantitative one in which he counted and categorized soldiers' value references with little regard to the context in which they were written. I, on the other hand, have evaluated soldiers' religious comments with reference to the context in which soldiers made them. See Michael Barton, *Goodmen: The Character of Civil War Soldiers* (University Park: Pennsylvania State University Press, 1981) 24, 91–110.

[10] William M. Cash and Lucy Somerville Howorth, eds., *My Dear Nellie: The Civil War Letters of William L. Nugent to Eleanor Smith Nugent* (Jackson: University Press of Mississippi, 1977) 41.

To demonstrate that the Civil War had a maturing effect on the faith of these Confederate Christian soldiers, one must first define the characteristics of spiritual maturity. In his Second Letter to Timothy, the Apostle Paul identified several attributes of a model soldier of Christ. These have been restated by theologian Charles C. Ryrie as unwavering religious conviction, exhibiting strong faith in God, focusing on matters of the spirit, and godliness in service to others. Overall, the nine soldier-Christians in this study did indeed exemplify these characteristics. Early on, as well as throughout the war, these Christians read their Bibles, associated with other Christian soldiers, attended religious services and regularly communed privately with God. The realization that they had little control over the circumstances of war or the well-being of their families moved these men to rely on God. Their experience was that God proved faithful, thus strengthening their trust or faith. Furthermore, these men grew in their emulation of the virtues of Christ. Their outlook on life and worship took on new significance. They exhibited more humility and they sought to serve God more actively. It was during the postwar era, however, that these Christian veterans fulfilled formal roles as the Lord's institutional servants. Without exception, the men in this study who survived the war returned home and took up leadership positions in their local churches, where they served faithfully until their deaths.[11]

---

[11] Charles Caldwell Ryrie, *The Ryrie Study Bible* (Chicago: Moody Press, 1978) 2 Tim 2:2–26.

Chapter 1

FAITH UNTESTED BY FIRE
LIFE AND FAITH IN THE
ANTEBELLUM SOUTH

My brethren, count it all joy when ye fall into divers temptations; Knowing this, that the trying of your faith worketh patience. But let patience have her perfect work, that ye may be perfect and entire, wanting nothing.—James 1:2–4 (KJV)

Alfred Tyler Fielder

Alfred Tyler Fielder was forty-seven years old in April 1861 when Confederate forces occupying Charleston, South Carolina, bombarded Fort Sumter into submission. Traveling soon thereafter to Camp Brown, Tennessee, he enlisted as a private in the Friendship Volunteers, Company B, 12th Tennessee Infantry Regiment. The Volunteers, who were local boys from the vicinity of Fielder's adopted hometown of Friendship, Tennessee, welcomed him into their fold. By the spring of 1863, his leadership abilities proven, they elected him their captain. Captain Fielder, whose regiment was mustered into the Army of Tennessee, fought in several engagements and suffered wounds at Missionary Ridge and Atlanta. He survived the conflict and returned home to Friendship, where he remained until his death in 1893.[1]

Fielder was born in Caswell County, North Carolina, in March 1814. At the age of eighteen he married Isabell Tate, also of Caswell County. The couple migrated to West Tennessee in 1835 and settled in the vicinity of Friendship, located in Dyer County. In 1836, Fielder's newly widowed mother, Susannah, followed him to Tennessee and settled near him in Dyer County.[2]

The soils of Dyer County are notably fertile. The bottom-lands near the Mississippi River are alluvial, while areas to the east are a dark, rich loam. Crops such as cotton, corn, wheat and tobacco grew well in the county. Most residents were tillers of the soil, and Fielder was no exception. He operated a modest farm of about sixty improved acres, on which he grew wheat and corn primarily, but also a little cotton. As the years went by, he grew increasingly dependent upon slave labor to plant and harvest the crops. By 1860, he owned twelve slaves.[3]

In Friendship, Fielder became a respected community leader. Before the town was founded in 1853, a post office was located in his home and Fielder served as the area's first postmaster. The Dyer County Court regularly called on him to serve as an election judge and venireman. Voters in Dyer and Lauderdale counties elected

---

[1] Ann York Franklin, ed., *The Civil War Diaries of Capt. Alfred Tyler Fielder, 12th Tennessee Regiment Infantry, Company B, 1861–1865* (Louisville KY: self published, 1996) 1, 7, 152, 189, 248; Compiled Service Records, 12th Tennessee Infantry, National Archives, Washington DC.

[2] Franklin, *Fielder Diaries*, 248.

[3] *History of Tennessee from the Earliest Time to the Present; Together With an Historical and a Biographical Sketch of Gibson, Obion, Dyer, Weakley and Lake Counties* (Nashville: Goodspeed Publishing Company, 1887) 842, 845 (hereafter cited as *History of Dyer County*); Eighth Census, 1860, Manuscript Returns of Productions of Agriculture, Dyer County, Tennessee, 59; Seventh Census, 1850, Manuscript Returns of Productions of Agriculture, Dyer County, Tennessee, 801; Seventh Census, 1850, Manuscript Returns of Slaves, Dyer County, Tennessee, 886; Eighth Census, 1860, Manuscript Returns of Slaves, Dyer County, Tennessee, 207. For average farm sizes in Tennessee in 1860, including Dyer County, see Stephen V. Ash, *Middle Tennessee Society Transformed, 1860–1870: War and Peace in the Upper South* (Baton Rouge: Louisiana State University Press, 1988) 5–8.

Fielder, a Democrat, as their representative to the House of Representatives in the Thirty-First Tennessee General Assembly, 1855–1857.[4]

In matters of religion, Fielder possessed characteristics associated with those of a mature Christian. Although his religious past is sketchy because no prewar writings or church records exist, it can be pieced together from other sources. His wartime diary tells us that his father and mother were devout believers and long-time members of a Methodist church in North Carolina. Each morning and evening, his father gathered the family around the hearth to pray. Nurtured by godly parents, Fielder experienced a conversion at an early age and claimed Christianity as his own. In December 1861, a few months after enlisting in the Confederate army, he acknowledged his mother's impact on his life when he wrote, "all I am may be attributed to her advi[c]e and prayers."[5]

Once he had settled in West Tennessee, Fielder attended a small Methodist church called Mt. Zion. The church was founded in 1832—the result of a Methodist camp meeting—and met in a one-room log cabin. Camp meetings proved to be an effective way to minister to the sparsely settled regions during the early nineteenth century. People throughout the area would travel to meeting sites, pitch camp, hear the preaching and socialize over a period of several days. Methodists, Baptists and Presbyterians all used camp meetings—sometimes even jointly—during the Second Great Awakening (mid-1790s–1837). This period of notable religious revivalism in the United States had its beginnings in Kentucky in the mid-1790s, quickly spreading to all points on the American

---

[4] *History of Tennessee from the Earliest Time to the Present; Together With an Historical and a Biographical Sketch of Lauderdale, Tipton, Haywood and Crockett Counties* (Nashville: Goodspeed Publishing Company, 1887) 837 (hereafter cited as *History of Crockett County*); Nancy C. Wallace, ed., *History of Friendship, Tennessee 1824–1986* (n.p., n.d.) 43, Tennessee State Library and Archives, Nashville; Historical Records Survey, Tennessee, *Minutes of the County Court of Dyer County, 1848–1852* (Nashville, 1942) 32, 69, 164, 274; Robert M. McBride and Dan M. Robison, *Biographical Directory of the Tennessee General Assembly*, 2 vols. (Nashville: Tennessee State Library and Archives and the Tennessee Historical Commission, 1979) 2:1031–32.

[5] Franklin, *Fielder Diaries*, 21, 160–61.

compass—especially the rural and wilderness areas. Most evangelically-minded clergy and churches used camp meetings and revivalism to stoke the fires of religious fervor throughout the antebellum era.[6]

Fielder remained an ardent Methodist and a spiritual pillar of his local church during the antebellum period. The Quarterly Conference of Mt. Zion's district elected him to the Board of Trustees of Mt. Zion during the 1850s. His election to this position of leadership testifies to his piety and faithfulness, for candidates were nominated by pastors who were not likely to offer a name without thoughtful consideration. Indeed, Fielder's pastor, Rev. T. D. Harwell, knew him very well and they corresponded frequently throughout the war. Fielder's own words suggest his devotion to the tenets of the Methodist faith. In 1863, upon hearing that his chaplain was organizing a Christian Association in his regiment, Captain Fielder expressed his disdain for such an organization and his intention not to join: "I am a member of the M. E. C. South and [I] am willing to be governed by its rules and this association...might adopt some rule contrary to those of the Church to which I have the honor to be an humble member." Fielder demonstrated his devotion to the Methodist Church in his actions as well. In 1859, "in consideration of the love and affection they have to and for the Methodist Episcopal Church, South," Fielder and his mother deeded at no charge two acres to the church for the construction of a new "house or place of worship...to preach and expand God's Holy Word

---

[6] *The History of the Mt. Zion Methodist Church* (n.p., n.d.) 1, Mary Alice Badget personal paper, Friendship, Tennessee; Samuel S. Hill, *Southern Churches in Crisis* (New York: Holt, Rinehart and Winston, 1966) 62–63; Anne C. Loveland, *Southern Evangelicals and the Social Order, 1800–1860* (Baton Rouge: Louisiana State University Press, 1980) 32, 68, 72–75; Walter B. Posey, *Religious Strife on the Southern Frontier* (Baton Rouge: Louisiana State University Press, 1965) 6; Dickson D. Bruce, *And They All Sang Hallelujah: Plain-Folk Camp-Meeting Religion, 1800–1845* (Knoxville: University of Tennessee Press, 1974) 3–4; John B. Boles, "Evangelical Protestantism in the Old South: From Religious Dissent to Cultural Dominance," in *Religion in the South*, ed. Charles Reagan Wilson (Jackson: University Press of Mississippi, 1985) 14; Donald G. Mathews, *Religion in the Old South* (Chicago: University of Chicago Press, 1977) 50–51.

therein." After a new church building was constructed, Fielder served as its superintendent. He remained a trustee of Mt. Zion until his death in 1893.[7]

William Lewis Nugent

Colonel William Lewis Nugent, as he was affectionately known from 1865 until his death in 1897, in fact never exceeded the rank of captain during the war. Beginning his military service soon after the war began, he obtained a position as inspector-general for the state of Mississippi. Desiring a more active role, he resigned this position and in March 1862 enlisted in Company D, 28th Mississippi Cavalry, quickly rising to the rank of second lieutenant. During the first two years of the war, the 28th Cavalry was assigned to the Department of Mississippi and East Louisiana, remaining in the Mississippi Delta for most of 1862 opposing Federal raids. In mid-1863 the regiment cooperated with General Joseph E. Johnston in his unsuccessful attempt to raise the siege of Vicksburg. In September 1863, Brigadier General Samuel W. Ferguson, the former commander of the 28th Mississippi Cavalry, promoted Nugent to captain. General Ferguson appointed the new captain to his staff as assistant adjutant-general, a position in which Nugent served for the remainder of the war.[8]

Nugent was, like Alfred Fielder, a mature Christian before the war. He described himself as a "sober-sided Methodist." Born on 12 December 1833 in Opelousas, Louisiana, Nugent grew up on his family's sugar plantation. His father, John Pratt Nugent, was an accomplished attorney, parish judge and devoted Christian.

---

[7] *The Doctrines and Discipline of the Methodist Episcopal Church* (New York: Nelson & Phillips, 1876) 215; Franklin, *Fielder Diaries*, 24, 46–47, 114, 164; Susanna W. Fielder and Alfred T. Fielder to A. W. Swift and Others, 10 February 1859, Deed Book L, 1858-1859, 350, Register of Deeds Office, Dyer County, Tennessee; *Mt. Zion Methodist Church*, 1.

[8] William M. Cash and Lucy Somerville Howorth, eds., *My Dear Nellie: The Civil War Letters of William L. Nugent to Eleanor Smith Nugent* (Jackson: University Press of Mississippi, 1977) 41n, 51n, 93, 96, 110–13, 126–27; Compiled Service Records, General and Staff Officers, National Archives, Washington DC; Compiled Service Records, 28th Mississippi Cavalry; Stewart Sifakis, *Compendium of the Confederate Armies: Mississippi* (New York: Facts On File, 1995) 53.

Methodist Bishop Charles Galloway once described Nugent's father as "an earnest Christian and an ardent Methodist," who in addition to writing several books on the law, authored one on theology. Nugent's mother, Anne, was also a devout Methodist. Anne's public role in her local church, like that of most evangelical women of the antebellum South, probably amounted to holding women's Bible studies, praying and exhorting those seeking Christ, particularly during camp meetings. Her role within her own family, however, was another matter altogether. Anne devoted much time to instructing her children in religious matters. According to one of Nugent's brothers, when it came to religion, "she gave it to us all." Anne Nugent continued to instruct her children after they were grown. In 1859, after William had moved east to Greenville, Mississippi, his pious mother entreated him to remember the Lord's promises: "O what a privilege to feel that we are the children of God and can claim his blessing at any time and in any place and yet how often our faith is too weak to reach out and take the cup of blessing that is ever ready for us."[9]

It is no surprise that Nugent, having been raised in such a religious environment, became the "sober-sided Methodist" he considered himself to be. While attending a camp meeting, eleven-year-old William professed faith in Christ and joined the Methodist Church. At fifteen, he continued his family's long affiliation with Methodist institutions of higher learning, leaving home to attend Centenary College, in Jackson, Louisiana. Attending a school well-known for its rambunctious students, Nugent not only remained

---

[9] Cash and Howorth, *My Dear Nellie*, 24–25; Jackson (Mississippi) *Clarion-Ledger*, 18 January 1897; *Biographical and Historical Memoirs of Mississippi*, 2 vols. (Chicago: Goodspeed Publishing Company, 1891) 2:515; Charles B. Galloway, *Colonel William L. Nugent* (n.p., n.d.) 4, Mississippi Department of Archives and History, Jackson; Christine L. Heyrman, *Southern Cross: The Beginnings of the Bible Belt* (New York: Alfred A. Knopf, 1997) 166; Bruce, *And They All Sang Hallelujah*, 76, 86; Mathews, *Religion in the Old South*, 101–14; C. J. Nugent to Charles Galloway, 5 September 1898, Charles B. Galloway Papers, Wilson Library, Millsaps College; Anne L. Nugent to William L. Nugent, 3 April 1859, Lucy Somerville Howorth and William M. Cash Papers, Capps Archives and Museum, Delta State University, Cleveland, Mississippi.

steadfast in his faith but also excelled academically. During his time there he edited the school newspaper and tutored other students. At his graduation, he delivered the salutary in Latin and an oration entitled "The Bible, the Foundation of Government."[10]

Soon after graduating from Centenary in 1852, nineteen-year-old William traveled to Washington County, Mississippi, and settled in Greenville, a river town in the fertile Mississippi Delta. He joined the household of Abram F. Smith, a local attorney and planter, who hired Nugent to tutor the Smith children, including young Nellie, whom William would later marry. Continuing his affiliation with the church of his childhood, Nugent joined the Lake Lee Methodist Church near Greenville. A small church, Lake Lee more than likely shared an itinerant pastor with other Methodist churches in the Greenville area, which meant that preaching took place regularly yet on less than a weekly basis. Such circuit-riding between charges (congregations) was common among the Methodists of the sparsely-populated sections of the Old South. Extant records suggest that Nugent had no leadership role in Lake Lee Church prior to the Civil War, which is understandable considering his age and his short period of membership before the war.[11]

---

[10] Cash and Howorth, *My Dear Nellie*, 24–25; C. J. Nugent to Charles Galloway, 5 September 1898, Galloway Papers; Jackson (Mississippi) *Clarion-Ledger*, 18 January 1897; "History of Millsaps College" (typescript), Howorth and Cash Papers; Arthur Marvin Shaw, Jr., "Rampant Individualism in an Ante-Bellum Southern College," *Louisiana Historical Quarterly* 31 (October 1948): 877–96; William H. Nelson, *A Burning Torch and a Flaming Fire: The Story of Centenary College of Louisiana* (Nashville: Methodist Publishing House, 1931) 128, 386; Galloway, *Colonel William L. Nugent*, 7–8.

[11] Greenville (Mississippi) *Times* 23 January 1897; Cash and Howorth, *My Dear Nellie*, 11, 33; Greenville District Quarterly Conference Minutes, 1867–1881, 20 November 1868, First Methodist Church, Greenville, Mississippi. Although this conference occurred after the war, Nugent attended as a steward of Lake Lee Church, which suggests that he had been a member of the church for some time. It is a safe assumption that Lake Lee operated on a circuit considering that during this time First Methodist Church in Greenville, a much larger church, did so. See Nell Thomas, *This is Our Story…. This is Our Song: First United Methodist Church, Greenville, Mississippi, 1844–1994* (Greenville MS: Burford Brothers Printing, 1994) 8–10. The use of itinerants to minister to widely-scattered settlements is described in Hill, *Southern Churches in Crisis*, 62–63. Nugent is listed neither in the antebellum

After teaching for two years, Nugent commenced reading law under Abram Smith and in 1856 entered into a partnership with him. Evidently Smith drummed up most of the legal work for the firm, for when the Smith family was absent on a summer tour in 1860, Nugent had little to do. The fledgling attorney attested to his financial plight in a letter to Nellie, in which he remarked that she should enjoy herself on her tour since "it may never again be your good luck married as you will be soon to a poor young lawyer."[12]

In addition to practicing law, Abram Smith owned a prosperous cotton plantation valued at $30,000 in 1850. Smith relied on slave labor to produce the cotton, and by 1850 he had acquired sixty-one slaves. Though he owned no slaves himself, Nugent supported the institution. He used Smith's servants freely and, in fact, one of them accompanied Nugent as a servant throughout the war.[13]

Nugent was a devout, serious-minded Methodist, a fact obvious to those close to him. Writing to him in 1859 about his brother Clarence, who was visiting him in Greenville, his mother remarked: "I...hope his stay up there may prove as advantageous to him as Thomas's was...knowing that your influence with them is great." Undoubtedly, Nellie took notice of Nugent's strong religious convictions. Having grown close to Nellie while tutoring her, he asked for her hand in marriage and in 1860 they became engaged. Nugent realized that he had his work cut out for him, for his future wife was only sixteen and adventurous. Considering the summer tour as her last opportunity for amusement before the bonds of marriage—and quite possibly her husband's strict religious beliefs—took hold of her, Nellie set out to have a good time. In fact,

---

Greenville District Quarterly Conference Minutes nor the Mississippi Annual Conference minutes for that period; both list him during the postwar period.

[12] Cash and Howorth, *My Dear Nellie*, 6, 19, 32.

[13] Seventh Census, 1850, Manuscript Returns of Free Inhabitants, Washington County, Mississippi, 249; Seventh Census, 1850, Manuscript Returns of Productions of Agriculture, Washington County, Mississippi, 831; Seventh Census, 1850, Manuscript Returns of Slaves, Washington County, Mississippi, 508. Unfortunately, no Eighth Census manuscripts exist for Washington County, Mississippi. For examples of Nugent's interactions with the slaves, see Cash and Howorth, *My Dear Nellie*, 8, 8n, 11.

during the first month of her trip, she was much too occupied to write him. News of her activities, however, soon filtered back to Nugent. Upon learning that she had attended a dance, he wrote her, "I should like to know whether it is *really a pleasure* to you, the fiancee of a poor, sober-sided Methodist lawyer. If this be the case, I presume you have soberly determined to surrender your connection with the Church." And, with a question steeped in the tradition of Methodist Arminianism, he inquired about her salvation: "Do you propose not to be among the throng?" Having instructed Nellie for so long as her teacher, Nugent informed Nellie that he now intended to help her "assimilate your opinions to mine."[14]

During Nellie's prolonged absence in the summer of 1860, Nugent faced one of the biggest trials of his life to that time. Without the one he loved, he lamented, "I sometimes almost feel weary of life itself!" It was a foretaste of what he would experience during the war. Missing his fiancee and concerned for her safety, Nugent prayed daily for her and placed his trust for her protection in "He who tempers the wind." Nellie returned home in September 1860, and the two were married soon thereafter. As a devout Christian, Nugent no doubt returned thanks to God for Nellie's safe return and learned more about trusting in the Lord. Within a year, Nugent marched off to war and would again find it necessary to rely wholly upon God for a sense of peace and comfort over circumstances clearly beyond his control.[15]

---

[14] Anne Nugent to William Nugent, 3 April 1859, Howorth and Cash Papers; Cash and Howorth, *My Dear Nellie*, 6, 17, 25. Arminianism was the belief held by Methodists that salvation was available to all, not just the "elect" as Calvinists maintained. See Thomas A. Langford, *Methodist Theology* (Peterborough UK: Epworth Press, 1998) 6–7; J. Paul Williams, *What Americans Believe and How They Worship* (New York: Harper & Brothers, Publishers, 1952) 279–80; Hill, *Southern Churches in Crisis*, 63; E. Brooks Holifield, *The Gentlemen Theologians: American Theology in Southern Culture, 1795–1860* (Durham: Duke University Press, 1978) 187–91. Evidently Nellie had yet to make a profession of faith, for in 1864 Nugent wrote, "There is, in my opinion, but one thing needed to make you all that the most enobled imagination could picture, and that is the pure religion of our Lord and Savior, Jesus Christ." See Cash and Howorth, *My Dear Nellie*, 205.

[15] Cash and Howorth, *My Dear Nellie*, 8, 12, 19, 26; Myra Smith diary, 24 September 1860, Susie Trigg Papers, William Alexander Percy Memorial Library,

William Nelson Pendleton

Another of the Old South's mature Christians, William Nelson
Pendleton, was mustered into the Rockbridge Artillery in May 1861
at fifty-one years of age and entering his twenty-fourth year as an
Episcopalian clergyman. During his years of Christian service before
the war, Parson Pendleton had served churches in Newark,
Delaware, and Baltimore and Frederick, Maryland, before arriving in
Lexington, Virginia, in 1853 to take over as rector of Grace
Episcopal Church. By the time of the Civil War, he had behind him
two and one-half decades of scriptural meditation, preaching and
caring for a congregation.[16]

Having had no intention of participating in the military aspects
of the war, William Pendleton nevertheless found himself drawn into
the conflict. In April 1861, with the officers and cadets from the
nearby Virginia Military Institute gone, a company of volunteers
from Washington College called on Parson Pendleton to drill them
in infantry and artillery tactics. He wrestled with a dilemma: he
considered it his duty to defend his country, but he had a duty to
God as well. Although he intended his assistance to be only
temporary, Pendleton reluctantly accepted when elected to the
captaincy of what became the elite Rockbridge Artillery. He had
decided to serve in a "double capacity of soldier and minister of
Christ." During the war, he preached regularly to the troops.[17]

General Joseph E. Johnston soon recognized Captain
Pendleton's abilities and elevated him to his staff as chief of artillery
and, in March 1862, promoted him to brigadier general. After
General Robert E. Lee replaced Johnston in mid-1862, General
Pendleton retained his position as chief of artillery in the Army of

---

Greenville, Mississippi.

[16] Susan P. Lee, *Memoirs of William Nelson Pendleton, D.D.* (Philadelphia: J. B.
Lippincott Company, 1893) 7, 69, 84, 90; Grace Episcopal Church, Lexington,
Virginia, Vestry Minutes, 1840–1913, 14 July 1853, Robert E. Lee Memorial
Church, Lexington, Virginia.

[17] Lee, *Memoirs of Pendleton*, 137–38, 142–43, 191.

Northern Virginia. Largely an administrative position, Pendelton held it for the duration of the war.[18]

Pendleton was born on 26 December 1809 and raised on his family's estate in rural Caroline County, Virginia. His antebellum religious history resembles that of the Prodigal Son in Jesus' New Testament parable. Living in an era in which there were few schools in the Virginia countryside and no Episcopal church nearby, Pendleton's mother taught her children Bible verses and hymns as well as how to read and write. In 1826, sixteen-year-old William left home and enrolled in the military academy at West Point. His studies and experiences at the academy led him to question the faith of his childhood. He eventually abandoned the religious principles his mother had taught him. After graduating fifth in the class of 1830, Pendleton received his appointment to the rank of second lieutenant in the 4th Regiment of Artillery. Soon thereafter, he married Miss Anzolette Page of Virginia and settled into life in the army. En route to his assignment at Fort Moultrie in Charleston Harbor, Lieutenant Pendleton contracted a debilitating case of fever. He suffered greatly but recovered fully. Deciding that providence had been at work in his survival, the young lieutenant turned back to the God of his childhood and experienced a genuine religious conversion. Soon after, in a letter home, Pendleton pondered whether to employ his abilities in a new profession: "[I] might turn whatever abilities God has given me to the highest use...in studying and proclaiming the holy truths of Christianity."[19]

Pendleton's conversion experience, his reliance on faith in Christ for salvation and his tolerance of other Protestant denominations identify him as an evangelical Episcopalian or Low Churchman. Although the High Church and evangelical parties within the nineteenth-century Episcopal Church were at one

---

[18] Douglas Southall Freeman, *Lee's Lieutenants: A Study in Command*, 3 vols. (New York: Charles Scribner's Sons, 1943) 2:615, 707; Compiled Service Records, General and Staff Officers.

[19] Luke 15:11ff; Lee, *Memoirs of Pendleton*, 16, 18, 26–28, 30, 33–40; Ezra J. Warner, *Generals in Gray: Lives of the Confederate Commanders* (Baton Rouge: Louisiana State University Press, 1959) 234.

concerning the fundamental doctrines of the Church and the
significance of the *Book of Common Prayer*, the guidebook for worship
in the Church, they differed on interpretation and emphasis. High
Churchmen emphasized salvation as a journey and the role that the
church, the sacraments and the ministers played in it; evangelicals
believed firmly that faith in Christ alone was sufficient for salvation.
In the early nineteenth century, evangelical Episcopalians began to
exert considerable influence within the Episcopal Church,
particularly in Virginia.[20]

While in the army, Pendleton's religious convictions and
commitment continued to grow. In 1832, Bishop William Meade,
one of the leaders of the evangelical movement in the Episcopal
Church and later Pendleton's close friend, performed Pendleton's
confirmation ceremony. While he was stationed at Fort Hamilton,
near New York harbor, Pendleton's commitment to attend religious
services grew. On Sundays, he frequently endured the inconvenience
of traveling into New York City to attend services; on days when
travel was impossible, he led a Bible study at the fort.[21]

---

[20] The terms Low Churchman and evangelical were frequently used
interchangeably during this period. See E. Clowes Chorley, *Men and Movements in
the American Episcopal Church* (New York: Charles Scribner's Sons, 1946) 44; and
James Thayer Addison, *The Episcopal Church in the United States, 1789–1931* (New
York: Scribner's, 1951) 90. It is clear from his conversion experience and his close
association with Bishop William Meade, a well-known leader of the evangelical wing,
that Pendleton was an evangelical or Low Churchman; and his daughter labels him
as such in Lee, *Memoirs of Pendleton*, 88. The characteristics of the High Churchmen
and evangelicals are described in Robert W. Prichard, *The Nature of Salvation:
Theological Consensus in the Episcopal Church, 1801–73* (Urbana: University of Illinois
Press, 1997) 3, 24–29; Chorley, *Men and Movements*, 60–61, 71–76, 86, 168–93;
Addison, *Episcopal Church in the United States*, 89–90; W. Norman Pittenger, *The
Episcopalian Way of Life* (Englewood Cliffs NJ: Prentice-Hall, 1957) 22–24, 72,
131–43; Diana H. Butler, *Standing Against the Whirlwind: Evangelical Episcopalians in
Nineteenth-Century America* (New York/Oxford: Oxford University Press, 1995) 4,
13.

[21] In the confirmation ceremony, one expresses one's commitment to Christ and
receives the Holy Spirit through the Bishop's "laying on of hands." See David E.
Sumner, *The Episcopal Church's History: 1945–1985* (Wilton CT: Morehouse-Barlow,
1987) 207. For information on Pendleton's confirmation and his religious activities at

Seized by a desire to benefit his fellow man, Lieutenant Pendleton resigned from the army in 1833 and engaged in several civilian occupations before settling down as a parish rector in 1847. From 1833 to 1837, he taught at Bristol College in Pennsylvania. It was there that he learned a significant lesson in trusting the Lord regarding matters beyond his control. The college had financial problems during his tenure there, about which Pendleton wrote to his wife: "All this is in the hands of God. He will direct that which is best for His own honor." While in Pennsylvania, Pendleton continued to grow spiritually as he meditated on Scripture and read religious commentaries in his spare time.[22]

During the summer of 1836, struggling financially himself, Pendleton accepted an offer to supervise a railroad engineering party surveying a track from southwestern Virginia into North Carolina. This position, although a temporary one, was arduous and proved to be a foretaste of what he would experience during the war. Subjected to long absences from loved ones and danger in the form of disease, Pendleton responded much the same way he would during the war. He prayed often for himself and his family, committing himself and their well-being into the hands of "an all-directing Providence."[23]

Traveling frequently through rural areas of Virginia and North Carolina, Pendleton often found himself on Sundays without access to an Episcopal church. This was another taste of things to come. As he would do two and a half decades later, Pendleton attended whatever church was available in these circumstances, although at times he exercised some choice in the matter. While he was working near Danville, Virginia, for example, he found himself with a choice between two local evangelical churches, one Presbyterian and one Baptist. Accustomed to the educated clergy of the Episcopal Church, he chose to attend the Presbyterian church which also adhered to an educated clergy and a more formal style of worship. On another

---

Fort Hamilton, see Lee, *Memoirs of Pendleton*, 49, 51. Bishop Meade's role in the evangelical movement is described in Chorley, *Men and Movements*, 42–44.

[22] Lee, *Memoirs of Pendleton*, 55–62.

[23] Ibid., 62–64.

occasion in rural Virginia, however, Pendleton attended what he described as a "homely" Baptist church.[24]

Pendleton emerged from the difficult summer of 1836 with a better understanding of the Lord's purpose for him. In a letter to his wife he wrote, "I have come to the conclusion…that God required of

---

[24] For examples of Pendleton's attendance at the services of other denominations, see Lee, *Memoirs of Pendleton*, 63–66. Samuel Hill points out that many of the common folk associated the Episcopal Church with England and found its unemotional, liturgical worship lacking. See Hill, *Southern Churches in Crisis*, 53–55. The high educational standards required of Presbyterian ministers are described in Loveland, *Southern Evangelicals*, 28; and Mathews, *Religion in the Old South*, 85. See also Butler, *Standing Against the Whirlwind*, 11–12. Interdenominationalism, i. e., persons of one denomination attending religious services of another, was, as Pendleton illustrates, common in the antebellum South. This is not to say that competition for members and doctrinal differences did not exist, for indeed they did. Walter Posey in *Religious Strife*, for example, argues that religious Southerners in the nineteenth century were in fact very denominational. He maintains that competition between the evangelical denominations generated friction and "extreme antagonism." Competition for members, however, was not the only factor contributing to the antipathy between the evangelical denominations. E. Brooks Holifield, in *Gentlemen Theologians*, contends that while many historians label evangelicalism as anti-intellectual and overly-emotional, the evangelical ministers devoted much thought to such weighty doctrinal issues as baptism, predestination and the Lord's Supper or Holy Communion.

According to Donald Mathews in *Religion in the Old South*, evangelicals regardless of denomination shared many characteristics and interests. They acknowledged the importance of the Bible, emphasized the necessity of a salvation experience and worshipped similarly. Matthews acknowledges that competition and friction existed between the evangelical denominations, but insists that the relations between them were mostly cordial. Perhaps the best illustration of interdenominationalism is the protracted meeting or the camp meeting. Deeming the salvation of souls to be more important than doctrinal issues, ministers of different denominations put aside their differences and cooperated during these meetings. And, as Pendleton's case demonstrates, antebellum Christians frequently attended services that were most convenient, including Catholic Mass, although the motivation here was often curiosity. For Christian soldiers who found themselves far away from their regular church services, denominationalism took on even less significance. See Posey, *Religious Strife*, xiii–xv, 9, 12; Holifield, *Gentlemen Theologians*, 3, 165–85, 187–98; Heyrman, *Southern Cross*, 154; Mathews, *Religion in the Old South*, 132–33, 242; Hill, *Southern Churches in Crisis*, 76–77, 94–99; Lewis O. Saum, *The Popular Mood of Pre-Civil War America* (Westport CT: Greenwood Press, 1980) 36, 39, 42, 44; Loveland, *Southern Evangelicals*, 66, 77.

me to preach the Gospel...He can, and often does, use the weakest and most unworthy of His servants to promote the salvation of men."[25]

The continuing financial difficulties at Bristol College proved too much and in 1837 the college closed its doors. In that same year, Pendleton accepted another professorship at Newark College in Delaware. Having been ordained by Bishop Meade, Pendleton engaged in preaching at two small churches near Newark. The bishop, however, had other plans for Pendleton. In 1839 the senior cleric induced Pendleton to return to Virginia as headmaster of a church school in Alexandria. Burdened by the school's pecuniary difficulties, however, Pendleton resigned, much to the regret of the board of trustees and students, who lauded his Christian character. After a short stint teaching and preaching in Baltimore, Pendleton landed in 1847 at All Saint's Episcopal Church in Frederick, Maryland, where he became rector.[26]

During Pendleton's tenure at All Saint's, his religious faith continued to mature. Freedom from routine teaching duties afforded him more time for his personal religious studies and ministry. He led a daily devotional for his family and also provided religious instruction for his children. In addition to four services a week at the church, he ministered to the inmates of the local jail and almshouse. Catastrophe also served to test and strengthen Pendleton's faith: in 1849 his second daughter, Lucy, contracted fever and died. Her passing drew Pendleton nearer to Christ. In a letter to his wife, he recalled how Lucy loved to play the piano and revealed how the recent tragedy ultimately served to deepen his own faith: "The music fit for heaven, the Song of the Lamb, is her delight now; Lord, let no murmuring mingle with our mourning.... Lord help us to live near Thee."[27]

Parson Pendleton labored on as rector of All Saint's Church until 1853, when a disagreement with the vestry over the physical

---

[25] Lee, *Memoirs of Pendleton*, 66.
[26] Ibid., 66–67, 69, 72, 81–90.
[27] Ibid., 90, 96, 99.

condition of the church prompted him to resign. Convinced that the church building was not a true reflection of the congregation's wealth, Pendleton set out to have a new church built. Unable to persuade the vestry to collect the necessary funds, Pendleton took his argument to the pulpit. On a Sunday in January 1853 he preached a scathing sermon titled "The Lord's House—as It Should Be and as It Is," in which he listed point by point the problems with the present church building and criticized the apathy of the congregation in this matter. Furthermore, he printed his sermon and circulated it among the congregation. Not receiving the response he desired, Pendleton tendered his resignation and left Frederick in July 1853. Ironically, a few years after his departure, a new, costly edifice was erected in place of the old one.[28]

In the fall of 1853 Grace Episcopal Church in Lexington, Virginia, called Pendleton as rector. Realizing that he would have an opportunity to minister to the students attending Washington College and the Virginia Military Institute, he accepted the position despite its modest salary. Pendleton had long held an interest in ministering to students and had been an unsuccessful applicant for the chaplaincy of West Point in 1846. After arriving in Lexington, he began a college ministry and was soon holding two services a week at VMI and morning services at Washington College. Pendleton's efforts bore fruit: by the fall 1861, Grace Church had added seventy-six new members, including nearly sixty students.[29]

His salary proving insufficient, Pendleton decided to supplement it and accepted a position as an agent for an interdenominational organization called the American Sunday School Union (ASSU).

---

[28] Ibid., 99–102; pamphlet, "The Lord's House—as It Should Be and as It Is: A Sermon," 30 January 1853, William Nelson Pendleton Papers, Southern Historical Collection, University of North Carolina, Chapel Hill.

[29] Grace Episcopal Church, Vestry Minutes, 13 June, 14 July 1853; George M. Brooke, Jr., *General Lee's Church* (Lexington VA: News-Gazette, 1984) 14–18, 24; William N. Pendleton to President James K. Polk, 11 December 1846, Pendleton Papers; Martin P. Burks, E. Pendleton Tompkins, and John D. Letcher, eds., "A Short History of the Protestant Episcopal Church, at Lexington, Rockbridge County, Virginia," (typescript) 18, Washington and Lee Miscellaneous Collection, Leyburn Library, Washington and Lee University, Lexington, Virginia.

Formed in 1824, the ASSU sought to plant and nurture Sunday schools throughout the nation. As an agent for the ASSU, Pendleton traveled for two and a half years throughout the country and met with other clergymen on Sunday-school business. The travel and absence from loved ones quickly wearied him. A few months after accepting the position he wrote his wife: "I am longing for the day when I can start homeward. Absence can be borne as a duty, but it is a hard trial." During this time of trying service, Pendleton evinced an ever-deepening faith, as a letter to his wife from Philadelphia illustrates: "Dear love, lean more confidingly on the tender mercy of a covenant Saviour and unfailing friend.... I more humbly and steadily serve God, His Spirit helping me. So will you, my beloved wife."[30]

Fatigued by his work with the American Sunday School Union, Pendleton resigned the position in 1857. To augment his meager salary at Grace Church, he opened a school in the rectory and crowded the pupils into a cramped attic dormitory. In 1860, in addition to his own family of seven, Pendleton housed twelve young men whose ages ranged from fourteen to seventeen and who hailed from several Southern states. Pendleton operated a small farm to help feed his family and students. He used the services of his three slaves—one male and two females—to help with the workload. Except for a four-year interruption during the Civil War, Pendleton

---

[30] Lee, *Memoirs of Pendleton*, 107, 108–10, 112–13; Edwin W. Rice, *The Sunday-School Movement (1780–1917) and the American Sunday-School Union (1817–1917)* (1917; reprint, New York: Arno Press & the New York Times, 1971) 79–87. Sunday schools had existed since the late eighteenth century as centers for teaching basic reading and writing, but between 1810 and 1830 a new type of Sunday school spread rapidly across the country. In these, teachers focused primarily on Bible-based instruction that was expected eventually to bring about a religious conversion. Nationwide enrollment grew to approximately 8 percent of white children by 1832. For more on the transformation of nineteenth-century Sunday schools, see Anne M. Boylan, *Sunday School: The Formation of An American Institution, 1790–1880* (New Haven: Yale University Press, 1988) 6–11, 28.

remained in Lexington and served as rector of Grace Church until his death in 1883.[31]

Edward Owings Guerrant

Edward ("Ned") Owings Guerrant's military service began in February 1862. Having promised his father and friends that he would not enlist in the Confederate army as a private, he joined the staff of fellow Kentuckian, Brigadier General Humphrey Marshall. The frail Guerrant was well-suited for his position as the general's secretary. General Marshall's command was responsible for defending a vital link in the Virginia and Tennessee Railroad that ran through southwestern Virginia. Guerrant served the general faithfully. In December 1862 he was elevated to the position of assistant adjutant-general and promoted to captain. After Marshall resigned in June 1863 to enter the Confederate Congress, Captain Guerrant served Marshall's successors conscientiously. Among those successors was the legendary General John H. Morgan, with whom Guerrant served a short stint that ended with Morgan's death in September 1864. After Morgan died, Guerrant and his brigade remained for the most part in southwestern Virginia under the command of Colonel Henry L. Giltner.[32]

Guerrant, unlike Pendleton, Nugent, and Fielder, was a spiritual neophyte when the Civil War began. Ned Guerrant was born on 28 February 1838 in Sharpsburg, Kentucky, to Dr. Henry Guerrant and his wife Mary. He grew up in a Christian home and there received his first instruction in matters of religion. Recalling his mother long

---

[31] Lee, *Memoirs of Pendleton*, 118–19; Eighth Census, 1860, Manuscript Returns of Free Inhabitants, Rockbridge County, Virginia, 8; Eighth Census, 1860, Manuscript Returns of Productions of Agriculture, Rockbridge County, Virginia, 71; Eighth Census, 1860, Manuscript Returns of Slaves, Rockbridge County, Virginia, 194.

[32] Edward O. Guerrant diary, 11 and 13 February 1862, Edward O. Guerrant Papers, Southern Historical Collection, University of North Carolina, Chapel Hill; J. Gray McAllister and Grace Owings Guerrant, *Edward O. Guerrant: Apostle to the Southern Highlanders* (Richmond: Richmond Press, 1950) 26–54; William C. Davis and Meredith L. Swentor, eds., *Bluegrass Confederate: The Headquarters Diary of Edward O. Guerrant* (Baton Rouge: Louisiana State University Press, 1999) 4–6.

after the war in his memoirs, Guerrant described her as a tender yet eloquent preacher: "She told the story more sweetly and lovingly than some mighty preachers, I have heard." His mother passed away in the early 1850s, but evidently Dr. Guerrant continued to emphasize religion, for records show that young Ned regularly attended the local Presbyterian church while residing at home in 1856. Dr. Guerrant's religious commitment may have been motivated partly by the wishes of his late wife, for it was not until September 1859 that he himself was admitted to the Presbyterian Church by the public profession of his faith.[33]

After his wife's death in 1850, Dr. Guerrant remained in his modest home in Sharpsburg and devoted himself to practicing medicine and raising his family. To assist with caring for his six small children, he relied on black servants. By 1860, he had acquired three female slaves. Ned himself never owned slaves, but he likely sanctioned the institution, for he grew up in a household with slaves and never voiced any concerns about the "peculiar institution."[34]

The Guerrant family placed a premium on education, and in the fall of 1856 eighteen-year-old Ned traveled to Danville, Kentucky, where he enrolled at Centre College, a Presbyterian school

---

[33] McAllister and Guerrant, *Edward O. Guerrant*, 1; Edward O. Guerrant, *The Soul Winner* (Lexington KY: John B. Morton & Company, 1896) 21; Guerrant diary, 6, 19 January and 3, 10, 24 February 1856. Guerrant ended his 1856 diary soon after these entries and resumed it when he arrived at Centre College in the fall of 1856. Dr. Guerrant's admission to the Presbyterian Church is noted in the Presbyterian Church, Sharpsburg, Kentucky, Register of Members, 1848–1930, 11 September 1859, Presbyterian Historical Society, Montreat, North Carolina. See also Guerrant diary, 11 September 1859.

[34] According to the 1850 and 1860 censuses, he claimed no agriculture productions and his real estate value remained at a modest $600 in both 1850 and 1860. See Seventh Census, 1850, Manuscript Returns of Free Inhabitants, Bath County, Kentucky, 106; Eighth Census, 1860, Manuscript Returns of Free Inhabitants, Bath County, Kentucky, 75. Mary Guerrant's date of death is listed as 6 January 1850 in the Presbyterian Church, Sharpsburg, Church Register, 135. Guerrant's slaves are listed in the Seventh Census, 1850, Manuscript Returns of Slaves, Bath County, Kentucky, 287; Eighth Census, 1860, Manuscript Returns of Slaves, Bath County, Kentucky, 87; McAllister and Guerrant, *Edward O. Guerrant*, 7–8.

administered by the Kentucky Synod. For many young men in the antebellum era, college was a time of vulnerability that made them more susceptible to religious conversion. During the spring of 1857 a revival swept through Centre College and sparked dozens of conversions, including Guerrant's. While attending revival services at First Presbyterian Church of Danville, Guerrant, burdened by the weight of his sin, "prayed earnestly that God would forgive my sins." Examined by the Session of Second Presbyterian Church of Danville, he joined the church by profession of faith and was baptized.[35]

After his conversion, Guerrant became an earnest follower of Christ. Only illness or bad weather kept him from attending worship services in Danville. He often attended services of other denominations when a Presbyterian church was not accessible. By attending church and regularly associating with fellow Christians, Guerrant avoided the main pitfall new converts face: backsliding. Losing one's first religious ardor occurred frequently after the post-conversion euphoria wore off and could be avoided only through constant self-examination and the nurturing fellowship of other religious persons. Guerrant, having embraced the assurance of salvation for himself, desired the same for others and shared his faith privately when opportunities presented themselves. In addition to

[35] Guerrant diary, 31 October 1856; McAllister and Guerrant, *Edward O. Guerrant*, 12–15. The Synod was a regional governing body within the Church's hierarchy composed of the Presbyteries in a specific geographical area. Most power within the Presbyterian Church, however, rested with the Presbyteries that were made up of the ministers and one elder from each church within a geographical district. There existed within each local congregation a Session (comprised of elected elders along with the pastor), that oversaw the functioning of the church; and a body of deacons, who superintended the church buildings. For a description of the Presbyterian hierarchy, see Williams, *What Americans Believe*, 202–203; see also Randall Balmer and John R. Fitzmier, *The Presbyterians* (Westport CT: Greenwood Press, 1993) 15. The Centre College revival was part of a larger one within the Presbyterian Church in 1857–1858. See McAllister and Guerrant, *Edward O. Guerrant*, 17–18; Loveland, *Southern Evangelicals*, 88; Ernest T. Thompson, *Presbyterians in the South*, 3 vols. (Richmond: John Knox Press, 1963–1973) 1:469–70. Guerrant's conversion is noted in the back of Guerrant diary, vol. 41; and Second Presbyterian Church, Danville, Kentucky, Session Minutes, 1852–1969, 27 March 1857, Presbyterian Historical Society, Montreat, North Carolina.

attending Sunday worship, he regularly participated in Bible study in the college chapel on Sunday mornings before services. At times when no organized Scripture study was held, he meditated on the sermon notes he had recorded, studied his Bible, or read other religious books.[36]

Guerrant's postconversion diary suggests that his thoughts were often occupied with the workings of the Almighty, even in the smallest of matters. Once, upon awakening to a beautiful day, he recorded, "Delightful day. All nature seems a living breathing monument of God's goodness and greatness." Ruminating on prayer and its power, Guerrant wrote, "Prayer moves the Arm that moves the Universe...prayer is the greatest privilege man can have." His religious reflections were not, however, limited solely to his diary. In December 1858, he delivered an address in the college chapel titled "The Promises of God," which he printed and circulated among the student body.[37]

Sensing that the Lord was "calling" him to be a preacher, Guerrant decided prior to his graduation in 1860 that he should attend seminary and enter the ministry. Unlike their Baptist and Methodist brethren, Presbyterians seeking to enter the ministry were required to obtain a classical education, graduate from a theological seminary and endure a rigorous examination conducted by a local Presbytery. Although the establishment of their own denominational colleges during the 1820s and 1830s provided more opportunities for an educated clergy, Baptists and Methodists relied first and foremost on an individual's sense of "calling" to preach and treated formal

---

[36] Guerrant diary, 9 January, 13 February and 10 July 1859. On backsliding and the sharing of faith see Loveland, *Southern Evangelicals*, 2, 8, 13, 15–16. Examples of Guerrant sharing his faith are in Guerrant diary, 18 March 1860. For his private meditations, see ibid., 16 January, 6, 13 February, 6 March, 23 October, 19 November 1859; and 20 January, 9 February 1860.

[37] Guerrant diary, 6 May, 19 November 1859; and 18 March 1860; pamphlet, "The Promises of God," in Edward O. Guerrant Family Papers (microfilm), King Library, University of Kentucky, Lexington.

academic education as a secondary—and sometimes unwelcome—
qualification for ministry.[38]

Guerrant returned home to Sharpsburg after graduation and
taught school while awaiting the beginning of the seminary's fall
semester. In October 1860, he returned to Danville and enrolled in
the theological seminary there. Confined to his bed for several weeks
by an illness he contracted soon after arriving in Danville, a
disappointed Guerrant withdrew from the seminary, vowing to
resume his studies in the fall of 1861. He could not know that twelve
years would elapse before he would return to his theological studies.[39]

Felix Pierre Poché

Though he was a patriotic Confederate, Felix Pierre Poché did
not enter Confederate service until July 1863. He organized a
company of local volunteers early in the war but failed to have it
attached to a regiment, and Confederate authorities disbanded it in
October 1862. Disappointed but undaunted, Poché signed on as a
volunteer aide in the commissary department of Brigadier General J.
J. A. Alfred Mouton's brigade in the Trans-Mississippi Department.
Poché served Mouton, and his successor, Brigadier General Henry
Gray, until September 1864. In December he took command of a
company of partisan rangers who operated near the Mississippi River
in southern Louisiana. Poché continued to serve in this role, with
only moderate success, until 12 May 1865.[40]

Poché, like Guerrant, was a spiritual neophyte when the war
broke out. He was born on 18 May 1836 in St. James Parish,
Louisiana, to the Creole family of Pierre and Marie Poché.

---

[38] Guerrant diary, 22 January and 6, 19 April 1860; Loveland, *Southern Evangelicals*, 24–28; Mathews, *Religion in the Old South*, 85–86.

[39] Guerrant diary, 28 June, 9 July, and 2, 8, 20 October 1860; McAllister and Guerrant, *Edward O. Guerrant*, 24–25.

[40] Edwin C. Bearss, ed., *A Louisiana Confederate: Diary of Felix Pierre Poché*, trans. Eugenie Watson Somdal (Natchitoches LA: Louisiana Studies Institute, Northwestern State University, 1972) v, 244; Patricia L. Faust, ed., *Historical Times Illustrated Encyclopedia of the Civil War* (New York: Harper & Row Publishers, 1986) 321, 515; Napier Bartlett, *Military Record of Louisiana* (Baton Rouge: Louisiana State University Press, 1964) 37–44.

Bordering the Mississippi River in Louisiana between New Orleans and Baton Rouge, St. James Parish possessed rich, alluvial soil and was characterized by a climate suitable for growing sugar cane. Pierre Poché operated a small sugar plantation of 40 improved acres where, in 1859, he produced 40,000 pounds of sugar cane and 4,000 gallons of molasses. Producing sugar was very labor-intensive. Harvesting and grinding the cane, in particular, required round-the-clock attention. To assist him in this work, Pierre relied on slave labor, and according to the 1860 census he owned five slaves. It was in this environment that young Felix grew up and spent his boyhood.[41]

The Poché family enjoyed a long affiliation with the Roman Catholic Church. This is not surprising considering the ubiquitous presence of the Church in southern Louisiana during the mid-nineteenth century. Much of the Church's strength in the area could be attributed to the French-speaking Creole population, who were so numerous that the weekly Thibodaux (Louisiana) *Sentinel* published bi-lingual newspapers until 1900. The local Catholic diocese's church records suggest that the Poché family was devoutly Catholic. Beginning with Felix's grandparents, the Pochés long attended St. Michael's Catholic Church located in nearby Convent. Evidently the family began attending the church soon after it was founded in 1809, for one of their children was baptized there that year. It was there that Pierre married Marie Melacon in June 1835, and there that Felix was baptized in August 1836. Three of Felix's siblings were likewise baptized at St. Michael's; and Pierre was buried at St. Michael's cemetery after his death in June 1859.[42]

---

[41] New Orleans *Times-Picayune*, 17 June 1895; Thibodaux (Louisiana) *Sentinel*, 16 September 1865; Eighth Census, 1860, Manuscript Returns of Productions of Agriculture, St. James Parish, Louisiana, 21; Joe G. Taylor, *Louisiana: A Bicentennial History* (New York: W. W. Norton & Company, 1976) 58, 64–65; Eighth Census, 1860, Manuscript Returns of Slaves, St. James Parish, Louisiana, 38; *Biographical and Historical Memoirs of Louisiana*, 2 vols. (Chicago: Goodspeed Publishing Company, 1892) 2:315.

[42] Samuel S. Hill, Jr., *Religion and the Solid South* (New York: Abingdon Press, 1972) 162; Randall M. Miller, "The Failed Mission: The Catholic Church and Black Catholics in the Old South," in *Catholics in the Old South: Essays on Church and Culture*, ed. Randall M. Miller and Jon L. Wakelyn (Macon GA: Mercer University

To understand the devoutness of the Pochés, one must understand the perception of the Roman Catholic Church by its members. In the Gospel According to Matthew, Christ says to Peter: "I say also unto thee, that thou art Peter, and upon this rock I will build my church." Catholics believe that by these words, Christ established the Catholic Church with Peter as its first titular head. Therefore, unlike evangelical Protestants, Catholics maintain that theirs is not just one of several Christian denominations, but the one, true Church. In light of this, devout Catholics believe that it is their duty to accept and follow, without questioning, the basic teachings of the Church.[43]

Catholics believe that mankind is burdened under the weight of Adam's original sin and insist that human beings must rely on God's grace to lift the weight of that sin. According to Catholic theology, God linked his mercy and saving grace to seven external or observable signs called sacraments. The seven sacraments of the Church are: Eucharist or Communion, baptism, penance, confirmation, anointing of the sick, ordination, and marriage. As the sole dispenser of these sacraments, the Church is the sole dispenser of the means of grace. As long-time Catholics, the Pochés undoubtedly attended Mass regularly and partook of the sacraments, for these were not only required by the Church but also considered indispensable to salvation.[44]

Press, 1983) 151; Thibodaux (Louisiana) *Sentinel*, passim; *Diocese of Baton Rouge, Catholic Church Records*, 18 vols. (Baton Rouge: Diocese of Baton Rouge, Department of Archives, 1982–95) 3:704. Information in the front of volume 3 lists St. Michael's Church as established in 1809. Felix was baptized approximately three months after his birth, which appears to have been the standard practice for Catholics in that diocese. See ibid., 5:492; 6:524–25; 9:439.

[43] Matthew 16:18; Williams, *What Americans Believe*, 16, 20. Poché's own words confirm his adherence to this belief. After attending one Mass, he wrote, "It is in these moments of happiness and of rapture of divine joy that the Christian feels in the bottom of his heart the truth of the Catholic Church." See Bearss, *Louisiana Confederate*, 71.

[44] Williams, *What Americans Believe*, 43–45; Karl Rahner, *The Church and the Sacraments*, trans. W. J. O'Hara (New York: Herder and Herder, 1963) 19, 21, 25–26, 40.

Considering it important that his sixteen-year-old son receive a Catholic education, Pierre sent Felix to Bardstown, Kentucky, in 1852 to attend St. Joseph's College. St. Joseph's, founded by Jesuits in 1819, became a favorite boarding school for Catholics in antebellum Louisiana. Poché was for the most part a serious-minded student. He attended to his studies assiduously and earned good marks in conduct and diligence. Yet, at the same time, he appeared to take his religious responsibilities lightly. The boys were expected to be present at Mass. Poché apparently attended more or less regularly, for in his antebellum diary he recorded such phrases as "Had mass and benediction as usual." On more than one occasion, however, several of the boys, including Poché, skipped Mass and slipped down to the river to enjoy a morning or late afternoon swim. When he was in attendance, Poché occasionally assisted in Mass by serving the priest at the altar. He may have considered it more of an obligation than a privilege, for one time after Mass he wrote in his diary "I had to serve Mass."[45]

After graduating from St. Joseph's in 1855, Poché remained in Bardstown and embarked on a legal career. His mentor was Kentucky ex-governor Charles A. Wickliffe, who was so impressed by a college oration of Poché's he had heard that he invited the young man to study law in his office. After he completed his studies and was admitted to the Kentucky bar in 1858, Poché returned to Louisiana and read law under Judge J. J. Roman, who practiced in Thibodaux in Lafourche Parish, near St. James. Admitted to the Louisiana bar in 1859, Poché practiced law for a short time in Thibodaux. During this time he struggled financially: according to the 1860 census, he had no real estate, no slaves and valued his personal property at only $150. Wanting to be closer to his widowed mother and family after his father's death in 1859, Poché moved back to St. James Parish in

---

[45] *Memoirs of Louisiana*, 2:315; Katherine Bridges, "A Louisiana Schoolboy in Kentucky: Felix Pierre Poché's Diary, 1854," *Louisiana Studies* 10 (Fall 1971): 187–88; Felix P. Poché diary, 25–26, 28 June, 18, 25–26 July 1854; and passim, Eugenie Watson Somdal Papers, Watson Library, Northwestern State University, Natchitoches, Louisiana.

1860 and practiced law there until he joined the Confederate army in 1863.[46]

While there are few records regarding Poché's religious faith during the time between his graduation from St. Joseph's and his military enlistment, those that do exist suggest that he increasingly became more devout. For one thing, having settled again in St. James Parish, he was able to attend Mass at the church of his childhood, St. Michael's. Quite possibly he resumed attending services with the members of his family who still resided in the community. Moreover, in July 1860 he married Sélima Deslatte, a graduate of Sacred Heart Convent and a devout Catholic. Felix and Sélima undoubtedly attended Mass together and shared similar religious commitments, for when she visited him during the war, they spent part of their time together reading the Liturgy of the Mass. The most telling sign of his increased Catholicity, however, is the rapidity with which Poché had their first child baptized. Marie Marguerite was born on 17 February 1862 and baptized at St. Michael's the very next day. Unlike the evangelical denominations that view baptism solely as a sign of rebirth or regeneration, the Catholic Church teaches that every child is tainted with original sin at the moment of conception. Consequently, unless a person's soul is purified through the sacrament of baptism he or she cannot enter into heaven. By having his daughter baptized soon after her birth, Poché was presumably ensuring her eternity in heaven were she to die in infancy.[47]

---

[46] New Orleans *Times-Picayune*, 17 June 1895; *Memoirs of Louisiana*, 2:315; Eighth Census, 1860, Manuscript Returns of Free Inhabitants, Lafourche Parish, Louisiana, 61. Although Poché owned no slaves, he evidently had access to his father's, for one accompanied him as a servant during the war. See Bearss, *Louisiana Confederate*, 205–206.

[47] *Diocese of Baton Rouge*, 9:438–39. On Sélima's influence, Poché wrote, "it is to the saintly influence that comes from her pure heart to which I owe all my religious fervor." See Bearss, *Louisiana Confederate*, 50, 71, 178–79, 182. For Baptist views on baptism, see O. C. S. Wallace, *What Baptists Believe* (Nashville: Southern Baptist Convention Sunday School Board, 1913) 151–57; and Holifield, *Gentlemen Theologians*, 166–75. For Presbyterian views, see Balmer and Fitzmier, *Presbyterians*, 14. For Methodist views, see James E. Kirby, Russell E. Richey, and Kenneth E. Rowe, *The Methodists* (Westport CT: Greenwood Press, 1996) 165, 178, 252. The significance of baptism for Catholics is explained in Williams, *What Americans*

Hiram Talbert Holt

Believing that "every one should be at his post at this time to defend his country," Hiram Talbert Holt enlisted as a private in the Suggsville (Alabama) Grays early in 1861. When the conflict began in April he was already on duty, manning the ramparts of Fort Morgan at Mobile Bay. Except for a short stint at Fort Pillow, Tennessee, during the spring of 1862, Holt remained in the Mobile area until April 1863, when his regiment, the 38th Alabama Infantry, reinforced the Army of Tennessee at Tullahoma. Holt, who had received a promotion to sergeant, fought in the desperate engagements of that army until his death near Dalton, Georgia, in February 1864.[48]

Holt was, like Guerrant and Poché, a Christian neophyte at the war's outset. Choctaw Corner, lying in the northernmost part of Clarke County, Alabama, was his home. At the time of his birth, 16 July 1835, it was a thriving little community of small farmers and planters who engaged mostly in the production of cotton. Although not one of Alabama's black-belt counties, Clarke had a sizable slave population, almost equal in number to the county's white population. The northern part of Clarke was hillier than other parts of the

---

Believe, 43–44; and Roderick Strange, *The Catholic Faith* (New York/Oxford: Oxford University Press, 1986) 86–88.

[48] Jack G. Dewitt to Talbert Holt, 18 May 1861 (typescript), Robert Partin Papers, Draughon Library, Auburn University, Alabama. The date Holt enlisted in the Suggsville Grays is unknown, but the 7 March 1861 issue of the *Clarke County Journal* lists him as a private in the company. His service record shows that he enlisted 1 April 1861 but this must have been when his regiment, the 2nd Alabama (later consolidated with the 38th Alabama), was mustered into Confederate service, since Holt was garrisoned at Fort Morgan long before then. See Compiled Service Records, 2nd Alabama Infantry. Holt's service record does not record his promotion to sergeant, but in a letter to his wife he said that he was acting sergeant major. See Talbert Holt to Carrie Holt, 22 August 1862, Partin Papers. Other information on his service is in Talbert Holt to Carrie Holt, 13 April 1863, Partin Papers; and Robert Partin, "A Confederate Sergeant's Report to His Wife During the Campaign from Tullahoma to Dalton," *Tennessee Historical Quarterly* 12 (December 1953): 308.

county and the farms there were on average smaller. One of these small farms belonged to Talbert Holt's father, Lewis.[49]

Information on Lewis Holt and his family in the antebellum years is sketchy. What evidence there is indicates that he and his wife, Sarah, migrated to Alabama and settled in the vicinity of Choctaw Corner about the time of the War of 1812. There he acquired a small farm on which he grew corn and raised livestock, particularly swine and sheep. Lewis owned one slave. By 1850 the Holts had seven children. When his two boys—John and Talbert—came of age, Lewis gave each some acreage, while retaining a portion for his own needs. John, the older son, prospered: by 1860 his farm was valued at $3,000 and he had nine slaves. Talbert, however, split his time between farming and teaching school, and evidently struggled as a farmer. According to the 1860 census, he produced no crops. In a letter to his wife from Fort Morgan in early 1862, Holt acknowledged their indigence: "Although we are poor, yet with our love to sustain each other, by the blessing of God we will come out of poverty and live oh! how happily."[50]

---

[49] Holt manuscript, 13, Partin Papers; John S. Graham, *History of Clarke County* (Greenville SC: Southern Historical Press, 1994) 6, 201; David S. Akens, "Clarke County to 1860" (M.A. thesis, University of Alabama, 1956) 41, 70–72, 75, 87; T. H. Ball, *A Glance into the Great South-East, or, Clarke County, Alabama, and Its Surroundings, from 1540 to 1877* (1882; reprint, Tuscaloosa: Willo Publishing Company, 1962) 248–50.

[50] Holt manuscript, 5, Partin Papers. Lewis Holt's farm in 1850 consisted of 80 improved acres and 140 unimproved acres, the value of which was $1,500 according to the Seventh Census, 1850, Manuscript Returns of Productions of Agriculture, Clarke County, Alabama, 865. The Seventh Census, 1850, Manuscript Returns of Slaves, Clarke County, Alabama, 142, lists Lewis as owning one male slave. Although the Holts had seven children, only six resided on the family farm in 1850—Talbert and five sisters. See Seventh Census, 1850, Manuscript Returns of Free Inhabitants, Clarke County, Alabama, 206. Lewis, John, and Talbert all lived next to each other in 1860. The census manuscripts indicate that Lewis' generous gift to his sons was given sometime during the 1850s, for his real estate value decreased significantly between 1850 and 1860. See Eighth Census, 1860, Manuscript Returns of Free Inhabitants, Clarke County, Alabama, 581. John Holt owned nine slaves in 1860, while Lewis still owned one. See Eighth Census, 1860, Manuscript Returns of Slaves, Clarke County, Alabama, 439. According to the Eighth Census, 1860, Manuscript Returns of Productions of Agriculture, Clarke County, Alabama, 6, Talbert produced

Talbert owned no slaves and no clear record of his thoughts on the subject exists. It is nevertheless likely that he sanctioned the institution of slavery. Not only was he raised in a slave-holding family, he married into one; his father-in-law owned four slaves. More tellingly, after Talbert and his wife settled on their own farm, his father and older brother continued to use slave labor on their farms which were next to his own. Finding his family's slaves available, Holt may well have employed them on occasion for some task on his own farm.[51]

Illiterate himself, Talbert's father saw to it that his son received a good education. How long Talbert attended school is unknown, but his 1858 teaching contract suggests that he attended for a number of years and was an excellent pupil, for in it he agreed to teach eleven subjects, including Latin, algebra, metaphysics and philosophy. He was apparently a strict disciplinarian: his list of classroom rules prohibited talking, moving about and fighting. Rule number six prohibited boys and girls from fraternizing. Talbert, however, must have exempted himself from this last rule. He courted and, in September 1859, married one of his pupils, Carrie. Talbert's wife was the daughter of his pastor, L. L. DeWitt.[52]

Because the relevant church records have been destroyed, very little is known about the Holt family's religious background. Evidently, within a few years after arriving in Alabama, Lewis and Sarah joined the New Hope Baptist Church. The 1848 Bethel Baptist Association Minutes list Lewis Holt as a deacon and lay-delegate from that church. Lewis must have been a well-respected and pious member of the church for a number of years to have attained such an

---

no crops but did claim twenty-five swine, two cows, and one horse. Talbert's admission was made in Talbert Holt to Carrie Holt, 11 February 1862, Partin Papers.

[51] Eighth Census, 1860, Manuscript Returns of Slaves, Clarke County, Alabama, 444.

[52] That Lewis was illiterate is indicated by his inability to write his name on the probate records of his son John. See Estate of John Holt, 12 December 1865, Deed Book M, 1864–1866, 161, Probate Office, Clarke County, Alabama. For more on Talbert's duties as a teacher, see Talbert Holt school contract, 16 October 1858 (typescript); and Holt manuscript, 7, both in Partin Papers.

important leadership position. Unlike the more hierarchical Presbyterian and Methodist Churches, in the Baptist faith each congregation managed its own affairs and had a loose affiliation, if any, with other churches or associations. With no Presbytery or District to oversee them, deacons and other lay-leaders, as well as the congregation as a whole, played a more prominent role in Baptist churches than in other denominations. Furthermore, as a church leader, Lewis undoubtedly saw to it that his entire family attended services regularly. The little evidence available about Talbert's spiritual progression indicates that he experienced a conversion and joined the Baptist Church sometime in 1860, a few months after his marriage to Carrie. Moreover, it is clear that by the time he left Choctaw Corner for Fort Morgan in the spring of 1861, his faith had developed considerably. The religious reflections he included in his wartime letters were those of a serious-minded and devout Christian believer.[53]

Giles Buckner Cooke

On 17 April 1861, the day his home state of Virginia seceded from the Union, Giles Buckner ("Buck") Cooke enlisted in the state's military forces at Norfolk. Later that month he took part in a raid on the Norfolk Naval Yard in which the Rebels captured a large supply of gunpowder. After escorting the powder to Richmond, Cooke joined the staff of Brigadier General Philip St. George Cocke as aide-de-camp, thus beginning a four-year stint as a Confederate staff officer. He served as assistant adjutant-general or inspector-general

---

[53] *Minutes of the Twenty-Eighth Annual Meeting of the Bethel Baptist Association, South Alabama… in Clarke County, 1848* (Tuscaloosa: n.p., 1848) 1. In Baptist churches, the entire congregation met as necessary to discuss church business, elect deacons and pastors, and discipline members. The role of local Baptist congregations in the governing of their churches is further illustrated in Wayne Flynt, *Alabama Baptists: Southern Baptists in the Heart of Dixie* (Tuscaloosa: University of Alabama Press, 1998) 24, 36–49. In Talbert's obituary, published in the *Clarke County Journal*, 5 May 1864, his chaplain stated that Holt had been a member of the Baptist Church for four years. Furthermore, it was common practice for Baptist churches to admit only those who had made a profession of faith. See Williams, *What Americans Believe*, 249.

on various generals' staffs, including those of Braxton Bragg, Samuel
Jones, P. G. T. Beauregard and Robert E. Lee. As a member of Lee's
staff, Cooke—who had risen to the rank of major—endured the siege
of Petersburg, suffered wounds at the Battle of Sayler's Creek and
witnessed the surrender of the Army of Northern Virginia.[54]

Early in the war the prospect of death greatly troubled Cooke.
In May 1861 he attended an Episcopal service in which he heard
"one of the most appropriate sermons I ever heard in my life" on the
peace of mind found in Christ. Within two weeks, Cooke professed
faith in Christ and took "up the cross of my Lord and Saviour."[55]

Unlike the six Christians previously described, Cooke was a
wartime convert. He preserved an extensive wartime and postwar
chronicle of his life. For the antebellum period, however, no such
autobiographical record exists. The story of Cooke's life before 1861
can be pieced together only from other sources.

Buck Cooke was born 13 May 1838 in Portsmouth, Virginia.
His father, John Kearns Cooke, owned fifteen slaves and operated a
lumber mill in Portsmouth valued at $19,400 in 1850. His father's
business success afforded young Buck a good education. He attended
some of the best private schools in Portsmouth before departing for
the Virginia Military Institute in 1855.[56]

At VMI some of Buck's preconversion personality was unveiled.
A former VMI executive officer, William Couper, remembered the
young man in a letter to Cooke's biographer and nephew

[54] James M. McPherson, *Battle Cry of Freedom: The Civil War Era* (New
York/Oxford: Oxford University Press, 1988) 279; Giles Buckner Cooke diary, 19,
24, 29 April 1861; and 6, 9 April 1865, Giles Buckner Cooke Papers, Virginia
Historical Society, Richmond; Compiled Service Records, General and Staff
Officers.
[55] Giles B. Cooke questionnaire, 3, Giles B. Cooke folder, Virginia Military
Institute; Cooke diary, 19 May and 2 June 1861.
[56] Cooke questionnaire, 1, Cooke folder; Seventh Census, 1850, Manuscript
Returns of Free Inhabitants, Norfolk County, Virginia, 181; Seventh Census, 1850,
Manuscript Returns of Slaves, Norfolk County, Virginia, 329. Evidently, operating
the lumber mill was John Cooke's primary occupation, for he does not appear in the
1850 Manuscript Returns of Productions of Agriculture for Norfolk County. Cooke
attended four private schools before attending Virginia Military Institute. See Cooke
questionnaire, 1, Cooke folder.

as—delicately speaking—one "who had lots of pep." Cooke evinced a
carefree attitude toward his studies. He spent four unimpressive years
at the institution, graduating twenty-second out of twenty-nine in the
class of 1859. He did, however, best most of his classmates when it
came to demerits. His count in that field far exceeded the average for
the class. Cooke's generally lackadaisical attitude often got him into
trouble. In addition to frequent pranks, such as barking like a dog in
class when the instructor's back was turned, he had occasional
confrontations with professors. Once, in Professor Thomas J.
Jackson's class, an angry dispute erupted between Cooke and Jackson
after the student had completed a problem incorrectly on the
blackboard. Soon afterward, Cooke stormed out of the classroom.
(Cooke never forgot the encounter. Following his conversion, the
former student apologized to the former professor when he saw him
in a Confederate camp after the Battle of First Manassas.) Cooke's
escapades, however, went beyond classroom gags. On more than one
occasion he and some of his fellow cadets, disguised in civilian
clothes, slipped away from the Institute and into town where they
drank to the point of intoxication. As a result of his repeated
misconduct, Cooke lost what rank he had attained at VMI and was
dismissed at least once, only to be reinstated later.[57]

Graduating from VMI in July 1859, Cooke decided to become
an attorney and read law under Congressman Roger Pryor in
Petersburg, Virginia. To defray his expenses there, Cooke taught in a
private school. He remained in Petersburg until the war broke out in
1861.[58]

Little is known about Cooke's religious history up to 1861.
Although he was an Episcopalian and undoubtedly attended services
while at VMI (the cadets regularly marched to Sunday services in

---

[57] William Couper to Giles B. Palmer, 22 March 1940, Cooke Papers; 1859 class
ranking, Cooke folder; Giles B. Cooke Biography, by Giles B. Palmer, (typescript),
chaps. 2 and 3; Minutes of Board of Visitors, Virginia Military Institute, 1 July 1857;
F. H. Smith to John K. Cooke, 27 May 1858; and John K. Cooke to F. H. Smith, 31
May 1858, all in Cooke Papers.
[58] Cooke questionnaire, 2, Cooke folder; Cooke biography, chap. 3, Cooke
Papers.

town), he had neither been baptized nor confirmed in the Church. Indeed, his actions while at VMI suggest strongly that he was not much concerned with religion.[59]

Alexander Tedford Barclay

Barely seventeen years old in June 1861, Alexander Tedford ("Ted") Barclay enlisted as a private in the Liberty Hall Volunteers, Company I, 4th Virginia Infantry. This company was composed almost exclusively of students, recent graduates and professors from Washington College in Lexington, Virginia. The 4th Virginia, along with four other Virginia regiments, constituted the "Stonewall Brigade," that won renown at First Manassas. Serving as a private for most of the war, Barclay earned a promotion to lieutenant in April 1864 but hardly had time to assume the duties of his new office before his capture during the Spotsylvania campaign in May 1864. He spent the remainder of the war in a Union prison camp.[60]

During the spring of 1862, Barclay experienced a religious conversion. He wrote to his sister shortly after the Battle of Kernstown: "The voice of a Mother and Sister, the early death of a brother, [and] two bloody battlefields all warn me of the shortness and uncertainty of life." Concerned about his spiritual condition, Barclay discussed the subject with Hugh White, a fellow Volunteer and the son of his home-church pastor. Soon after his conversation with White, Barclay made public his profession of Christian faith.[61]

Little information exists about Barclay during the antebellum period. Ted was born on 16 May 1844 at Sycamore, the family's plantation near Lexington. His father, Alexander Barclay, was considered one of the foremost citizens of Lexington, his ancestors having been some of the earliest settlers in Rockbridge County. Alexander died in 1848 and Ted's mother, Mary Elizabeth Barclay,

[59] Cooke biography, chaps. 2 and 4, Cooke Papers.
[60] Lexington (Virginia) *Gazette*, 15 May 1874; Compiled Service Records, 4th Virginia Infantry; Faust, *Encyclopedia of the Civil War*, 724.
[61] Charles W. Turner, ed., *Ted Barclay, Liberty Hall Volunteers: Letters from the Stonewall Brigade, 1861–1864* (Rockbridge VA: Rockbridge Publishing Company, 1992) 60; Lexington (Virginia) *Gazette*, 15 May 1874.

raised him and his siblings on the plantation. Barclay's antebellum life revolved around his family and their home in Rockbridge. After the death of his father, Ted took on much of the responsibility for overseeing the family's fifteen slaves and superintending the plantation's agricultural production, which was markedly diverse. According to the 1860 census, the Barclays grew wheat, corn, clover, potatoes and fruit on their three hundred acres of improved farmland. In addition, they owned several horses, cows, swine and sheep. The plantation produced a significant amount of butter and wool. Ted enrolled in Washington College in 1859 and attended there until the summer of 1861, when he withdrew to enlist in the Liberty Hall Volunteers.[62]

The Barclays were long-time members of the venerable Presbyterian Church of Lexington. Alexander Barclay assumed a church leadership position in 1843 when he was elected elder. In the Presbyterian Church, elders and the pastor made up the Session, which concerned itself with such important duties as the organization of worship, admission of new members and church discipline. To have attained such a position testifies to Alexander's piety and faithfulness, for elders were elected by their fellow church members and examined by the Session. Other Barclays served in leadership positions in the church as well. Ted's older brother, John, was elected deacon on the same ballot as VMI professor Thomas J. Jackson in 1857. Although there is no record that Ted was admitted to the Presbyterian Church before his conversion in the spring of 1862, his family's stature in the congregation suggests that the Barclays were faithful members and attended services regularly. In an address delivered at the completion of a postwar renovation of the church, Ted confirmed as much when he lovingly recalled his childhood

---

[62] Lexington (Virginia) *Rockbridge County News*, 2 December 1915; Presbyterian Church, Lexington, Virginia, Register of Members, 1775–1920, 72; Eighth Census, 1860, Manuscript Returns of Slaves, Rockbridge County, Virginia, 210; Eighth Census, 1860, Manuscript Returns of Production of Agriculture, Rockbridge County, Virginia, 100; *Catalogue of Washington College, Lexington, Virginia, for the Collegiate Year Ending June, 1860* (Richmond: MacFarlane & Fergusson, 1860) 5.

pastor, under whose guidance "many of us...grew to manhood and womanhood."[63]

Robert Augustus Moore

Approximately six weeks after the war began, Robert A. Moore traveled from Holly Springs, Mississippi, to nearby Corinth and enlisted as a private in the Confederate Guards, Company G, 17th Mississippi Infantry Regiment. The 17th Mississippi belonged to the hard-fighting Barksdale Brigade that participated in a number of battles as part of the Army of Northern Virginia. Moore served most of the war as a common soldier, evidently garnering the respect of his comrades-in-arms who elected him a second lieutenant in July 1863. Lieutenant Moore, however, would not enjoy his new position long: he was killed in action during the Chickamauga campaign in September 1863.[64]

During the winter of 1862–63, Moore participated in the large-scale revivals at Fredericksburg, Virginia. Weighed down with sin, he prayed for mercy and received Christ: "I have to-night found Christ in the pardon of my sins. Oh! what a relief.... I can recommend the atoning blood of Christ to all."[65]

Moore was born 2 July 1838 in Marshall County, Mississippi. Cotton was the chief product of this north Mississippi county. By 1850 Robert's father, Austin, had acquired a one hundred sixty acre farm on which he engaged primarily in growing that crop. The elder Moore evidently enjoyed some success and by 1860 he had more than doubled the size of his farm, expanding his cotton production by 235 percent. Enslaved blacks comprised a majority of Marshall County's

---

[63] Oren F. Morton, *A History of Rockbridge County, Virginia* (Staunton VA: The McClure Company, 1920) 177; Robert F. Hunter, *Lexington Presbyterian Church, 1789–1989* (Lexington VA: self published, 1991) 18, 23–24; Presbyterian Church, Lexington, Virginia, Register of Members, 72, 88, 111; Balmer and Fitzmier, *Presbyterians*, 15. Barclay delivered his address in 1899 after the renovation of the Lexington Presbyterian Church. For excerpts of his address, see Hunter, *Lexington Presbyterian Church*, 108–10.

[64] Compiled Service Records, 17th Mississippi Infantry.

[65] James W. Silver, ed., *A Life for the Confederacy: As Recorded in the Pocket Diaries of Pvt. Robert A. Moore* (Jackson TN: McCowat-Mercer Press, 1959) 135–36.

population and it is no surprise that the Moores owned as many as fifteen persons.[66]

Information about Moore's prewar life is scant. He evidently spent most of it on the family's plantation. He probably attended one of the area's local academies, for his penmanship and literacy indicate that he was relatively well-educated. It is possible that his desire was to be a planter; by the time he was twenty-one, Robert was serving as his father's overseer.[67]

The Moores attended the Wesley Chapel Methodist Church near Holly Springs. The church was established in 1845, just eight years after the Moores first arrived in the county. The church register suggests that his father and mother may have been charter members. As long-time members of the Methodist Church, Robert's parents presumably provided a Christian home for their children. Robert's own words testify to the piety of his father, who evidently instructed him regarding religious matters. On a Sunday in June 1861, after a dress parade in camp, Private Moore recorded in his diary: "It seemed very strange to see men out with guns on the Sabbath. Pa does not allow us to handle a gun on Sunday." The fact that during the 1850s several of the Moore children, including Robert, joined Wesley Chapel suggests not only that the Moore family attended church regularly, but that the parents emphasized the importance of church membership. It should be noted, however, that unlike most other evangelical denominations, the nineteenth-century

---

[66] Ruth Watkins, "Reconstruction in Marshall County," in *Publications of the Mississippi Historical Society*, ed. Franklin L. Riley, 12 (1912): 155–56; *Biographical and Historical Memoirs of Mississippi*, 2:464; Silver, *A Life for the Confederacy*, 10; Seventh Census, 1850, Manuscript Returns of Productions of Agriculture, Marshall County, Mississippi, 121; Eighth Census, 1860, Manuscript Returns of Productions of Agriculture, Marshall County, Mississippi, 19. The 1850 slave schedule indicates that Austin Moore owned fifteen slaves, but he is not listed in the 1860 slave schedule. Since his agricultural production increased dramatically between 1850 and 1860, however, it is safe to assume that his slave holdings increased as well and that his omission from the 1860 schedule was a census-taker's error. See Seventh Census, 1850, Manuscript Returns of Slaves, Marshall County, Mississippi, 26.

[67] Silver, *A Life for the Confederacy*, 10; Eighth Census, 1860, Manuscript Returns of Free Inhabitants, Marshall County, Mississippi, 62.

Methodist Church did not require a profession of faith as a prerequisite for admission. Believing that the ultimate objective was to lead persons to repentance and a profession of faith, Methodists frequently admitted "seekers" as conditional members of the Church—enjoying full fellowship within congregations, if not the entire range of membership privileges—in order to help them along to a conversion. Predictably, other evangelical denominations criticized the Methodists for allegedly embracing low admission standards and the willingness to admit just about anyone into the life of the Church.[68]

Despite having being raised in a Christian home and his membership in the Methodist Church, Moore implied in his diary that he was not the ardent Methodist he appeared to be. Away from home, possibly for the first time, he seems to have succumbed to temptations, particularly drinking. His propensity to sin, however, would not endure.[69]

During the antebellum period, Alfred Fielder, William Nugent and William Pendleton all exhibited characteristics consistent with those delineated by the Apostle Paul in Second Timothy. As long-time Christians, these men encountered many opportunities for their

---

[68] Wesley Chapel listed its admissions chronologically, with Austin and Elizabeth admitted as the seventh and eighth members, respectively. See Wesley Chapel Methodist Church, Holly Springs, Mississippi, Church Register, 1837–1936 (microfilm), Mississippi Department of Archives and History, Jackson. Moore's observation of the Sunday dress parade is recorded in Silver, *A Life for the Confederacy*, 28–29. The church register lists Robert's two sisters, Zenobia and Martha, as members 50 and 115, respectively, and it shows Robert as number 250. During what was traditionally a six-month probationary period, the "seekers" met weekly for religious instruction, and the class leaders reported their progress to the pastor. Although technically the probationers were not professing Christians, they were expected to conduct themselves as such. Admission requirements for the nineteenth-century Methodist Church are explained in *The Doctrines and Discipline of the Methodist Episcopal Church*, 87; Kirby, *Methodists*, 177–79; Williams, *What Americans Believe*, 278.

[69] The fact that Moore attended services in the army before his conversion supports the supposition that he attended church regularly at home. See Silver, *A Life for the Confederacy*, 28, 36, 40, 42, 48, 54, 60. His drinking is noted in ibid., 51, 56, and his religious conversion is described in ibid., 136.

faith to grow during the prewar period. Nugent and Pendleton learned to rely on God for that which was beyond their control, something they would do often during the war. Furthermore, these men remained steadfast in their faith and exhibited a degree of personal sanctity. Fielder demonstrated his piety and love for the Methodist Church when he deeded a portion of his family's property for a new church building. Nugent's devoutness was likewise unquestionable. Hearing of Nellie's adventures while on her trip, Nugent not only criticized them but also resolved to assimilate her beliefs to his own. Meanwhile, Pendleton's faith grew as he endured the difficulties of life, including financial hardship and the death of a loved one.

All but Nugent, the youngest of the three, played an active role in their churches. Fielder served as a trustee at Mt. Zion Church and as superintendent of the new building; and Parson Pendleton rendered godly service as rector. This is not to suggest that these men were the perfect model Christians, for they also exhibited attributes unbecoming of Christians. In his disagreement with the vestry of All Saint's Church, Pendleton acted proudly and belligerently. Nugent's reaction to Nellie's adventures could be characterized as both angry and judgmental. Perhaps what is most interesting about their antebellum faith is that during hardships encountered, these Christians turned to and relied on God. As God proved faithful in their circumstances, their willingness to trust in him increased. This poses an interesting question: if these antebellum hardships—which seem slight when compared to adversity inherent in warfare—strengthened the faith of Christians, how much more would faith increase as a result of the tribulations endured in four years of civil war?

Edward Guerrant, Felix Poché, and Talbert Holt were younger and less mature Christians than the immediately preceding trio. Guerrant and Holt, raised in religious families, underwent salvation experiences that elevated them to a higher state spiritually. Poché, raised in a devout Catholic family, engaged in some shenanigans during his college years that give the impression he may have taken his religious responsibilities lightly. After he graduated, settled into his law practice and married a devout Catholic, he exhibited a renewed faith. During the 1850s, the religious faith of these men took on new meaning, but their ages and spiritual development were such that they could not be characterized as mature Christians. They had yet to undergo many of the experiences that test and build a Christian's faith over a lifetime.

It is in the stories of Giles Cooke, Ted Barclay and Robert Moore that the most dramatic impact of war on one's faith is vividly illustrated. These men attended church regularly before the war, were well-versed in the doctrine and discipline of their churches and probably conducted themselves morally for the most part. They were not, however, true Christians as defined by their own denominations. As with tens of thousands of other Confederate soldiers, the adversity and uncertainty of war incited within these three men a desire to be something more than "pew-warmers," to move beyond their spiritual complacency and attain the solace and assurance only a profession of believing and committed faith in Christ could bring.

Chapter 2

A Firm Foundation
Justification of War and
Steadfastness in Faith

Watch ye, stand fast in the faith, quit you like men, be strong.
—1 Corinthians 16:13 (KJV)

Hundreds of thousands of Southerners took up arms during the Civil War to defend the Confederate cause, as did the nine men who are the focus of this study. As Christians, however, they had to reconcile their participation in the war with their religious convictions. They resolved this dilemma by defining the war as just, a matter of self-defense against Northern aggression; it was their duty to fight. Like most other antebellum white Southerners, these men believed that the institution of slavery was ordained by God. These convictions persuaded the nine and most other Confederates that God blessed their cause and sanctioned their participation in the war.

When the six men who were already Christians arrived in the Southern army camps, they were overwhelmed by the abundance of immorality. Vice flourished among the soldiers, especially at the outset of the war. Drinking, gambling, swearing and stealing were common. Despite the pervasive immorality characterizing their new environments, these six Christians maintained their religious beliefs and continued their religious activities. They attended services, read their Bibles and prayed regularly. When the exigencies of war impeded these practices, they found other ways and opportunities to commune with God. The three soldiers who experienced wartime conversions also became unwavering in their convictions after professing faith. They too went out of their way to hear preaching, study Scripture and commune with God. As the war progressed, each of these nine soldiers remained steadfast in faith and demonstrated evidence of spiritual growth.

These nine Christian soldiers fought in the Civil War because they believed that the Southern cause was just. They viewed Yankees as invaders who intended to conquer the South and subjugate its people, a view they maintained throughout the conflict. Reverend William Pendleton, a mature Christian, considered his enemies "misguided" and earnestly prayed for them; but he wrote, "never, never, never would I submit to their iniquitous domination." Demoralizing Federal successes in the West in early 1862 led Pendleton, who was in winter quarters near Centreville, Virginia, to warn his wife: "Let people understand that not only degradation awaits the entire South, but utter ruin and misery if we ever yield. Our men will be imprisoned, banished, and butchered, our women insulted, dishonored, and reduced to the lowest condition, and what is left of our country will be ground to powder."[1]

December 1862 found Tennessean Alfred Fielder near Murfreesboro, Tennessee, with a Union army between him and his home. Learning that Yankees had been to his farm in Friendship and had confiscated his slaves, an incensed Fielder wrote in his diary: "They are stealing our property burning our houses and endeavoring by every pos[si]ble means to sub[ju]gate us and make of us hewers of wood and drawers of water and place over us such task masters as they may see fit." When a Union force was advancing on General Braxton Bragg's Confederates near Murfreesboro later that month, Fielder commented in his diary: "Our enemies are said to be

---

[1] Susan P. Lee, *Memoirs of William Nelson Pendleton, D.D.* (Philadelphia: J. B. Lippincott Company, 1893) 136–37, 171; William Pendleton to Anzolette Pendleton, 23 February 1862, William Nelson Pendleton Papers, Southern Historical Collection, University of North Carolina, Chapel Hill.

advancing upon us with heavy force with the intent to Subjugate or Kill us and [we are] not…willing to submit to the rule of a tyrant."[2]

William Nugent, having been apart from Nellie for three years, was wearied by their separation. In the fall of 1864 he wrote that although he longed to be with her,

> a cruel, relentless war is waged for our annihilation, and unless we present a bold front to the enemy, contesting every inch of ground, we may expect nothing but vassalage and slavery all our lives. Our rights and privileges will be totally destroyed and military governors and Yankee judges will govern us, while our lands will be parcelled out among a horde of foreign adventurers and mercenary soldiers.[3]

A war of Northern aggression necessitated protecting one's native land. At Winchester, Virginia, just prior to General Stonewall Jackson's legendary Shenandoah Valley campaign, Ted Barclay wrote his sister and told her that he had yet to re-enlist but assured her that he would continue fighting, "so long as the abominable flag of despotism hovers over a fort on Southern soil. Rather would I have my bones rot on the hillside than live a slave for it would be the most degraded slavery." Robert Moore also was fighting to protect his home against Yankee invaders. In January 1862 he concluded that the Rebels had much to celebrate in "driving from our soil the ruthless invader who is seeking to reduce us to abject slavery." Edward Guerrant was fighting to free his home state of Kentucky from the "most despotic and cruel tyranny." In February 1865, as the end loomed near for the South, Guerrant remained defiant: "submission! N-e-v-e-r. With a thousand years between each letter and Eternity before the period!"[4]

[2] Ann York Franklin, ed., *The Civil War Diaries of Capt. Alfred Tyler Fielder, 12th Tennessee Regiment Infantry, Company B, 1861–1865* (Louisville KY: self published, 1996) 94, 96. For Fielder's other comments about Northern aggression, see ibid., 42, 52, 74.

[3] William M. Cash and Lucy Somerville Howorth, eds., *My Dear Nellie: The Civil War Letters of William L. Nugent to Eleanor Smith Nugent* (Jackson: University Press of Mississippi, 1977) 196.

[4] James W. Silver, ed., *A Life for the Confederacy: As Recorded in the Pocket Diaries of Pvt. Robert A. Moore* (Jackson TN: McCowat-Mercer Press, 1959) 91. For Moore's

These men, convinced that the war's root cause was Northern aggression, concluded that the South was fighting in self-defense. In their view, such a stance was scriptural. Although most of the men in this study quickly resolved any reservations they may have had about serving, the mature Christians—Nugent and Pendleton in particular struggled with reconciling their participation in the conflict and their religious convictions. Further along in their spiritual development, these men recognized inconsistencies between the conduct of war and the teachings of Christ. Nugent, overwhelmed by patriotic feelings early in the war after observing a parade of volunteers in Vicksburg, wrote Nellie: "I feel that I would like to shoot a Yankee, and yet I know that this would not be in harmony with the Spirit of Christianity, that teaches to love our enemies and do good to them that despitefully use us and entreat us." He maintained his belief that war, under most circumstances, violated God's laws; however, he believed that fighting in self-defense was an exception. Struck by war's devastation while marching through Middle Tennessee in May 1863, Nugent wrote from Spring Hill,

> War, pestilence and famine usually succeed one another in the order named; and are doubtless intended to remind us that the first is utterly inconsistent with the duties we owe the Supreme Being.... War is altogether an unmixed evil, and can never be justified unless in self-defense; and the only thing that can at all reconcile me to our war is the fact of its being for our homes and friends, our altars and our liberties.[5]

---

other remarks about Northern aggression, see ibid., 14, 97, 137. See also Charles W. Turner, ed., *Ted Barclay, Liberty Hall Volunteers: Letters from the Stonewall Brigade, 1861–1864* (Rockbridge VA: Rockbridge Publishing Company, 1992) 56–57, 135; and Edward O. Guerrant diary, 20 December 1861; 8 March 1862; 15 February, 29 April 1863; and 12 February 1865, Edward O. Guerrant Papers, Southern Historical Collection, University of North Carolina, Chapel Hill

[5] Cash and Howorth, *My Dear Nellie*, 45–46, 109. For Nugent's other comments about his fighting in self-defense, see ibid., 70–71, 87, 129, 148. Christ said, "Love your enemies, bless them that curse you, do good to them that hate you, and pray for them which despitefully use you, and persecute you" (Matt 5:44, KJV). He also said, "Blessed *are* [emphasis mine] the peacemakers: for they shall be called the children of God" (Matt 5:9, KJV).

Pendleton, too, realized the religious dilemma posed by the war. Having reluctantly decided to become captain of the Rockbridge Artillery, he wrote in May 1861: "Thus to take part in the dreadful work of death is to me much the severest trial of my life. Loving peace, praying for peace, preaching peace…I find myself, in the very name of the Prince of Peace, obliged to see my own dear country subdued, disgraced, and ruined, and my wife and daughters exposed to brutal outrage worse than death." After much reflection and prayer, he concluded that "defensive war cannot on gospel grounds…be condemned." Despite his belief the war was justified, the parson continued to be bothered by his decision to serve. He admitted to his daughter in a November 1862 letter: "It is a strange position for a servant of the Prince of Peace and a minister of the gospel of Peace…. I trust the blessing of the Peacemaker will not be denied me…. He sees that I desire in all sincerity to be a faithful soldier of the Cross, while trying also to be a useful soldier of a much-wronged country."[6]

As a mature Christian, Fielder too must have encountered a sense of inconsistency between war and Christianity. He appeared to have resolved any dilemmas recognized by July 1861, for there are no references to it in his diary. Manning the trenches surrounding Corinth, Mississippi, in May 1862, just days before General P. G. T. Beauregard evacuated the strategic railroad town, Fielder wrote that he and other Southerners were fighting "for our homes, our wives and our families and all that is sacred and all we want [is] to be let alone."[7]

Private Talbert Holt, a Christian neophyte, also may have pondered the incongruity of killing and Christianity. After two monotonous months at Fort Morgan, Holt wrote to Carrie in May 1861, "I hope that the white flag of peace may soon be unfurled wafting us backward to our homes to hear of wars no more. Why

---

[6] William Pendleton to unnamed correspondent, 1 and 28 May 1861; to Alexander Pendleton, 19 February 1862; to Anzolette Pendleton, 23 February 1862; and to unnamed daughter, 27 November 1862, all in Pendleton Papers.

[7] Franklin, *Fielder Diaries*, 52.

should man war upon his brother? But so it is and our duty is to drive our invaders back from our homes." Evidently he quickly put to rest any reservations he may have had regarding military service, for he was at his post defending Mobile Bay before the bombardment of Fort Sumter.[8]

The Christian Confederate soldiers in this study believed they were upholding the legacy of the American Revolution. They maintained that Lincoln was a tyrant, as was King George eighty-five years before. They made frequent references to liberty and freedom in their writings. These men held that the Confederacy was the true heir to the nation established by the Founding Fathers. On 4 July 1863, enjoying a furlough among friends near Pattonsville, Virginia, Guerrant reflected on the historic date:

> [America] died…[in] 1861—aged 85 years! Left one heir and glorious offspring, - in Dixie! Clothed in garments dyed in blood that youthful Child of Freedom (C. S. A.) stands today in proud and lofty defiance of the Tyrant's tremendous power…. This is the anniversary of her mother's birth, a day made memorable by a great and gallant people, and its memories disgraced by a degenerate offspring.

This conception of the North undoubtedly served to motivate Guerrant to enlist in the Confederate army and helped him justify his

---

[8] Talbert Holt to Carrie Holt, 3 May, 17 July 1861; and 5 February 1862 (typescript), Robert Partin Papers, Draughon Library, Auburn University, Alabama. Other soldiers in this study also believed that they were fighting in self-defense. See Silver, *A Life for the Confederacy*, 24, 26, 101; Turner, *Letters from the Stonewall Brigade*, 143; Edwin C. Bearss, ed., *A Louisiana Confederate: Diary of Felix Pierre Poché*, trans. Eugenie Watson Somdal (Natchitoches LA: Louisiana Studies Institute, Northwestern State University, 1972) 3–4, 142; Guerrant diary, 20 December 1861; 13 November 1862; 31 January and 15 February, 29 April, 14 May 1863; and 5 April 1865; Giles Buckner Cooke diary, 17 May 1862, Giles Buckner Cooke Papers, Virginia Historical Society, Richmond; Lee, *Memoirs of Pendleton*, 136–37, 142–43, 191. Self-defense was the motivation of many Confederates. See James M. McPherson, "Afterword," in *Religion and the American Civil War*, ed. Randall M. Miller, Harry S. Stout and Charles Reagan Wilson (New York/Oxford: Oxford University Press, 1998) 410; James M. McPherson, *For Cause and Comrades: Why Men Fought in the Civil War* (New York/Oxford: Oxford University Press, 1997) 21; Steven E. Woodworth, *While God Is Marching On: The Religious World of Civil War Soldiers* (Lawrence: University Press of Kansas, 2001) 121, 128–32.

participation in the conflict. As he prepared to depart for the army in late 1861, he recorded in his diary: "Resistance to Tyrants is Obedience to God."[9]

These Christian Confederate soldiers also considered themselves to be true Americans. Captain Guerrant consistently noted in his diary significant days in American history, such as George Washington's birthday and the Fourth of July. On Washington's birthday in 1862, Guerrant wrote: "The ever memorable and glorious Anniversary of Washington's Birth Day. Strange.... What thoughts of mingled amazement and sorrow crowd our minds and burden our memories, as we reflect upon the past and present,: upon the labors of Washington and our Revolutionary sires...now overthrown."[10]

Meanwhile, near Leesburg, Virginia, hundreds of miles to the east, the 17th Mississippi was quartered for the winter. Early on the cold winter morning of Washington's birthday, Union artillery across the Potomac River began firing, about which Moore wrote in his diary: "The enemy commenced the firing of a salute very early this morning celebrating the anniversary of the birthday of George Washington, the fruits of whose labor they are now attempting to destroy."[11]

Fielder echoed these sentiments. On 4 July 1863 he reflected on the significance of the day: "This day 87 years ago our revolutionary ancestors signed what is called the 'Declaration of Independence' which embraces a goodly number of our grievances and breathes the sentaments of a number of us their children and grand-children." Believing that his regiment was about to be ordered to Virginia, Holt informed Carrie of his imminent departure from Alabama. Trying to offset this worrisome news, he encouraged her: "Would you, Carrie, if you could, recall me? No! No! But with the fire and spirit of '76

---

[9] Guerrant diary, 20 December 1861; and 4 July 1863; William C. Davis and Meredith L. Swentor, eds., *Bluegrass Confederate: The Headquarters Diary of Edward O. Guerrant* (Baton Rouge: Louisiana State University Press, 1999) 301–302.

[10] Guerrant diary, 22 February, 4 July, 21 August, 13 November 1862; and 30 January, 22 February 1863.

[11] Silver, *A Life for the Confederacy*, 26, 101, 103.

you will point me, though with tearful eyes, to the invaders of our soil and say fight till the last of your blood."[12]

For some, the sense of duty was overpowering. Concerned about the recent surrender of Port Hudson and possible Union incursions near his home, Felix Poché volunteered to serve with Brigadier General J. J. A. Alfred Mouton's brigade in southern Louisiana. He wrote that "it almost broke my heart to part with my dear Sélima, and...my little Maggie.... But still the voice of duty to my country was more imperative." Lieutenant Fielder too had strong feelings regarding duty. In December 1862, when his regiment and another were consolidated, he was given the option of continuing to serve or returning home to recruit. Although he had had no furlough for ten months, he chose to stay and serve in the consolidated regiment.[13]

Furthermore, these soldiers were critical of those men who could serve but did not. Nearly nine months after his arrival at Fort Morgan, Private Holt looked forward to the expiration of his one-year enlistment and planned to return to farming in Choctaw Corner. He wrote Carrie in December 1861, "It is a good thing to have a clear conscience, this I've got, I've done *my duty*. Now let some others...do theirs." Holt's sense of duty, however, was strong. Despite the desire to return home, he re-enlisted in March 1862. Recovering from fever in an infirmary in Marietta, Georgia, during the Atlanta campaign, Nugent wrote in a letter to Nellie that there was a "sense of depression continually working away at my heart"

---

[12] Franklin, *Fielder Diaries*, 26, 52, 127; Talbert Holt to Carrie Holt, 4 June, 22 July 1861; and 4 June 1862, Partin Papers. For other comparisons to the Revolutionary period, see Cooke diary, 16 May 1862; and 25 December 1864; Cash and Howorth, *My Dear Nellie*, 159; William Pendleton to unnamed correspondent, 1 May 1861; and to unnamed correspondent, 28 May 1861, both in Pendleton Papers; James M. McPherson, *What They Fought For, 1861–1865* (Baton Rouge: Louisiana State University Press, 1994) 9–12, 27–30; Reid Mitchell, *Civil War Soldiers* (New York: Viking Penguin, 1988) 2, 20–23; Charles Reagan Wilson, "Religion and the American Civil War in Comparative Perspective," in Miller, Stout, and Wilson, *Religion and the American Civil War*, 396.

[13] Bearss, *Louisiana Confederate*, 4–5, 91. Major General Nathaniel P. Banks's plans to conquer Lafourche Parish, near Poché's home, are described in Christopher G. Peña, *Touched by War: Battles Fought in the Lafourche District* (Thibodaux LA: C. G. P. Press, 1998) 354–56.

because large numbers of men were fighting and suffering. Only "a sense of duty and the sacredness of our cause" helped him maintain his resolve. In the final days of the war the men's sense of obligation had not abated. On 9 April 1865, unaware that General Lee had just surrendered the Army of Northern Virginia, Captain Fielder expressed his desire to continue serving (even as a private) if his position were eliminated in a consolidation of regiments.[14]

These nine men had little to say in their wartime journals and letters about slavery. During the three decades prior to the war, white Southerners had grown to accept the view that the institution was ordained by God. They argued not only that slavery had existed in biblical times, but also that the Bible sanctioned the institution: had it not instructed slaves to obey their masters? Northern clergymen, however, criticized slaveownership. They maintained that although servitude had existed during biblical times, American slavery was much worse and violated the "spirit" of the Bible. Disturbed by Northern ministers' characterization of slaveholding as sinful, Southern Christians parsed the Scriptures to justify it. Convinced that slavery was God-ordained, Southerners concluded that Northern religion was corrupted by politics and therefore displeasing to God. Indeed, most white Southern Christians likely agreed with Pendleton, who characterized Northern churches as "most unchristian." Well before the outbreak of hostilities, the sectional religious debate over slavery was passionate and fierce. Ultimately,

---

[14] Talbert Holt to Carrie Holt, 13, 25 April, 5 May, 2 December 1861; and 5 February, 4 June 1862, Partin Papers. Holt re-enlisted in the 38th Alabama Infantry Regiment. The 2nd Alabama was disbanded in May 1862. See Compiled Service Records, 38th Alabama Infantry, National Archives, Washington DC. Evidently Holt also criticized his brother-in-law, Jack Dewitt, for not serving. See Jack G. Dewitt to Talbert Holt, 18 May 1861; and Talbert Holt to Carrie Holt, 16 July, 2 December 1861, all in Partin Papers. See also Cash and Howorth, *My Dear Nellie*, 53, 185–86. Others indicated their strong sense of duty as well. See Guerrant diary, 20 January, 17 November 1862; Cooke diary, 16 May 1862; Lee, *Memoirs of Pendleton*, 143; William Pendleton to unnamed correspondent, 31 May 1861, Pendleton Papers; Franklin, *Fielder Diaries*, 225. On "duty" as a motivator for Civil War soldiers on both sides, see McPherson, *For Cause and Comrades*, 22–25; and McPherson, *What They Fought For*, 11–12.

these led to to a split in the Methodist, Baptist, and Presbyterian Churches.[15]

What little these nine men did say about slavery, however, further confirms the presumption that they supported the institution. Parson Pendleton maintained that slavery was not "inherently and

---

[15] William Pendleton to unnamed correspondent, 1 May 1861, Pendleton Papers; W. G. Bean, *Stonewall's Man: Sandie Pendleton* (Chapel Hill: University of North Carolina, 1959) 35. In the early 1800s, Southern evangelicals had criticized slave ownership but eventually abandoned such criticism to gain more acceptance among Southerners. See Christine L. Heyrman, *Southern Cross: The Beginnings of the Bible Belt* (New York: Alfred A. Knopf, 1997). A discussion of Southern Christians' reaction to Northern attacks and their reliance on Scripture to justify slavery is in Woodworth, *While God Is Marching On*, 16–20; Donald G. Mathews, *Religion in the Old South* (Chicago: University of Chicago Press, 1977) 152, 155, 157–59; Eugene D. Genovese, "Religion in the Collapse of the American Union," in Miller, Stout, and Wilson, *Religion and the American Civil War*, 74, 78; Anne C. Loveland, *Southern Evangelicals and the Social Order, 1800–1860* (Baton Rouge: Louisiana State University Press, 1980) 258–59; George M. Fredrickson, "The Coming of the Lord: The Northern Protestant Clergy and the Civil War Crisis," in Miller, Stout, and Wilson, *Religion and the American Civil War*, 114; Randall M. Miller, "Catholics in a Protestant World: The Old South Example," in *Varieties of Southern Religious Experience*, ed. Samuel S. Hill (Baton Rouge: Louisiana State University Press, 1988) 117; Heyrman, *Southern Cross*, 27, 249; John B. Boles, "Evangelical Protestantism in the Old South: From Religious Dissent to Cultural Dominance," in *Religion in the South*, ed. Charles Reagan Wilson (Jackson: University Press of Mississippi, 1985) 29. The Apostle Paul wrote, "Servants, be obedient to them that are *your* [emphasis mine] masters according to the flesh, with fear and trembling, in singleness of your heart, as unto Christ" (Eph 6:5, KJV). On the views of Northern ministers, see Bertram Wyatt-Brown, "Church, Honor, and Secession," in Miller, Stout, and Wilson, *Religion and the American Civil War*, 92; Mark A. Noll, "The Bible and Slavery," ibid., 43–44, 47, 64–65; Samuel S. Hill, ed., *Religion in the Southern States: A Historical Study* (Macon GA: Mercer University Press, 1983) 395. On the sectional splintering of the churches in the antebellum era, see James E. Kirby, Russell E. Richey and Kenneth E. Rowe, *The Methodists* (Westport CT: Greenwood Press, 1996) 30–37; Mathews, *Religion in the Old South*, 160–63; Samuel S. Hill, *The South and the North in American Religion* (Athens: University of Georgia Press, 1980) 62–63; Randall Balmer and John R. Fitzmier, *The Presbyterians* (Westport CT: Greenwood Press, 1993) 254; Ernest T. Thompson, *Presbyterians in the South*, 3 vols. (Richmond: John Knox Press, 1963–73) 1:352–63, 564; Genovese, "Religion in the Collapse of the American Union," 78–79; John W. Kuykendall and Walter L. Lingle, *Presbyterians, Their History and Beliefs* (Atlanta: John Knox Press, 1978) 80; William W. Manross, *A History of the American Episcopal Church* (New York: Morehouse-Gorham Company, 1950) 290–92.

odiously sinful" as some Northern ministers had claimed, but was in fact God-ordained. He likely sermonized frequently on the topic from the pulpit before the war. His wife, Anzolette, took over superintending the slaves during his absence and even added to the family's holdings. In December 1862, Anzolette wrote her husband that she had purchased a female slave for $700.00. When she admitted to her husband that the slaves had become intractable, an angry Pendleton responded that he had asked a friend to stop by and threaten the slaves. About the most troublesome slave, he wrote: "he shall be sold and his wife and child hired out until it is proper to send them to their master. They may rest assured of this!"[16]

The others left less than Pendleton for the record, but their support for slavery was nevertheless evident. En route to Richmond with Brigadier General Humphrey Marshall and his staff, Guerrant observed slaves working in the fields but thought little of it: "They were all polite and well dressed, and apparently happy." Furthermore, upon hearing that several runaway slaves had been seen near Bristol, Virginia, Guerrant (who was recovering from illness at a friend's nearby plantation), raised a company of men and searched for them to no avail.[17]

In December 1864, Brigadier General Samuel Wragg Ferguson's brigade was near Perrysburg, South Carolina, where he and other Confederates were observing Union general William T. Sherman's army, which had just occupied Savannah, Georgia. Discouraged at the South's slender prospects for victory, Captain Nugent, one of Ferguson's staff officers, contemplated a South without slavery: "Without slavery little of our territory is worth a cent and there can be no peace as long as the alternative of abolition is presented to us." Poché's writings indicate that although he sanctioned the institution, he was willing to abandon it for Southern

---

[16] Anzolette Pendleton to William Pendleton, 11 December 1862; and William Pendleton to Anzolette Pendleton, 20 May 1863, both in Pendleton Papers. In an 1880 letter to a Northern minister, Pendleton defended slavery and referred to several Bible verses that he believed demonstrated God's approval of the institution. See William N. Pendleton to Rev. A. T. Irving, 27 January 1880, ibid.

[17] Guerrant diary, 2 May and 7 September 1863; and 18 June 1864.

independence. Responding to a rumor that France and England planned to recognize the Confederacy in exchange for the abolition of slavery, Poché remarked, "As for me I adhere to slavery as we have had it, but...I would make peace at the cost of abolishing slavery."[18]

Convinced that their cause was just and that Southerners were more pious than their enemy, these Confederate Christians concluded that God favored the South and that the Confederacy would surely triumph. Early battlefield victories and other encouraging news served to confirm that God favored their cause. After the Confederate victory at First Manassas in July 1861, Nugent wrote Nellie from a Mississippi riverboat: "I suppose you have heard of the great victory at Manassas Gap. The Federalists were defeated and chased for miles.... If God be for us, as I firmly and conscientiously believe he is—who can prevail over us?" Hearing of Rebel successes at Harper's Ferry and Alexandria, and that France and England had sided with the Confederacy—all false

---

[18] Cash and Howorth, *My Dear Nellie*, 117, 125, 129, 132, 229; Bearss, *Louisiana Confederate*, 115, 195, 208. See chapter 1 for information on each man's links to the institution of slavery. It was during the debate over slavery that Catholics gained acceptance in Southern society. Under attack from Northern abolitionists, white Southerners looked with suspicion upon anyone or anything in the South that appeared alien. One institution that garnered suspicious glances was the Catholic church. In a region dominated by evangelical Protestantism, the Church attracted criticism because of its doctrines and practices: its hierarchy was anti-democratic; its members were "loyal" to a foreign power; many of its priests were foreign-born; and the priests' pledge to celibacy was considered unnatural and inconsistent with Southern masculinity. Nevertheless, Southern Catholics, such as Felix Poché, on the whole defended slavery and supported secession, thus winning social acceptance from their fellow Southerners. See Walter B. Posey, *Religious Strife on the Southern Frontier* (Baton Rouge: Louisiana State University Press, 1965) 85, 92, 97; Miller, "Catholics in a Protestant World," 115, 117–21, 126; Randall M. Miller, "A Church in Cultural Captivity: Some Speculations on Catholic Identity in the Old South," in *Catholics in the Old South: Essays on Church and Culture*, ed. Randall M. Miller and Jon L. Wakelyn (Macon GA: Mercer University Press, 1983) 13–14, 18; Jon L. Wakelyn, "Catholic Elites in the Slaveholding South," 239; and Randall M. Miller, "The Failed Mission: The Catholic Church and Black Catholics in the Old South," *Catholics in the Old South*, 153, 155; Randall M. Miller, "Catholic Religion, Irish Ethnicity, and the Civil War," in Miller, Stout, and Wilson, *Religion and the American Civil War*, 263; Bearss, *Louisiana Confederate*, 115, 130–31, 208.

rumors—Holt wrote in May 1861: "All things go well with us. God is on our side."[19]

Early setbacks in the war, however, aroused some concern. After the fall of Fort Donelson in February 1862, Guerrant admitted that it was a blow to the Confederate cause, but added: "'In God is our trust.' 'He doeth all things well'. I can never believe that He will permit a brave and patriotic people—fighting for these rights which *He* gave them, to be subjugated by a fanatical mob animated by the most diabolical hate and revenge."[20]

When it came to religious piety and moral uprightness, these nine Christian Confederate soldiers were akin to being strangers in a strange land. Those who had entered the war as Christians criticized the sinful activity they observed in the camps and endeavored to remain steadfast in moral behavior and religious conviction. Although the soldiers who experienced wartime conversions may have engaged in iniquitous behavior prior to their professions, they became unwavering in their faith afterwards. Each of the men gained an increased sense of devotion to their faith as the war progressed. Especially for those who had embraced religious belief prior to the war, routines such as attending worship services, reading Scripture and prayer took on new meaning during the four-year struggle.[21]

---

[19] Cash and Howorth, *My Dear Nellie*, 43, 46, 77, 90; Talbert Holt to Carrie Holt, 11 April, 29 May 1861, Partin Papers.

[20] Guerrant diary, 20 December 1861; 16 February, 8 March, 13 September, 8 October 1862; and 29 June, 28 July 1863. See also Silver, *A Life for the Confederacy*, 127; Turner, *Letters from the Stonewall Brigade*, 83, 86, 115, 128; Franklin, *Fielder Diaries*, 98; William Pendleton to Anzolette Pendleton, 8 July 1861, Pendleton Papers; Cooke diary, 3, 6 September 1862; and 5 May 1863.

[21] There seems to be a consensus among historians that Confederate soldiers at the outset easily succumbed to the temptations of camp. Drew Gilpin Faust even noted that initially the "army presented a moral picture that was 'dark indeed.'" See Drew Gilpin Faust, "Christian Soldiers: The Meaning of Revivalism in the Confederate Army," *Journal of Southern History* 53 (February 1987): 68–69. See also Bell I. Wiley, *The Life of Johnny Reb: The Common Soldier of the Confederacy* (Baton Rouge: Louisiana State University Press, 1943) 36–58, 174–75; Woodworth, *While God Is Marching On*, 177–89; James I. Robertson, *Soldiers Blue and Gray* (Columbia: University of South Carolina Press, 1988) 172–73; Larry Daniel, *Soldiering in the Army of Tennessee* (Chapel Hill: University of North Carolina Press, 1991) 115;

Alfred Tyler Fielder

Alfred Fielder, a mature Christian, made specific note of immorality's prevalence in the Confederate camps. In Columbus, Kentucky, on Christmas day in 1861, Fielder was highly critical of many who spent the sacred day drinking: "The Cause of sobriety, virtue, and piety have comparatively few advocates in the army but as for myself though it may be unpopular—I am determined by God's grace to advocate them all and remonstrate with those who say and act differantly." Fielder apparently found few who took his advice, for two days later he remarked: "I further intend to talk less (because it anoys some) and think more as it may be more profit to myself and less anoyance to others."[22]

Fielder did not completely isolate himself from his fellow soldiers but associated mainly with other godly men in camp, especially the regiment's chaplain. He attended prayer meeting nearly every night in the chaplain's tent during his first few weeks in the army. He also enjoyed the fellowship of other Christian soldiers in camp. After attending a prayer meeting at Dalton, Georgia, in February 1864, he and "several of the boys repaired to our quarters and spent an hour in social conversation after which we had prayers." Furthermore, he reconsidered participating in the regiment's Christian Association and became a member of that group in June 1863. In addition to his regular attendance at the meetings, Fielder also prepared and read an essay on the power of prayer for the association. Fielder came to enjoy the fellowship of the Association immensely, often attending meetings of other regiments' Christian Associations as well.[23]

Fielder made it his intent to conduct himself morally and avoid any activity that could bring reproach to himself or to the cause of

---

Gardiner H. Shattuck, Jr., *A Shield and Hiding Place: The Religious Life of the Civil War Armies* (Macon GA: Mercer University Press, 1987) 96.

[22] Franklin, *Fielder Diaries*, 24–25.

[23] Ibid., 1–8, 18, 35, 37, 40, 59, 92, 114, 121, 134, 136–37, 148, 151, 163, 165, 174, 247. Fielder also attended church frequently with other religious persons, see ibid., 35, 110, 169.

Christ. In December 1862 he noted regretfully in his diary, "I played two games of Fox and Geese…last night and am sorry that I indulged even that much and intend to do so no more, not because the sin of it, but because it is a useless profitless amusement." Even though his influence on others was limited, Fielder was determined to stand firm in his faith: "I this day resolve in my heart to live more prayerful and let others do as they may; as for me I will still try to serve God and get to heaven."[24]

William Lewis Nugent

William Nugent also encountered impious behavior among the soldiers in his command. In a letter to Nellie from Spring Hill, Tennessee, in May 1863, he admitted the difficulty of remaining true to his religious convictions in camp: "You have no idea how demoralizing camp life is and how difficult it is for one to preserve his consistency of life and his inward purity of heart. Oaths, blasphemies, imprecations, obscenity are hourly heard…. Still, by the grace of God, I am enabled to live somewhat up to my professions, tho' not as much as I would desire." He nevertheless exhibited steadfastness in the presence of his less pious comrades. As one of General Ferguson's staff officers, he was often present at parties held for the staff. Nugent, who had criticized Nellie for dancing on her summer tour in 1860, wrote her about one party, remarking that while several of the officers drank and danced, he passed the time conversing. Nugent's determination to remain firm in his convictions grew stronger during the war. In July 1864 he wrote, "I am not unmindful of my allegiance to the Great God, who has so mercifully protected me, and with His help, I purpose remaining steadfast in my purpose to love, honor, and obey Him." [25]

---

[24] Ibid., 21, 25.

[25] Cash and Howorth, *My Dear Nellie*, 109, 191; William Nugent to unnamed correspondent, no date, Lucy Somerville Howorth and William Cash Papers, Capps Archives and Museum, Delta State University, Cleveland, Mississippi.

William Nelson Pendleton

In his letters home, Parson William Pendleton seldom commented on the sinful activity he undoubtedly observed in camp. He evidently was successful in maintaining the standards of piety and behavior his Christian faith led him to believe were appropriate. In a letter to his wife written near Centreville, Virginia, in December 1861, Pendleton described a "drinking match" attended by his fellow officers, remarking: "Rejoice that I was out on duty when it began." His commitment to faith is also evident in the fatherly advice offered his son, Sandie, in August 1862: "You [have told] your mamma that camp-life is destroying your religious character. Take care of this, my dear boy. Watch and pray! If you do not make opportunities for prayer regularly you will spiritually die. Let nothing prevent this."[26]

Edward Owings Guerrant

The Christian neophytes in this study also endeavored to maintain their newfound faith when faced with camp-life immorality. Vice appears to have permeated every Confederate camp, even those on the periphery like General Marshall's small command in southwestern Virginia. In February 1862, a few days after arriving in camp, Edward Guerrant recorded his first impressions of army life: "[There is] much noise—great confusion—: Profane swearing.... [I am] rather unfavorably impressed with the beauties of Camp life."[27]

According to Guerrant, "An abundance of money and no legitimate way to spend it" was the main cause of impious behavior. He opined that such circumstances furnished "temptations for the indulgence of vicious habits." He was, however, determined not to succumb to such temptations. Indeed, days later on his twenty-fourth birthday, Guerrant reaffirmed his commitment to Christ: "O may I celebrate it properly by renewing my vows and rededicating myself to the Great and Merciful God who created me as I am, and preserved me up to this time." His comments suggest that the presence of vice

---

[26] William Pendleton to Anzolette Pendleton, 3 December 1861, Pendleton Papers; Lee, *Memoirs of Pendleton*, 202.

[27] Guerrant diary, 5–6 February 1862.

among soldiers declined but little during the war and that he
probably never became inured to it. After eight months of service,
Guerrant wrote in his diary: "This life doesn't suit me. This secular,
vulgar, profane, wicked crowd—hurrying on in the red tide of war to
a common destiny and a common destruction is not my company. I
serve my country now at a great sacrifice to my self." Guerrant
pressed on with his duties and sought to isolate himself from the
impious soldiers. He associated with other Christians in camp and
often attended church with them.[28]

Hiram Talbert Holt

At Fort Morgan, where boredom was often a bigger adversary
than Yankee gunboats, immorality ran rampant. Talbert Holt, also a
Christian neophyte, wrote home to his wife in November 1861:
"Carrie this is the worst place I ever dreamed of in my life. You can
hear nothing but horrid oaths and blackguard as well as indecencies
of every kind…. There are also here all sorts of venereal diseases,
acquired by imprudent communications." This iniquitous behavior
showed few signs of abatement. In March 1863 he lamented,
"Sometimes I think I see a good change in the troops. I hear not so
much swearing and see not so much gaming, but then again it breaks
out in all its horror."[29]

Holt, like Guerrant, was determined to remain untarnished:
"Others…will return to their families as infidels having thrown off
religious restraint, ought you not to be happy then that…is [not] the
case with me! that I am well, that I still acknowledge the power and
love of God." Responding to a letter from his father-in-law, a Baptist
preacher, advising him to follow the teachings of Christ, Holt
remarked, "I…received pa's letter in which I found advice that was
good and which by the help of God I hope I have been following for
some time and still expect to follow." Indeed, it seemed that Holt had
little difficulty in maintaining his faith. He reported confidently in a

---

[28] Ibid., 9, 28 February, 9 March, 22 June, 28 October, 18, 30 November, 17
December 1862; and 3 May 1863; Davis and Swentor, *Bluegrass Confederate*, 42.

[29] Talbert Holt to Carrie Holt, 20 November, 12 December 1861; 10 March
1863, Partin Papers.

December 1861 letter that "I can live here so different from others while they are cursing and playing cards all around me. I can ly [*sic*] on my back in my bunk and hold sweet converse with my Savior." Renouncing sin and standing firm in the face of temptation were the foundation of Holt's faith. In an 1862 letter he explained this to Carrie: "I might ask, what constitutes Religion...I'll tell you, there must be a renouncing of Sin. Repentance and renouncing of Sin, under all the trials and temptations of life.... In other words Religion is a principle of the Soul living ever firm under all temptations." Holt did, however, succumb to at least one temptation, for which he expressed little remorse. On more than one occasion, he and some of the men in his company raided a local farm and stole watermelons. Although the men engaged in this activity partly to relieve boredom, he believed that their actions were justified because of privations in camp.[30]

Felix Pierre Poché

Felix Poché, like Guerrant and Holt, was critical of the vice he observed in camp. Joining General Mouton's staff in July 1863, he served in the Trans-Mississippi Department and encountered impiety similar to that reported in other camps. Having observed some of the men playing cards in January 1865, he remarked: "The young men who are loafing here will end up totally ruining their characters." Although he made no statements about maintaining his convictions, Poché demonstrated his devotion to Christ and the Church in his thoughts and actions. After attending Mass late in the war, he recorded his feelings: "I experienced sweet sensations at the sight of the minister of God at the foot of the altar renewing the Sacrifice of the Saviour on the Cross, especially as I had the good fortune of taking a part in the holy Sacrifice.... It is in these moments of happiness and of rapture of divine joy that the Christian feels in the bottom of his heart the truth of the Catholic Church."[31]

---

[30] Talbert Holt to Carrie Holt, 25 April, 2 December 1861; 23, 27 June, 29 July, 25 November 1862, ibid.

[31] Bearss, *Louisiana Confederate*, 71, 201.

Poché's position as an aide in the commissary department undoubtedly assisted in his efforts to remain steadfast. Traveling about procuring supplies, he was not only able to avoid the temptations prevalent in camp but also was free to visit and enjoy fellowship with the priests he had befriended during his travels. During these visits, Poché more often than not attended both confession and Mass.[32]

Robert Augustus Moore

Despite engaging in impious behavior prior to their conversions, the men in this study who made wartime professions of faith became unwavering in their religious convictions as well. Soon after the Battle of Ball's Bluff in October 1861, the 17th Mississippi Infantry regiment settled into winter quarters near Leesburg, Virginia. Robert Moore, who would not make a profession of faith until 1863, noted in his diary, "I think the majority of the men of our Regt. are becoming very wild & contracting many bad habits." He could not, however, resist the ubiquitous temptations found in camp and soon began drinking. During their stay near Leesburg, he and some of the boys occasionally slipped away from camp and ventured into town, where they procured strong drink. After one such trip, Moore acknowledged the popularity of whiskey among the men: "Found plenty of whiskey & brought a bottle home with us. It lasts but a short time in camp." Evidently his father was aware of Moore's propensity to drink, for when he visited his son in camp at Leesburg he brought Robert a bottle of whiskey. Robert's conversion, however, transformed him and afterwards he exhibited resoluteness in his newfound faith. Although he made no specific statements about abandoning his old ways, his actions and, in particular, his words were those of an earnest Christian. Soon after his conversion he wrote, "I hope to walk so as to never bring reproach on the cause of Christ."[33]

---

[32] Ibid., 15, 21, 24–26, 28, 30–31, 70, 75, 80, 84–85, 114, 116, 118–19, 161–63, 168.

[33] Silver, *A Life for the Confederacy*, 51, 56, 83, 96, 136.

Alexander Tedford Barclay

Ted Barclay was, like Moore, a wartime convert who struggled with the temptations in camp. In March 1862 he admitted to his sister, "I remain a hardened sinner. Sometimes I try to give myself to Christ but the world lures me on again and I am in the same old state." After he professed Christ, however, he criticized the immoral behavior he witnessed in camp, in particular that which he considered irreverent. A few days after Christmas in 1863, he wrote home: "Some of our officers disgraced themselves by getting drunk. Why is it the birthday of our Lord and Saviour should be especially set apart to be thus desecrated? Certainly it should be a day of rejoicing to us. But that it should be thus spent, how disgraceful and sinful." Like the others in this study, he was determined to stand firm in his religious convictions. His steadfastness was evident in a February 1864 letter to his mother, who had counseled him to remain true to Christ: "Do you think that I could for one moment think of returning to the beggarly elements of this world after enjoying the sweets of this Christian life?. . . I am exposed to great temptations still His grace is sufficient for me and I never cease to pray that He will keep me in the straight and narrow path that leadeth to heaven.... Oh, do not for one moment believe that I could be induced to forsake the cause of Christ." Like Fielder and Guerrant, Barclay sought to associate with religious persons and joined other Christians of the Stonewall Brigade in forming an interdenominational Christian Association. Its main purpose was to provide Christian fellowship for soldiers and combat the immoral influences prevalent in camp. Indeed, the preamble of the Association's constitution acknowledged that, "many members of the church... grow careless of their privileges and their duties; and many who are morally disposed, are led astray into current vices, through the want of some appropriate medium, by which christian influences may be thrown around them.... [W]e do propose to throw as many strengthening influences around the weak." Barclay not only regularly attended the meetings, but he also served a stint as president.[34]

Giles Buckner Cooke

Giles Cooke, who made a profession of faith early in the war, seldom commented about the immorality in camp. As an inspector general he spent much of his time traveling and had little interaction with common soldiers. Although Cooke's absence from camp undoubtedly removed him from many of the temptations found there, he likely would have remained steadfast in his faith whatever his position. Like several other Christian soldiers in this study, he fraternized with similarly-minded officers and often attended church with them. Furthermore, on his twenty-fourth birthday in May 1862 he reflected about his past misdeeds and revealed a resoluteness in his new-found faith: "Oh, how misspent have over 23 yrs of my life been. When I look back upon the sin that I have committed and the evil that I have done in this world, it fills my heart with sadness." Cooke asked God to lengthen his life so he could right the wrongs he had done "by living a purer, a holier and more useful life."[35]

The Christian soldiers in this study furthermore exhibited steadfastness by continuing many of their religious practices from the antebellum era. One of these was a desire to worship. Each of these men, regardless of his spiritual maturity, longed to attend divine services. In the absence of preaching or when duties prevented their attendance at services these soldier-Christians either communed privately with God or noted their disappointment in their writings. Moreover, as the war continued, their devotion to worship increased. This was caused partly by their inability to hear preaching as regularly as they would have liked. Before the war these men

---

[34] Turner, *Letters from the Stonewall Brigade*, 34, 60–61, 98, 120, 124, 129, 136, 138; *Constitution, By-Laws and Catalogue of Christian Association of The Stonewall Brigade* (Richmond: William H. Clemmitt Printing, 1864), in Richard Harwell and Marjorie Lyle, eds., *Confederate Imprints* (New Haven CT: Research Publications, 1974) microfilm, 4.

[35] Cooke diary, 13, 18 May, 20 July, 17, 31 August 1862; 3 May, 7, 14 June, 9 August 1863; 24 April, 28 August, 27 November 1864; and 1 January, 5, 12 February 1865.

encountered few impediments to their church attendance; however, during the war, the dearth of chaplains in some regiments, military duties, and army operations all hindered the ability of these soldiers to attend services. Therefore, attending divine worship became something of a privilege. Furthermore, soldiers had many war-related concerns, including the safety of loved ones and the possibility of death. Although their control over such matters was limited, they recognized God's power over them. Congregating with fellow Christians in the presence of God as well as listening to the ministers' discourses comforted these men and helped assuage their fears.

Alfred Tyler Fielder

Alfred Fielder, a lay-leader in his home church in Friendship, Tennessee, continued his antebellum practice of going to church and routinely attended religious services in camp. Indeed, on the first Sunday he was in camp he was present at services, although many other soldiers exhibited little interest in preaching. During the weeks in which there were no formal services, he often joined the chaplain in his tent for prayer meeting. Furthermore, he frequently endured inconveniences in order to worship. On a Sabbath day in camp in May 1862, Fielder, recognizing that the regimental chaplain was absent and that no preaching would occur, visited a nearby regiment and asked the chaplain to preach to his regiment that afternoon.[36]

Prevented by military operations from spending every Sabbath as he would have liked, Fielder often escaped from camp and sought a quiet, natural setting in which to worship. On a Sunday in November 1862 in Tullahoma, Tennessee, he recorded in his diary, "I have Just come in from a walk to the woods where I spent several hours in meditation and prayer Oh! I have thought of and prayed for dear friends at home." On a July 1863 Sabbath day in Chattanooga, Captain Fielder climbed Lookout Mountain to worship among the clouds. He noted in his diary that it was "one of the best places for reflection and meditation upon nature and natures God I ever saw—my mind was actively engaged almost all the time I was there in

---

[36] Franklin, *Fielder Diaries*, 1–2, 5–6, 8, 50, 108.

thinking of the great power and wisdom of him that spoke all things into existence and upholds all things by the word of his power." When he was prevented from attending Sunday services or communing privately, Fielder expressed disappointment. In December 1862, as General William S. Rosecrans's Union force advanced upon General Braxton Bragg's Confederates near Murfreesboro, Tennessee, he remarked, "This is a beautiful calm pleasant sabbath day and what a pitty it could not be spent in worship of God."[37]

His inability to attend religious services regularly engendered in Fielder a greater appreciation for and desire to worship. Recuperating from the wounds he received during the Battle of Atlanta, he reflectively noted in his diary, "I have thought much this morning of former sabbath privaliges when with my family I attended the house of God to worship in his temple but here I am away from home and . . . not able to get off my bed or scarcely turn my self in it, but my prayer is not my will but thine O God be done." Moreover, by early 1863 Fielder was often attending as many as three services on Sundays. On one Sunday, he recorded in his diary, "I trust that I have spent this day to profit having heard three sermons and indeavered to worship the God of my fathers in sincerity." Furthermore, inconveniences failed to prevent his attending worship services. Traveling home on furlough in 1864, Fielder attended divine services in several of the towns he passed through. In Selma, Alabama, he heard two sermons while awaiting his departure for Tennessee. His devotion to worship is further illustrated by his recording the scriptural references for the sermons he heard. This indicates not only his interest in the sermons but likely meant that he took notes as well and meditated on the ministers' words over and again. He also regularly evaluated the ministers' discourses and criticized those he found lacking, especially when he sought comforting words. Uneasy about an impending engagement near Murfreesboro, Tennessee, in December 1862, Fielder listened intently to a sermon delivered by his new chaplain but found it

---

[37] Ibid., 88, 96, 130, 139.

unsatisfying, for the minister "did not preach exceeding 10 minutes."[38]

William Nelson Pendleton

Reverend William Pendleton too remained steadfast in his desire not only to worship but also to preach. Remaining true to his commitment to serve in a double capacity as a soldier and a minister of Christ, the artillerist preached frequently to the troops: "It is good for me—I trust it is for others—for me thus to exercise my sacred calling while occupying this strange position." Indeed, his zeal for preaching was such that he often endured major inconveniences to do so. In Centreville, Virginia, in February 1862, Pendleton had a chapel constructed in camp because the local church was serving as a hospital. Even before it was completed, Pendleton held services in it.[39]

Although he regularly preached to his own men, Pendleton took advantage of opportunities to minister to those in other commands. On a Sabbath day near Richmond in 1862, Reverend Pendleton preached three services in three different commands. At times he was able to combine preaching and his duties. Conducting an inspection of the Army of Tennessee near Dalton, Georgia, in early 1864, he preached to an "immense congregation [that] was thoroughly attentive to the end." Furthermore, he frequently visited nearby local churches where he was often asked to preach, sometimes with little notice. During the ten-month siege of Petersburg, General Pendleton was a frequent guest preacher at the venerable St. Paul's Episcopal Church. (Giles Cooke, another Christian soldier in this study, frequented St. Paul's during the siege and heard him preach on a number of occasions.) When he was not presiding over his own services, Pendleton attended the services of other ministers. He was, however, highly critical of their sermons. Having listened to a sermon on the power of God, Pendleton took issue with the pastor for pointing out only the encouraging side of God. As the minister

---

[38] Ibid., 8, 70, 74, 78, 95, 104–106, and passim.
[39] Lee, *Memoirs of Pendleton*, 171, 191.

closed the service, Pendleton rose and addressed the congregation emphasizing that God would also judge men for their sins. Occasionally, he heard a sermon he liked. In early 1864 near Louisa Court House, General Pendleton listened to an eloquent sermon by a Methodist minister: "It was an earnest discourse from a devout, simple, active, and fearless mind, pleasingly as well as impressively delivered." He was so impressed that he not only took notes but also conveyed the main points to his wife in his next letter home.[40]

Pendleton longed to worship despite the military activity around him. Hindered in conducting or attending services during Union general Ulysses S. Grant's 1864 campaign, Pendleton remarked: "I hope to be privileged to attend worship somewhere this morning." And, when his duties prevented his attending services, he meditated on the Bible or read other religious books. When scriptural meditation was impossible on the Sabbath, he endeavored to keep his thoughts consistent with the spirit of the day. Having arrived in Fredericksburg on a Sunday in late November 1862, the artillerist was busy all day setting up camp and had no opportunity for worship: "It has been very little like God's holy day. I have tried to have my own mind exercised in harmony with the day."[41]

William Lewis Nugent

Others likewise desired to attend religious services regularly, but military operations prevented them from doing so. Traversing the state of Mississippi to repel Yankee raids, the 28th Mississippi Cavalry was constantly on the move. As a result, William Nugent was seldom able to attend church services or preaching in camp. In a letter to Nellie in 1863, he lamented his predicament: "I hear no sermons, hear none of the Songs of Zion, and am verily a stranger in a strange land." Evidently there was no chaplain in his regiment, for Nugent never mentioned preaching in camp. Nevertheless, he demonstrated an eagerness for worship. Traveling to Jackson,

---

[40] Ibid., 161, 189–91, 205, 229, 232, 272, 313, 317, 343, 359; William Pendleton to Anzolette Pendleton, 3 December 1861; and 3 May 1864, Pendleton Papers; Cooke diary, 19 June and 7, 28 August 1864.

[41] Lee, *Memoirs of Pendleton*, 235, 316, 336, 341.

Mississippi, in 1862, he passed an Episcopal church and "the tears filled up my eyes as I looked upon the House of God. When shall I again be privileged to go up to the Church to worship?" When opportunities for formal worship arose late in the war, Nugent hastened to take advantage of them. With his command stationary for a short time near Griffin, Georgia, in 1864, Nugent visited a local Methodist church and "listened to a fine sermon." Although he was unable to worship as he would have liked, Nugent suggested that his relationship with God suffered but little: "While I do not enjoy religion as I would like in the army, there are times when the little I have is a great comfort to me indeed."[42]

Hiram Talbert Holt

The Christian neophytes in this study also exhibited an eagerness for worship. Although Talbert Holt neglected to mention in his letters to Carrie that he regularly attended preaching, evidence suggests that he did so conscientiously. One of the few times he mentioned preaching was in November 1862 at Fort Morgan: "Carrie we have fine Sermons going on here every night! . . . Oh! how pleasant it is to hear the word of God." In a letter to Carrie after Holt's death in February 1864, Chaplain A. D. McCoy implied that Holt was a regular attendant at camp services: "I miss his presence very much at my meetings."[43]

As the war continued, Holt evinced an increased passion for worship. Near Chattanooga, Tennessee, in July 1863, he withdrew into the woods to commune with God: "I wanted to be away from the stir of camp, where I hear little else than vulgarity profanity and foolishness instead of the greatness, goodness, mercy, and majesty of our God. The trees were God's first Temples. . . . Then too is this

---

[42] Cash and Howorth, *My Dear Nellie*, 56, 113, 191, 220. For a list of Confederate chaplains and the regiments in which they served, see John W. Brinsfield et al., eds., *Faith in the Fight: Civil War Chaplains* (Mechanicsburg PA: Stackpole Books, 2003) 211–56.

[43] Talbert Holt to Carrie Holt, 13 April 1861; and 25 November 1862; A. D. McCoy to Carrie Holt, no date, all in Partin Papers.

place for me, here my confussed nerves become calm, my mind tranquil."[44]

Edward Owings Guerrant

Edward Guerrant, like Nugent, desired to worship but was unable to do so as he would have liked. Just weeks after arriving in camp, Guerrant wrote in his diary, "I have not heard a single sermon since I left home." Furthermore, he noted regretfully those Sundays on which there was no preaching. His longing to attend church was evident in early 1862 when a Sabbath day reminded him of home: "There is a heavenly calm, a peace & serenity about this day.... How recollection transports me back to those distant scenes.... Today I guess, Mr. George, preaches at Springfield. Would that the echo of his voice could reach Virginia." Marshall's brigade had only a handful of chaplains and the lack of preaching prompted Guerrant to travel into nearby towns for church, a practice he continued for the duration of the war. His diary suggests that he enjoyed the sermons he heard, for he often recorded the titles and scriptural references, possibly for later study. And evidently he listened closely, for he evaluated the sermons he heard. Like Pendleton, he criticized many but praised those that impressed him.[45]

Prevented by his duties from going to church every Sunday, Guerrant made time to commune with God. He disliked violating the Fourth Commandment, which prohibited working on the Sabbath, but often had to do so. After one such occurrence, Guerrant vented his anger in his diary: "Sweet sunny—Sabbath day. Day of rest.... Was called away from breakfast—to the duties of my office. Think I shall resign it or make them relieve me on the Sacred day. It is an undecided question in my mind—whether circumstances— (except of necessity) should ever force us to a violation of the Sabbath day." After completing his work, he rode out to a nearby mountain

---

[44] Talbert Holt to Harriet and Drucilla Holt, 19 July 1863, ibid.

[45] Guerrant diary, 16, 23 February, 9, 16, 23, 30 March, 6 April, 25 May, 22 June, 10, 20 July, 3, 24 August, 16, 23, 30 November, 7, 21 December 1862; 11 January, 26 April, 7 June, 26 July, 9, 23, 30 August, 27 September 1863; 29 May, 25 June, 25, 27 September 1864; and 19 February, 2 April 1865.

and meditated on Scripture. This became a common practice for Guerrant when his duties forced him to miss Sunday services. A few weeks later, Guerrant was again engaged in office work most of a Sabbath day but eventually "stole away and…. rode out into [the] country to enjoy the fresh air to 'hold communion with nature' & her God in all the various & majestic works that surround me here."[46]

Felix Pierre Poché

Felix Poché, like Guerrant, desired to attend divine worship and consistently went out of his way to do so. His position as an aide in the commissary department sometimes provided him opportunities to worship. Traveling throughout Louisiana procuring supplies, Poché routinely stopped in towns and attended Mass. In late 1864, he passed through Monroe, Louisiana, and visited the local Catholic church: "I went there and took advantage of the occasion to hear mass not knowing when I shall have another chance to do so." During his travels in southern Louisiana, Poché befriended the priests at St. Charles College, a Catholic school at Grand Côteau. Whenever his travels took him near there, he dropped in for confession and Mass. After one such visit, he recorded in his diary, "Oh! happy I felt when I knelt before Him…. Considering everything, and especially the chance of having received communion I am perfectly delighted with my visit at Grand Côteau College." Battling a persistent illness, Poché in mid-1864 obtained a furlough and spent several weeks recuperating at the college. There he attended Mass regularly and even began to assist in the services. Poché's participation in Mass increased noticeably during this time. He either attended or assisted in the services on twenty-four of the thirty-four days he resided at the college. When Poché's duties prevented him from going to Mass, he retired to his tent and read Mass privately. In the fall of 1864, Poché's wife, Sélima, traveled to her aunt's home in southeastern Louisiana to visit Felix, who planned to meet her there. During this visit, which lasted several weeks, the

---

[46] Ibid., 23 February, 9 March 1862. Guerrant also expressed his disdain for violating the Sabbath in ibid., 6 April, 31 August, 5, 12, 19 October, 21, 28 December 1862; 18 January, 12 April 1863; and 14 August, 18 September 1864.

couple was unable to attend Mass, but often repaired to their room and read Mass together.[47]

Those who made wartime professions of faith also made clear their desire to attend religious services. In fact, evidence suggests that each was present at preaching before conversion, although afterwards their devotion increased significantly.

Giles Buckner Cooke

Captain Giles Cooke, an 1859 graduate of VMI who attended services while at the Institute, continued his church attendance after joining the staff of Brigadier General Philip St. George Cocke in 1861. A sermon at one of these early war services stirred Cooke to reflect on his spiritual condition and resulted in his profession of faith in June 1861. After his conversion, Cooke adopted a rigorous routine that included (among other things) going to church every Sunday except when prevented by his duties.[48]

Like the others in this study, Cooke grew more religiously earnest during the war. Indeed, he often endured inconveniences in order to worship. As an assistant inspector general on various generals' staffs, he traveled frequently to other commands conducting inspections. During his travels, he sought out local churches, regardless of denomination, in which to worship. Indeed, he seized opportunities to hear preaching when they presented themselves. In his room in Chattanooga in July 1862, just prior to General Braxton Bragg's invasion of Kentucky, Cooke heard a church bell ringing. He followed the sound until he discovered its source: a church holding Wednesday night prayer meeting. He promptly joined in the worship. When formal worship was impossible, Cooke made time to commune with God. Once when sharing a room with a fellow officer, he retired to the closet for some time alone with God. And, during his frequent travels, he often read his Bible and Prayer Book on the

---

[47] Bearss, *Louisiana Confederate*, 8, 15, 79–80, 136–52, 163, 168, 175–79, 182, 194, 212–13, 215, 227, passim. Although the assistance he offered in Mass is unclear, it likely involved minor duties similar to that of an altar boy, such as lighting incense, ringing bells, handing wine to the priest, and the like.

[48] Cooke diary, 12, 19 May, 2 June, 7 July 1861; and passim.

railway cars. During the siege of Petersburg in 1864–1865, when Cooke served on General Robert E. Lee's staff, his increased fervor for worship was evident. On some Sundays, Cooke attended as many as three and four services. After one such Sunday, he remarked, "Oh that I could do my duty every day as well as I've . . . done it today."[49]

Cooke furthermore wanted to benefit from the religious services he attended. At Petersburg in late 1864, he noted after attending three services, "I trust that the holy Sabbath day has been profitably spent and that the services of the blessed day have been of benefit to my soul." He faithfully recorded the sermon titles, noted the scriptural references, and critiqued the sermons. On days when he was too busy to attend services, Cooke noted his disappointment in his diary. The fighting in May 1864 between Union general Benjamin Butler's troops and Confederate general P. G. T. Beauregard's force near Drewry's Bluff prompted Cooke, who was serving on Beauregard's staff, to remark, "Have not been able to spend the sabbath day as I would wish on account of active operations going on immediately on our front." Not to be deterred, he later walked into the woods and communed privately with God.[50]

Robert Augustus Moore

Robert Moore was, like Cooke, a wartime convert whose devotion to divine worship increased after his conversion. Continuing his family's prewar custom, Moore attended preaching in camp at the outset of the war, albeit intermittently, and he appeared to enjoy the services. His religious convictions, however, underwent a transformation after his conversion in February 1863. Prior to his profession of faith, Moore's notation of the church services he attended included little more than, "Have attended church today." Yet, just days after his conversion experience, he described a recent

---

[49] Ibid., 28 June, 5, 17, 30 July, 1 September 1862; 5 July 1863; 27 November, 18 December 1864; 8, 15, 22, 29 January, 19, 26 February, 5, 12, 19, 26 March 1865; and passim. Prayer Book is another name for the *Book of Common Prayer*.

[50] Ibid., 9 June 1861; 16, 18, 25 May, 1, 3–7, 23 June, 20, 27, 30 July, 2, 9, 16 November 1862; 27 March, 5 April, 27 September, 4 October 1863; 27 March, 3, 8, 10, 24 April, 22, 29 May, 18 September, 30 October, 6, 27 November 1864; and 5 March 1865.

service much differently: "Have been blessed with the privalege of meeting once more in the Lord's Sanctuary to worship." He furthermore was eager to worship. On an unusually calm Sunday near the Rapidan River in August 1863, Moore commented, "We have been blessed with a calm, quiet day in which to worship the Most High."[51]

Moore became steadfast in his new-found faith and often went out of his way to worship. Traveling home on furlough in March 1863, he sought out local Sunday services at a church in Lynchburg, Virginia; and on the way back to his command a few weeks later, he attended Sunday services at a Baptist church in Richmond. On the railway cars he studied Scripture and read religious books. In camp near the Rapidan River in August 1863, he noted in his diary, "Attend preaching in the brigade every night that the weather will admit."[52]

Alexander Tedford Barclay

Ted Barclay was, like Cooke and Moore, a wartime convert. It is unclear how often he attended religious services in camp prior to his conversion, but he likely was present at preaching often since he and his family had attended regularly before the war. His letters suggest that preaching occurred frequently, for he wrote his sister in June 1861, "We have religious services every night, having four parsons, better off than most companies." After his conversion in April 1862, Barclay's attendance at religious services increased, as did his devotion to worship. He often cited the titles and the biblical references of the sermons he heard, which suggests that he may have recorded the sermons' main points for study or meditation. Moreover, Barclay's own words attest to his growth in spiritual matters. In an 1864 letter to his sister he described partaking of the Lord's Supper at a recent church service: "I think it is delightful to have these points for renewed consecration of ourselves to the Lord. Oh, how devoted we should be. Every drop of blood in our veins

---

[51] Silver, *A Life for the Confederacy*, 28, 36, 40, 42, 48, 52, 54, 57, 60, 68–69, 77, 87, 118, 129, 132, 138, 160.

[52] Ibid., 139, 141–42, 157, 161.

should thank the Lord for this salvation, for He shed His blood for us." Captured during the Battle of Spotsylvania in May 1864, Barclay was sent to Fort Delaware. There he continued his attendance at religious services and steadfastly maintained his religious convictions. In a letter to his mother in July 1864 from the prison, he demonstrated great faith: "I hope you do not allow yourself any uneasiness on my account. Remember I have the same good God to watch over me and protect me here as on the battle field, and I still look to him for comfort and consolation."[53]

In addition to worship, the nine Christian soldiers in this study continued other religious habits from the antebellum period: Bible study, prayer, and in some cases spiritual encouragement. Those who were Christians when the war began not only assiduously continued these activities, but, on the whole, increased their devotion to them. Although the soldiers who experienced wartime conversions may not have continued many of their antebellum religious practices in earnest before their professions, they became unfaltering in them after. Each of the nine began reading Scripture and praying fervently, for in these activities he found hope and solace.

William Nelson Pendleton

Like he had done for years before the war, William Pendleton devoted a portion of each morning to Bible study and meditation. Even military operations failed for the most part to interrupt his morning routine. On the perilous retreat from Gettysburg in July 1863, he rose earlier than usual to have time for his daily devotional. In addition to his preaching and devotional, Pendleton regularly held "family worship" services for his staff and led his men in daily prayer. "I have arranged for general prayer in camp every evening under the open sky in good weather," he wrote in May 1861. He considered prayer an essential component of his religion and it grew more

[53] Turner, *Letters from the Stonewall Brigade*, 20, 23–26, 30, 96, 98, 136, 138, 147, 149; Janet B. Hewett, Noah Andre Trudeau, and Bryce A. Suderow, eds., *Supplement to the Official Records of the Union and Confederate Armies: Record of Events.* 80 vols. (Wilmington NC: Broadfoot Publishing Company, 1994–1998) 70:767–71. (Hereafter cited as *Supplement to the OR.*)

important to him during the war. Concerned for loved ones at home as well as those in the army, General Pendleton wrote his wife from Gaines' Mill in June 1864: "I have never been more in prayer than during this campaign. Generally, indeed, during the storm of battle my mind is earnestly engaged in supplicating God's mercy upon our army, country, and cause, with special mention of our dearest ones. It is an immense relief to the spirit amid the perils and anxieties of such critical scenes.... I marvel how rational creatures can forego so great a privilege."[54]

As he had done during times of adversity in the antebellum era, Pendleton encouraged others spiritually during the war. The comfort he offered not only evinces his faith but also sheds light on his own beliefs. Responding to his wife's concern in 1862 about the vulnerability of the Shenandoah Valley, where his home lay, as well as her anxiety regarding him, Pendleton reassured her: "Of course I feel the hazard, but have very little shrinking.... If He sees fit to have my days cut short and your hearts smitten by such an affliction, He can make it work for good to us all, and will I am persuaded.... Keep a stout heart, trusting in God." He made similar comments to his daughter after she expressed concern for loved ones serving in the army: "It is therefore my darling a time for all of us to live peculiarly by faith, having our treasure in heaven and our hearts there also." His spiritual encouragement, however, was not meant solely for his family. Over the course of the war he addressed meetings of the regimental chaplains in which he counseled and exhorted them in their work. Pendleton's religious counsel even reached the highest places of the Confederate government. Concerned about President Jefferson Davis's failing health, the artillerist wrote him in April 1864 and told him that he prayed daily for him. He also encouraged Davis with the promises found in 1 Pet. 5:7, "Casting all your care upon him, for he careth for you."[55]

---

[54] Lee, *Memoirs of Pendleton*, 142–43, 184, 189, 296, 341; William Pendleton to Anzolette Pendleton, 4, 19 April 1862; 14 June 1863; 2 January 1865; and to unnamed correspondent, 1 July 1861, all in Pendleton Papers.

[55] William Pendleton to unnamed daughter, 25 February 1862, Pendleton Papers; Lee, *Memoirs of Pendleton*, 180, 255–56, 271, 301, 341; William Pendleton to

Alfred Tyler Fielder

Alfred Fielder fervently continued his prewar religious practices
as well. Although there are no extant records that indicate how
frequently he engaged in Bible study before the war, Fielder was a
pious lay-leader in his home church and likely meditated on
Scripture often. What is clear is that once in the army, he read the
Bible fervently. Moved by the uncertainty inherent in war as well as
the sinfulness he observed in camp, Fielder immersed himself in the
Bible during his first week in the army. Just six days after his arrival
he read the three chapters in Matthew that constitute Christ's
Sermon on the Mount. In these verses, Christ instructed his
followers how to live godly lives.[56]

The prospect of death also prompted him to seek solace in
God's Word. After a desperate first day of fighting at the Battle of
Shiloh in April 1862, a thankful Fielder led the men in his company
in worship: "at the suggestion of Jas Hammons I read the 71 Psalm
give out and sing two verses of the hymn Commencing 'God of my
life whose gracious power' Knelt down and tryed to return
Thanksgiving and prayer to God." Near Chattanooga, Tennessee, in
August 1863, with the pickets exchanging fire continuously, Fielder
recorded in his diary, "I spent some time of this day in reading the
Scriptures meditation and prayer for myself and family Kindred
friends and Country yes and for my enemies." Furthermore, war
generated in Fielder an insatiable desire to learn more about God. In
1864 he set out to read the Bible from beginning to end. Less than
six weeks later, he had completed the task: "I finished reading the
bible through since I was wounded having commenced it about the
7th of August." Fielder continued to study Scripture throughout the

---

Jefferson Davis, 23 April 1864, in *The Papers of Jefferson Davis*, vol. 10, Lynda L.
Crist, Kenneth H. Williams, and Peggy L. Dillard, eds., (Baton Rouge: Louisiana
State University Press, 1999) 365.

[56] Franklin, *Fielder Diaries*, 1. Christ's "Sermon on the Mount" is in the Gospel
According to Matthew, chapters 5–7.

war. In addition to the Bible, he read other religious books he could borrow and even carried a hymn book.[57]

Fielder, like Pendleton, conversed regularly with God. At the outset of the war Fielder's prayers seemed to be little more than a continuation of his prewar religious routine, for early in his diary he noted, "As has been my custom for years I offered my devotions to almighty God before closing my eyes to sleep." War-related adversity, however, soon replaced habit as the primary motivation for his prayers. Concerned about the fall of Forts Henry and Donelson in February 1862, the Tennessean offered prayers almost unceasingly: "for the last two or three days my mind has much run out in prayer for myself and family and my country and after laying down though fatigued and wearied my mind were much upon home my family and all my earthly possessions being between me and Lincolns army." Battle or its inevitability prompted even more frequent and earnest prayers. Although illness prevented him from participating in the Battle of Perryville, Fielder offered at least four prayers at that time for his comrades, his country, his family, and himself. Near Tullahoma, Tennessee, in late June 1863, Fielder, whose company was serving as skirmishers, wrote that the enemy was advancing on them and a battle appeared imminent. That night, "I endeavored to offer my devotions to Almighty God and Commit myself into his Care."[58]

Other soldiers recognized that Fielder was a man of God. Indeed, they repeatedly asked him to lead them in prayer during services, and he did so gladly in the hope that his efforts might accomplish some good among the men. During one of the regular prayer meetings in January 1863 at Tullahoma, the chaplain asked Fielder to lead the meeting, which he humbly did. Later he recorded in his diary, "I trust good was accomplished." On a warm July night in 1862 near Tupelo, Mississippi, Fielder was summoned by an old friend who was dying of pneumonia: "he grasped me by the hand

---

[57] Franklin, *Fielder Diaries*, 2, 6, 8, 28, 33, 41, 43, 58–59, 129, 135, 189, 192, 196–197. In Psalm 71, David seeks God's refuge and deliverance.

[58] Franklin, *Fielder Diaries*, 35–37, 40–41, 56, 82, 126.

[and] said he was going to leave me . . . and that he wanted to hear me pray one time more before he died[.] I kneeled down and tryed to pray as best I could . . . I staid with him for several hours." His friend died the next morning.[59]

William Lewis Nugent

In his letters to his wife Nellie, Captain William Nugent said little about his wartime religious practices; however, it is likely that this "sober-sided Methodist" continued many of his religious activities from the antebellum era. It is evident from his letters that he prayed fervently. Burdened by the hazards of military service and concern for loved ones left behind, Nugent laid petitions before what he described as "the rich throne of Heavenly Grace." The day after he arrived in the camp of the 28th Mississippi Cavalry near Vicksburg in March 1862, Nugent, who had previously served in a relatively safe position as inspector general for the state of Mississippi, wrote Nellie, "Yesterday evening & this morning I offered up my first military camp prayer for the preservation of my own life, if consistent with the will of God, and the assistance and comforting support of our Heavenly Father for my dear wife." In another letter to her just days later, he wrote, "I believe that God in his goodness, will bring me safely through the present troubles . . . but you, my darling one, have no unimportant part to play in it. . . . Prayer is the most powerful lever known in the administration of the moral government of man, and can secure to us all blessings consistent with God's will." Furthermore, Nugent prayed daily for his loved ones back home: "I feel, when I pray, for you as I do every day, that a good Providence will watch over and protect you & your little babe from all harm and danger."[60]

Although Nugent neglected to mention whether he read the Bible regularly, he undoubtedly did so. Concern for his family and himself, coupled with his inability to attend worship services as he would have liked, most likely led him to worship privately.

---

[59] Ibid., 3, 55, 59–60, 63, 103.
[60] Cash and Howorth, *My Dear Nellie*, 51, 54, 61, 83, 112, 131, 148, and passim.

Furthermore, his letters indicate that he was well-versed in Scripture: he frequently made references to the Bible in the encouragement he offered his young wife and former pupil. Seeking to cheer Nellie from Vicksburg in June 1862, Nugent referred her to God's promise in the book of Joshua: "God has said, 'I will *never* leave you nor forsake you.'"[61]

Nugent's exhortations to his wife began early in the war and lasted throughout the conflict. One of his first encouraging remarks occurred in December 1861 while he was serving as inspector general. He predicted a long and bloody conflict, yet urged Nellie to be "brave, my dear little wife, and if you have the assistance of the divine mercy & grace the true value of which misfortune alone teaches us properly to appreciate, 'all will be well!'" More important, however, were his comments late in the war, for while he intended them for Nellie, they indicate that his own faith had grown: "Oh! What a blessing it is to possess an elastic nature; one which no suffering can subdue, when sustained by the favoring smile of Divine Providence. It buoys us up; sustains us amid the most dreadful passages of life; and points, as an inducement to patience, to the 'Mansion not made with hands' beyond the surging billows of life's troubled sea." Perhaps the best testimony of his growing faith came in January 1865, when he wrote, "Were I not comforted continually by a firm belief that the promises of the Bible are true, I would often feel miserable on your account. As it is, I live on, work on, think on sustained by an unfaltering trust that he who numbers the hairs of our heads will surely care for my wife & my little child."[62]

Edward Owings Guerrant

The Christian neophytes, like the more mature Christians, carried on many of their prewar religious practices during the war. After his profession of faith in 1857, Edward Guerrant had regularly engaged in Bible study with other students at Centre College, meditated privately on Scripture and frequently read religious books.

---

[61] Ibid., 83, 85; Joshua 1:5.

[62] Cash and Howorth, *My Dear Nellie*, 48, 55, 83–84, 111, 120, 143, 156, 186, 204–205, 230–31.

Because his duties and the dearth of preaching in camp often hampered his attendance at preaching, Captain Guerrant placed even more importance on these other activities. When he could not attend church, he communed privately with God. On one such occasion he "rode out of town a little way—ascended the highest mountain I could find—took a view of the country and read two or three chapters in my Bible." How frequently Guerrant read his Bible is unclear, but his own words suggest that he read it assiduously, for in late 1862 he noted in his diary: "Tonight unpardonably neglected to read a page in my Bible."[63]

For Guerrant, reading Scripture usually meant in-depth Bible study, as this 1863 entry attests: "Read and noted some in Genesis and Matt today." Furthermore, as the war dragged on, he read Scripture related to the circumstances he saw unfolding around him. Disappointed with General Bragg's unsuccessful invasion of Kentucky in the fall of 1862 and the failure of Kentuckians to rise up and join with the Rebels, Guerrant meditated on three chapters in Psalms that describe the foolishness of man. In 1865, as the war drew to a close, Guerrant was drawn to the story of Job and his perseverance in times of adversity.[64]

Guerrant's passion for reading Scripture increased during the war. In May 1863, he wrote, "Commenced the New Testament and finished Genesis in the Old T. Both are *new* to me. I never read the Bible without discovering new truths and beauties I never saw before. O the depths of infinite wisdom contained within those familiar pages." A day later he echoed the sentiment: "[I] understand the Bible better than ever before!—A Great and Glorious Book." And his passion for reading God's Word continued late into the war. After engaging in Bible study one Sunday in March 1865, he noted in his diary: "I read the 10th of Job. *Most beautiful.*" Further evidence of this new appreciation for the Bible is that he began transcribing Bible

---

[63] Guerrant diary, 23 February, 9 March, 29–30 November, 4 December 1862; 2, 26 September 1863; and passim.

[64] Ibid., 25 October 1862; 22 February, 29 May, 26 August 1863; and 12 March, 3 April 1865. He read Psalms 12, 14, and 15.

verses. In the appendixes of some of his 1863 diaries, he recorded numerous quotations from Scripture, including each of the Ten Commandments.[65]

In addition to studying Scripture, Guerrant, like the mature Christians, prayed ardently during the war. As had the Bible, prayer took on new meaning for him. Now he was burdened not only with the prospect of death but also with concern for his loved ones back in Kentucky, who were living under the yoke of Yankee occupation. Guerrant prayed throughout the conflict for himself, his family and his country.[66]

Hiram Talbert Holt

Talbert Holt, another Christian neophyte, also persisted with many of his prewar religious practices. During the struggle he fervently prayed, earnestly read Scripture and consistently provided religious instruction to Carrie. Despite their relatively close proximity to each other (Fort Morgan was one hundred thirty miles south of Choctaw Corner), Holt expressed great concern for his wife's welfare. In May 1861 he wrote: "There has no letters come from any of you for the last 7 or 8 days I am getting very uneasy about you...Not a day nor night passes but what I pour forth the prayer of my soul's sincerest desire in your behalf, that he will alike shield you from disease calumy and want, that He will be a protector to you while [I] am away." Holt not only prayed earnestly for his wife but also requested that she pray for him: "Carrie let us commence on the 4th of August and pray for each other, friends and country at precisely one oclock, it will not prevent us from praying at other times, it will make our prayers more fervent to know that we are praying for each other at that very moment." Holt drew strength and comfort from his time in prayer and conversation with God. In an 1862 letter home, he wrote: "When I get afar down the hill of sadness and sorrow I fly to the communion of God who soon drives all my sorrows away in contemplating his divinity! his greatness! his

---

[65] Guerrant diary, 28–29 May 1863; and 12 March 1865. His religious references are in the back of volumes 13 and 15, both written in 1863.

[66] Ibid., passim.

truth! Which satisfy's me. For He is the good Shepherd and knoweth his sheep."[67]

Holt's faith in prayer grew during the war. The anxiety he exhibited for his loved ones was assuaged by God's faithfulness, which he acknowledged in an 1862 letter: "God has been good to me. I have always found you well in every way." His increased belief in the power of prayer was evidenced in 1863 when he offered spiritual advice to L. L. Dewitt, his long-time pastor and father-in-law. Evidently Dewitt had expressed concern about his sons serving in the army. Holt wrote his pastor and encouraged him: "Oh! What power in true prayer, you thus borrow strength from Him, who, is all strength. Then since we know of a surety that our God still hears and answers prayer, be not too much cast down, let not your soul be too much troubled, but only *Trust in God*, who will protect your dear distant ones for you."[68]

Although Holt's letters do not indicate how frequently he read the Bible, his command of Scripture suggests that he read it regularly. Until his death in February 1864, he repeatedly instructed Carrie in matters of religion and referred her to numerous verses in the Bible. These actions confirm not only that he knew Scripture well, but also that he wanted it to be the guide by which he and his wife lived. Indeed, Holt even admonished his wife when he believed that she had violated a biblical law. In a July 1861 letter to Carrie, Holt wrote her about their little girl: "I am glad she is so interesting to you. But the Scriptures Say 'Worship no idols above God.'" Furthermore, he recommended that Carrie turn to the Bible for encouragement and comfort. On his way back to Fort Morgan from home after a brief furlough in August 1861, Holt scribbled a quick

---

[67] Talbert Holt to Carrie Holt, 5 May, 27 July 1861; 26, 29 April, 25 November 1862; and 18 December 1863, Partin Papers.

[68] Talbert Holt to Carrie Holt, 29 April 1862; and to L. L. Dewitt, 19 December 1863, ibid.

letter to Carrie in which he said, "Remember to go to your Bible and your God for aid and consolation."[69]

Felix Pierre Poché

Confederate soldier and Roman Catholic Christian Felix Poché also steadfastly carried on with his antebellum religious customs. One of the practices he engaged in consistently was prayer. Like the other Christians in this study, Poché expressed concern for his family back home. A few days after he joined General Mouton's brigade, he wrote in his diary, "I hope... that God, seeing that I am unable to assist the two dear beings that he has given to my care, and placed under my protection, will guide them safely through their troubles." Furthermore, like the other Christian soldiers, Poché expressed concern for his own welfare, particularly when fighting appeared imminent. In March 1864 just before the battle for Fort De Russy during the Red River campaign, he wrote: "Soon the cannon will begin to rumble and belch forth their deadly missiles on that band of men and in a few minutes the ground will be covered with bloody corpses. And the very natural question would I be one of that number was followed immediately by the natural answer of probably yes. That is why after that answer I reflected a moment, and spent a few minutes in prayer."[70]

Poché remained faithful to the discipline of prayer and conversation with God throughout the war. By late 1864, war weariness augmented his other reasons for praying, and he petitioned God earnestly for peace. In February 1865, he recorded in his diary: "This morning arising at an early hour I arrived at the church, where I went to confession and received Holy Communion, which I offered to God in a special manner for the favor of an immediate peace, and to being soon reunited with my sweet little wife, whose absence makes me suffer so much."[71]

---

[69] Talbert Holt to Carrie Holt, 25 April, 12 May, 22 July, 2 September 1861; 16 June, 1, 13 December 1862; 19 January, 26 March, 20 April, 8 May 1863; and 17 February 1864, ibid.

[70] Bearss, *Louisiana Confederate*, 9, 13, 15, 64, 71, 77, 85, 94.

[71] Ibid., 136, 151, 187–88, 191, 201, 208, 211, 214.

There is no evidence that Poché read the Bible during his military service. Unlike the Protestant denominations, the nineteenth-century Roman Catholic Church held that Scripture was not self-explanatory and thereby required proper interpretation to the laity by the Church's sanctioned representatives: the priests. As a devout Catholic, Poché respected this rule but read the Liturgy of the Mass and a prayer book regularly. He also enjoyed reading other religious books.[72]

Giles Buckner Cooke

Those soldiers who made wartime professions of faith likewise exhibited steadfastness in their religious convictions following their embrace of Christianity. Following his conversion, Giles Cooke rarely failed to pray and read the Bible morning and evening. Although he did not mention the subject of many of his prayers, he petitioned God mostly for his own protection, especially in the face of impending battle. During the retreat of the Army of Mississippi to Corinth after the Battle of Shiloh in early April 1862, Captain Cooke was serving under General Bragg, a corps commander. As the Union forces advanced on them, Cooke recorded in his diary, "As the battle is drawing near I pray God to prepare me for whatever shall be my fate. Have mercy upon us Good Lord."[73]

Other concerns as well prompted Cooke to lift supplications heavenward. Referring to himself frequently as "wicked" or "unworthy," he regularly prayed for God's mercy. Having heard a good sermon at a church in Wytheville, Virginia, in 1863, Cooke wrote in his diary: "The weight of sin in me today is peculiarly heavy... but the Great Creator can even know how corrupt and sinful my weak nature is. May the Lord cleanse my unrighteous heart of all of it iniquities." As war weariness set in he also prayed earnestly for peace. In March 1865 in Petersburg, Virginia, he wrote, "Oh, that our prayers for peace and independence ascend to the Mercy Seat

---

[72] Ibid., 8, 49, 136, 175, 178–79, 182, 194, 212, 215; John A. Hardon, *The Catholic Catechism* (New York: Doubleday & Company, 1975) 22.

[73] Cooke diary, 30 April 1862; and passim.

today with fervancy and earnestness. May the Lord help us…and lead us in His own good time—to a lasting and honorable peace."[74]

An important component of Cooke's daily routine was reading. Each morning and evening he read both his Bible and Prayer Book. He also read other religious books when he had them. His routine was not performed perfunctorily; indeed, he evinced a genuine desire to worship and grow spiritually. Having lost one of his favorite religious books late in the war, he directed a statement to it in his diary: "I may never see you any more, but I trust that the lessons I have learned from you may be of benefit to my immortal soul." Relatively early in the war he pledged to read the entire Bible. In late April 1862, he wrote "Shall commence tonight at the Old Testament and read the blessed Bible regularly through. Commenced the New Testament a few days ago. I pray that God may implant its teaching deep in my heart."[75]

Although Major Cooke's position as inspector general required him to visit other commands, he seldom allowed the inconveniences of travel to hinder his daily practice. Wherever he was, Cooke made time to carry out his routine. He conversed with God and read his Bible in his quarters or on the railway cars en route to his next assignment. Even furloughs and illnesses failed to interfere with his daily habit. In December 1864 in Petersburg, Cooke was sick in bed but "did not forget to offer up a prayer in the morning to the Throne of Grace for the many mercies bestowed upon me and all those near and dear to me."[76]

---

[74] Ibid., 2 June 1861; 16 May, 1, 10, 29, 31 July, 4, 15, 24, 29–30 August, 6, 11, 13, 18, 24, 28 September, 8, 22–23 October, 18 November, 14, 20 December 1862; 3–4, 7, 23–24 January, 6 June, 19 July, 15 October, 22 November, 18 December 1863; 8 April, 20 May, 5 December 1864; and 5 January, 10, 31 March 1865.

[75] Ibid., 28 April 1862; and 12 December 1864.

[76] Ibid., 7–8, 28–29 June, 4–5, 12, 15, 19, 23, 29 July, 1–2, 20 September, 24 September–15 October, 18–19 October, 9–10 December 1862; 16 March–14 April, 17 May, 7 October 1863; and 4–27 January, 3, 22 February, 26 March, 5 December 1864. Cooke was promoted to major in December 1862. See Compiled Service Records, General and Staff Officers, National Archives, Washington DC.

Alexander Tedford Barclay

Ted Barclay, like Cooke, exhibited firmness in his convictions after his conversion. Although he said little in his letters about his religious activities (a year's worth of his letters immediately after his regeneration were lost), a description of his postconversion religious life can be pieced together from the extant records. Having been raised in a Christian home, he was undoubtedly accustomed to praying and reading the Bible. He continued to do so occasionally in the army prior to his profession. Indeed, concern for his family prompted him to pray for their protection before his conversion; but, on the whole, his letters suggest he seldom prayed. After his regeneration, however, Barclay's interest in religious matters increased, particularly, his interest in prayer. He prayed continually for his family back home. For example, in August 1863 he wrote his widowed mother, who was attempting to persevere under trying circumstances during his absence: "I know that you are troubled more than usual. God help you to sustain yourself under them all." He also evinced concern for his brother, whom he regarded as reckless: "I pray God to turn him from the error of his ways."[77]

Barclay also prayed that God would protect him during the numerous engagements in which he was involved. His letters demonstrate clearly his growing belief that God was faithful in answering prayers. Writing home after the Battle of Chancellorsville in May 1863, he admitted to his sister: "Feeling that perhaps at that time prayers were going up at home for our protection, I became almost unconscious of danger though men were falling thick and fast all around me." Even more telling was a February 1864 letter in which he encouraged his family to harbor no anxiety about his safety, for they all had prayed for him and "has He not promised to hear our prayers?"[78]

It is probable that Barclay read the Scriptures regularly following his conversion. He carried a Bible with him and appears to have read it conscientiously, for in an 1863 letter home he requested a

[77] Turner, *Letters from the Stonewall Brigade*, 61, 100.
[78] Ibid., 79, 124.

replacement: "My Testament got wet and is torn all to pieces. I have to borrow one when I want it."[79]

In addition to his fervency in worship and active membership in his brigade's Christian Association, Barclay began to exhibit characteristics of maturing faith. On at least one occasion he led the men in religious services: "I have just finished conducting our company prayer meeting.... Oh, that I could conduct it in such a manner as to impress upon some of our numbers to leave the ranks of sin and fly to God."[80]

Robert Augustus Moore

Robert Moore, like Cooke and Barclay, was a wartime convert who also exhibited steadfastness in faith after his conversion. Before he professed Christ as Savior and Lord in early 1863, his religious activities amounted to little more than attending services. His brief diary entries seldom commented on any of his spiritual practices. His post-conversion remarks, however, suggest that religious matters became more meaningful to him after his spiritual regeneration. On the retreat from Gettysburg, he made a diary entry affirming the importance of reading Scripture and prayer. On another occasion, after attending Sunday services in camp on 19 July 1863, Moore sought seclusion and "spent the day reading the Bible and in prayer.... How very sweet it is to commune with God. What a dear friend is Jesus to those who live in constant prayer with him."[81]

As Christians, each of the nine men who are the focus of this study had to reconcile killing and faith. Believing that Northern aggression provoked the war and that South was fighting in self-defense, each concluded that the war was just. Furthermore, these men considered it their duty to defend their country and repel the invaders. Under such circumstances, they believed that God would not condemn them for fighting. Indeed, they believed that God was on their side; not only was the war just, but slavery was sanctioned by Scripture.

---

[79] Ibid., 92–93.
[80] Ibid., 144.
[81] Silver, *A Life for the Confederacy*, 157.

During the war, these nine soldier-Christians were steadfast in their faith. Those who were Christians at the time of their enlistment, regardless of their spiritual maturity, maintained their religious convictions despite the prevalence of vice in the camps. Those who professed Christ during the war quickly became resolute in their faith. Although many soldiers in camp behaved impiously, these Christian soldiers not only expressed a determination to behave as required by their faith, but also sought ways to fulfill this lofty goal. They kept company with like-minded men and joined organizations such as regimental Christian Associations. Others were aided by their positions, which not only isolated them from the common soldier, but required them to travel away from camp. Throughout the conflict and whatever their immediate situation, these Christians remained true to their religious convictions.

Among the nine Christian Confederate soldiers, those who had practiced any form of religious discipline in the antebellum era continued the same during the war years. They attended worship, prayed and read Scripture. Some even offered spiritual direction to their loved ones back home. Those who had more mature faith, Fielder and Pendleton in particular, continued in their roles as spiritual leaders. As he did before the war, Pendleton preached regularly to the men in his command and in others, led his staff in worship and prayed daily with his men. Fielder also exhibited leadership in religious matters. He occasionally led the men in prayer and Bible study. Both men were respected for their piety. Nugent's religious activities are less certain. He held no leadership position in his home church before the war and may have done little to lead his comrades in spiritual matters.

The Christian neophytes did not become spiritual leaders in their camps, but they demonstrated firmness in their faith by continuing many of their antebellum practices. Like the mature Christians, they exhibited an eagerness to worship, read their Bibles, and prayed. They were stalwart, practical witnesses for the Lord to whom they had entrusted not only their lives and well-being, but those of their family and cause as well. The men who made wartime professions of faith in Christ also exhibited resoluteness in maintaining the standards required by their newly embraced evangelical Christian faith.

Each man, moreover, grew increasingly steadfast in his faith as the war dragged on. As opportunities to worship became increasingly scarce, each increasingly recognized worship as a privilege. Indeed, the men endured notable inconveniences in order to worship corporately or commune with God privately. The uncertainties of war drove the men to rely ever more closely on the providence of God. Exercising little control over their own fates or those of their loved ones, these soldiers of the cross relied on God to provide the protection they could not. As God proved faithful in answering the prayers lifted in faith and trust, their devotion to God increased.

Chapter 3

"INTO THE HANDS OF A FAITHFUL AND TRUSTY FRIEND" THE TRIALS OF WAR AND SOUNDNESS OF FAITH

"My grace is sufficient for thee: for my strength is made perfect in weakness." —2 Corinthians 12:9 (KJV)

Soldiers endured extraordinary adversity during the Civil War. The men who fought were deeply affected by the carnage and destruction they witnessed, the possibility of their own deaths and the prolonged separation from loved ones. The nine men who are the subjects of this book were no exception. Although numerous concerns troubled these Christian soldiers, they naturally exhibited the most anxiety about impending battles and the looming possibility of death. As their comrades fell by the thousands during bloody engagements at such places as Shiloh, Murfreesboro and Gettysburg, each man began to understand fully that he no longer exercised control over his own fate. Indeed, each turned to "Almighty God, the Ruler of the Universe" and relied on him for protection. As their God proved faithful in meeting their needs, the soldiers' devotion and trust in the Lord increased.[1]

---

[1] Giles Buckner Cooke diary, 4 June 1862, Giles Buckner Cooke Papers, Virginia Historical Society, Richmond.

Most of these fighting men of faith were also clearly concerned about loved ones left behind. No longer able to be present at home, to care for and personally protect their families, these Confederate soldiers of the cross prayed fervently that the Lord would watch over their families. Again, they readily acknowledged God's faithfulness in answering those prayers and their faith grew in proportion. Each man in this study had his faith tested and purified by the war. And at the end of the conflict, the surviving subjects exhibited attributes of a sound, maturing Christian faith.

Although Alfred Fielder, William Nugent, and William Pendleton arrived at the Civil War as mature, devout believers whose faith may well have been tested in the antebellum period, they learned new levels of trust in God through the more dramatic circumstances of the war. Soon after entering the army each man was open concerning his faith in God and earnestly prayed for the Lord's protection. Each drew great strength and abiding comfort from relying on God during their daily trials as soldiers. The faith that sustained these Confederate Christians as the war began became an ever stronger source of spiritual and emotional sustenance as the days of conflict and bloodshed followed one after another.

Alfred Tyler Fielder

A desire to come to blows with the enemy was common among unbloodied soldiers on both sides. Mature Christian soldiers like Alfred Fielder were no exception. When the 12th Tennessee was preparing to move to Columbus, Kentucky, in September 1861, Fielder wrote: "we are all excite[d] and anx[ious] desiring to be off." His initial sense of adventure, however, would not endure. In November 1861, soon after he arrived at Columbus, Fielder got his first taste of battle when his regiment participated in the effort to repel a small Union force advancing on Belmont, Missouri. The 12th Tennessee was deployed to reinforce the Confederates in the town. During the engagement, Fielder saw several of his friends fall and he himself "felt the wind from a ball brush my left lock or whisker." The next day he remarked in his diary, "Oh! how thankful to God I am that I am still spared and that I am what I am…. I do not remember to have ever seen a day in my life that I felt more thankful and more willing to submit to the will of providence." After his baptism of fire, Fielder was never again excited at the prospect of battle.[2]

The other battles in which he fought served only to reinforce Fielder's growing abhorrence of war. After the desperate fighting on the Union right in the Battle of Murfreesboro on 31 December 1862, Fielder wrote: "This day's battle was an awful one and will be talked and read of when my name shall have been quite forgotten." Again during that engagement he suffered a close call: a "coat sleeve pierced with a ball that graind my left arm and [I was] hit with two spent balls during the day." In August 1863 near Chattanooga, Tennessee, wearied greatly by the war, Fielder supplicated God's mercy for the battle that appeared imminent. He asked the Lord "in his providence [to] turn aside the threatened Cloud of war that now appears to be gathering about us and forbid the affusion of blood." Fielder persevered to the end of the war, suffering wounds during two major engagements: the Battle of Missionary Ridge and the Battle of Atlanta.[3]

Realizing that he had little control over his survival in battle, Fielder prayed ardently for protection. After each bloody battle, he quickly acknowledged God's faithfulness in sparing his life. Following the engagement at Shiloh in April 1862, he wrote, "I...passed the two days of the ever memorable Battle of Shiloah—the thousands that had been killed and wounded; and that I had passed through it all and was not seriously hurt my soul appeared to be almost melted within me in thankfulness to God for his preserving care."[4]

---

[2] Ann York Franklin, ed., *The Civil War Diaries of Capt. Alfred Tyler Fielder, 12th Tennessee Regiment Infantry, Company B, 1861–1865* (Louisville KY: self published, 1996) 4, 15–16; Christopher Losson, *Tennessee's Forgotten Warriors* (Knoxville: University of Tennessee Press, 1989) 33–35; *The War of the Rebellion: A Compilation of the Official Records of the Union and Confederate Armies,* 70 vols. in 128 pts. (Washington DC: 1880–1901) 3:306–10. (All citations hereafter are to series 1 unless otherwise indicated.)

[3] Franklin, *Fielder Diaries,* 98–99, 135, 141, 152, 189–90.

[4] Ibid., 44.

The impact of battle and the perception of the Lord's faithfulness in preserving his life engendered in Fielder a desire to become a more devout Christian. Offering his thanks to God for sparing him at Shiloh, Fielder pledged, "I intend to be a better man." He repeated the sentiment in January 1863 after having survived several more fiery engagements. Following the Battle of Murfreesboro, he wrote: "Thank God I have been spared to see the Commencement of an other year. Dear Lord help me to spend the future of my life more devoted than the past. It is my firm determination to do so." Recuperating from wounds he received during the Battle of Atlanta, Fielder noted: "I am quite feeble and have a poor apetite but my faith and trust is strong in God." The best testament to his strengthened faith, however, was made in March 1865 as the war drew to a close: "I have come up through many difficulties and dangers, but God's unseen hand has protected and shielded me thus far; for which I am thankful and feel in my heart willing to trust him in the future, believing his grace will be sufficient for me."[5]

William Lewis Nugent

After witnessing an enthusiastic parade of volunteers early in the war, William Nugent boastfully declared in a letter to his wife Nellie that he would like to "shoot a Yankee." In a less emotional setting, however, he was more pensive, even prophetic, about war. In mid-1861, just days before the engagement at Manassas, he wrote: "From present appearances this war will continue for sometime and every man will have to take up arms in defense of his country. The North seems to be as united as we." Months later, en route to Fort Pillow, Tennessee, Nugent expressed a similar sentiment: "My humble conviction is that we have not yet seen the beginning of the end of this war. Years will pass ere the smoking of the ruins will disappear.

---

[5] Ibid., 1, 8, 10–11, 14, 16, 21, 24, 26, 30, 36–37, 40, 43–44, 82, 99, 100, 108, 112, 126, 139, 141, 191, 214, 219.

Tears of anguish are yet to be shed, and homes remain to be destroyed."[6]

Like Fielder's, Nugent's detestation of war grew as the events he had predicted came to pass. The death and destruction he witnessed deeply affected him. Hurrying back to Mississippi with his cavalry regiment in early May 1863 to defend the state against Union invaders, Nugent penned a quick letter to Nellie from Spring Hill, Tennessee. In it he described the war-torn landscape of Middle Tennessee: "Broken and burnt fences, pillaged houses and untilled fields remind us of the presence of war in our midst; a war so devastating and dreadful. Horror of horrors is not a term expressive enough for war." The constant nearness of death made a deep impression on him as well. During the Atlanta campaign in the summer of 1864, Nugent described the harrowing bombardment of the city: "When one of these merciless missiles strikes down a fellow soldier by your side, the shock is terrible in the extreme. The sensation produced cannot well be described…. A spirit of awe and faintness almost overpowers you. I never want to see 'the like' again."[7]

Nugent, like other soldiers, recognized the hazards of military duty. Indeed, soon after receiving his appointment as inspector general for the state of Mississippi in July 1861, he wrote Nellie that he had composed a will, "in view of the uncertainty of life." As a devout Christian, Nugent turned to God for protection. In March 1862 he resigned his position as inspector and enlisted as a private in the 28th Mississippi Cavalry. Realizing that this new position would be far more dangerous, he prayed earnestly for God's protection. The day after he arrived in camp he wrote, "Yesterday evening and

---

[6] William M. Cash and Lucy Somerville Howorth, eds., *My Dear Nellie: The Civil War Letters of William L. Nugent to Eleanor Smith Nugent* (Jackson: University Press of Mississippi, 1977) 42, 46, 48.

[7] Ibid., 109, 200–201; Janet B. Hewett, Noah Andre Trudeau, and Bryce A. Suderow, eds., *Supplement to the Official Records of the Union and Confederate Armies: Record of Events*, 80 vols. (Wilmington NC: Broadfoot Publishing Company, 1994–1998) 32:421. (Hereafter cited as *Supplement to the OR*.)

this morning I offered up my first military camp prayer for the preservation of my own life."[8]

Trusting that God would shield him from the enemy's missiles brought comfort to Nugent. He firmly believed that divine providence controlled the affairs of men. In March 1862 he remarked, "We cannot all survive; and He who 'guides the whirlwind and controls the storm' can as well preserve us in the battle's front as beneath the shade of our own fig tree.... This is a sustaining thought to me and braces me up to a patient endurance of my present mode of life." Nugent's faith continued to assuage his fears throughout the conflict. Writing from Georgia in October 1864, he commented: "It is dreadful to contemplate the many, many dangers which continually surround us, and yet I do not feel alarmed, because my trust is in the great Ruler of the Universe."[9]

Throughout the war, Nugent maintained the belief that God would preserve his life. Anticipating his first major engagement in central Mississippi in June 1863, he wrote: "I believe and trust that I will be protected in the 'perilous edge of battle.'" And as he was spared time and again, he counted it as the Lord's faithfulness in protecting him. A close call during the battle for Atlanta, inspired these remarks: "The other day...I was reclining...under a pear tree preparatory to taking a nap, not suspecting the Yankees...when a shrapnel shot struck the tree under which I was lying and killed Capt. McGill who was standing by my side and quite touching me.... God has wonderfully manifested his love and mercy in my behalf."[10]

Nugent was grateful for God's faithfulness. In November 1863 he wrote Nellie: "If after our troubles are over we are privileged to reunite once more...we will have ample cause for pouring out our souls in adoration to God. So far I have mercifully been spared notwithstanding the dangers to which I have been frequently exposed, and I believe that I will survive the war."[11]

---

[8] Cash and Howorth, *My Dear Nellie*, 42, 51.

[9] Ibid., 51, 216. Nugent also expressed his trust in God for protection in ibid., 46, 61–62, 64, 76, 110–12, 144, 189, 196.

[10] Ibid., 110, 189.

[11] Ibid., 110–12, 119, 144, 189.

The letters Nugent wrote late in the war suggest that his wartime experiences strengthened his faith in God. Indeed, he seems to have learned much about relying on the Lord. During the continuous fighting and skirmishing of the Atlanta campaign, he observed that the horrors of war caused soldiers to have "a firm trust in the God of battles and a fixed purpose to abide [by] his holy will." Moreover, he applied the lessons he learned from his wartime experiences to other trials in life. In July 1864 he wrote: "There are so many sorrows in this world, so many difficulties, so many trials, that we need and must have encouragement and support from a higher source."[12]

William Nelson Pendleton

Reverend William Pendleton's reluctance to serve in the Confederate army was overcome by his sense of duty and a growing desire to defend his country. As a former professional soldier trained at West Point, Pendleton knew something of war and hoped that the South would be spared its great cost. Soon after the Confederates fired on Fort Sumter he prayed, "Almighty Father, spare the effusion of blood, frustrate evil counsels, order for our land conditions of peace." This was not to be, and in early May 1861 he agreed to take command of the Rockbridge Artillery, a battery recruited in and around Lexington, Virginia. Hours after accepting this position, Pendleton prayed for protection and guidance: "I go to the post of danger. Lord Jesus, go with me. Blessed Spirit, be my guide."[13]

The carnage Parson Pendleton saw during the war made a deep impression on him. The Battle of First Manassas in July 1861 was his initial significant engagement, and afterwards he prayed that he would not see another: "May God of his great mercy keep us from such a dreadful battle as the last. What an awful spectacle." In late

---

[12] Ibid., 179, 188.

[13] Susan P. Lee, *Memoirs of William Nelson Pendleton, D.D.* (Philadelphia: J. B. Lippincott Company, 1893) 137–38, 140, 143; William Pendleton to unnamed correspondent, 1, 28 May 1861; to Alexander Pendleton, 19 February 1862; to Anzolette Pendleton, 23 February 1862, all in William Nelson Pendleton Papers, Southern Historical Collection, University of North Carolina, Chapel Hill.

February 1862, when the Yankees began advancing up the Shenandoah Valley, Pendleton wrote his daughter, "The thought of more bloody battles is distressing." He never became inured to the appalling battlefield carnage he was forced to witness. After the Seven Days Battles in mid-1862, he found himself at a loss for words: "Oh, the awfulness of the different battle-fields! Language cannot describe it!" He was affected, in particular, by the bloody Battle of Fredericksburg in December 1862. The Yankees, he wrote, "suffered terribly. The ground was literally wet with the blood of the slain Yankees, awful to behold! On all the battlefields I have seen nothing like it."[14]

Well aware of the hazards of military service, Pendleton placed his trust in God for protection. In February 1862 he counseled his son Sandie, who was serving with General Stonewall Jackson's command, to do so as well: "Looking up therefore to our just Father, Merciful Saviour, and Holy Guide, we may go cheerfully on through whatever adversity he ordered for us." When his wife expressed concern for his safety, Pendleton replied, "God can cover my head as He has done before. If He sees fit to have my days cut short and your hearts smitten by such an affliction, He can make it work for good to us all." As Union forces massed across the Rappahannock River near Fredericksburg, Virginia, in late 1862, Pendleton again placed his trust in the Ruler of the Universe: "When I contemplate my own part in such a struggle, my feelings are solemn, yet trustful and hopeful. He who notes the fall of every sparrow holds in His hands my life on the battlefield as everywhere else."[15]

Like Fielder and Nugent, Pendleton acknowledged the Lord's merciful protection and expressed not only gratefulness but also a desire to become a more devout Christian. After the Battle of

---

[14] William Pendleton to Anzolette Pendleton, 30 July 1861; to unnamed daughter, 25 February 1862, both in Pendleton Papers; Lee, *Memoirs of Pendleton*, 199, 209, 247–48.

[15] William Pendleton to Sandie Pendleton, 19 February 1862; to unnamed daughter, 27 November 1862, both in Pendleton Papers; Lee, *Memoirs of Pendleton*, 180, 193. For Pendleton's other expressions of comfort, see ibid., 177, 180, 272, 341, 379, 385.

Spotsylvania in May 1864, Pendleton wrote home: "We have great cause for thankfulness in that…our lives have been spared. We have all been many times in the extremest dangers of hot battle, yet almost as by miracle not one has thus far received a scratch. Such protection from the hand of God ought to render us personally and more thoroughly devoted to His holy service." Pendleton was not immune to the consequences of warfare and, like Fielder and Nugent, also experienced close calls—brushes with injury or worse—in battle. One in particular occurred in Petersburg, Virginia, and profoundly affected him: "Saturday, George Peterkin and I were shielded again by the Almighty arm…[W]e escaped a shell by perhaps the sixth part of a second…A moment later for us, or earlier for it, and we must have been struck. I desire to be daily more grateful and devoted."[16]

Perhaps Pendleton's greatest trial during the war was the death of his son, Sandie, who was killed in action in September 1864 in the Shenandoah Valley. Someone of lesser faith might have faltered, but Pendleton yielded to what he perceived to be the will of God. He recalled the words Christ had uttered in the Garden of Gethsemane, of submission to a Will greater than his own, as an object lesson and comfort for his own time of grief. In a letter to his wife soon after receiving the news of Sandie's serious wounds, he wrote: "It has pleased God to permit a heavy grief to fall upon us. Our dear Sandie, [is] wounded…. Oh, how it extracts the bitterness from affliction to know that it is ordered by our Almighty Father as part of His boundless plan of righteousness and love!…Shall we not, therefore, submissively bow under His dealings? 'Father, not my will, but thine, be done.'" After Sandie died, his grieving father again demonstrated deep faith by encouraging the sorrowing family back home: "Our fallen nature finds it hard to realize how blessed they are whom God prepares and takes to Himself, and how peacefully we may walk with Him even in sorrow."[17]

The faith of the Christian neophytes was likewise strengthened during the war. Unlike the mature Christians in this study, these

[16] Lee, *Memoirs of Pendleton*, 331–32, 367–68.
[17] Ibid., 370–71, 376–77.

three young men had not yet been tested by the trials of life that strengthen one's faith. This was to change, however, as they endured the fiery maelstrom of war. Though comparatively "young in faith," Guerrant, Holt, and Poché relied on the Lord's protection and attributed the sparing of their lives to their God's faithfulness. As a result, their trust in God was strengthened. They, too, evinced Christian faith that was increasingly sound and mature as the terrible years of internecine bloodshed drew to a close.

Edward Owings Guerrant

During the antebellum period Edward Guerrant held a naive and romantic vision of war. As a youth he "loved to hear about battles." His first few weeks in camp, however, shattered his illusions. The reality of war became all too apparent in the privation, vice, illness and death that were commonplace during wartime. Just weeks after arriving at Brigadier General Humphrey Marshall's command, Guerrant noted in his diary, "These wars of men are terrible things. No one who has not seen can appreciate it. Its external paraphernalia is beautiful—grand—but its inward trials and hardships and suffering and danger and death is absolutely awful. Today another four soldiers died in town: far away from home."[18]

Although he served almost exclusively in southwestern Virginia, which was not a major theater of war, Guerrant participated in several battles that placed him in harm's way. Like most soldiers early on, he was excited about the prospect of fighting the enemy. As Marshall's brigade prepared to engage a small Union force near Princeton, Virginia, in May 1862, Guerrant described the camp as "full of bustle and excitement." His first taste of battle, however, was bitter. Following the Princeton engagement, he wrote: "Here and now for the first time in my life I heard the death song of the murderous Minnie ball—which whizzed all around us, sometimes in very uncomfortable proximity.... As we advanced...I saw for the first time the corpse of an enemy—the fruit of war, the food of the

---

[18] Edward O. Guerrant diary, 20, 22 February 1862; and the appendix of vol. 9, Edward O. Guerrant Papers, Southern Historical Collection, University of North Carolina, Chapel Hill.

grave—the victim of folly and madness…. I pray I may never see another such sight." His position as Marshall's secretary had offered him little protection from the hazards of battle: "[Today I] was engaged with Gen Marshall—writing orders, bearing dispatches, etc. etc. Sometimes in danger—sometimes more than the soldiers." The battle made a lasting impression on him, and months later he remarked that "my war spirit has never been so fierce since."[19]

Later battles served only to reinforce Guerrant's antipathy for war. In early November 1863, his command advanced on a small Federal force encamped near Rogersville, Tennessee. After a sharp engagement in which the Confederates were victorious, Guerrant rode over the battlefield in search of wounded soldiers. Again, the scenes disturbed him: "I want to see no more battle fields. The utter destruction of property and life…Horses shot dead at their hitching post, or rolling in the agonies of death…The dead and wounded men neglected lying there alone–alone–alone."[20]

The engagements he fought in and the carnage he saw reminded Guerrant that an enemy's minie ball could claim anyone's life at any moment, including his own. He consequently placed his trust in his heavenly father for protection. As the soldier perceived that God was faithfully preserving his life, Guerrant's spirit of gratitude and depth of faith grew. During the retreat of General Braxton Bragg's army from Kentucky in October 1862, Guerrant acknowledged the Lord's role in his survival: "Thankful that I am alive! It is more than I deserve! If I escape with my life, where thousands fall—I'll ask no more!"[21]

Brushes with death, in particular, engendered much reflection. Attempting to move into Kentucky on a raid in the spring of 1863, Marshall's command encountered a small Union force lying in wait in a strong defensive position. Guerrant and other members of the staff were riding forward to reconnoiter when a Yankee soldier "fired

---

[19] Ibid., 15–16 May 1862; and 31 January 1863. Guerrant suffered several close calls. See ibid., 10 October, 5 November 1863; and 10 May 1864.
[20] Ibid., 4–6 November 1863; *War of the Rebellion*, 31(1): 563–66.
[21] Guerrant diary, 27 October 1862.

a ball just over our head—[we] sought the friendly cover of our good old mother Earth." That evening Guerrant noted in his diary: "I have learned a lesson I shall not soon forget. That however far away we wander from that Father's house, his board, his care, whenever, cold, hunger or danger comes upon us we instinctively arise and go back. While treading the ground of death today, I could but take this solemn warning of my own derilection home to my life."[22]

Guerrant's faith in God clearly grew stronger over time. Following the Battle of Saltville in October 1864, he expressed the belief that the Lord would protect him in the future because God "had shielded me thus far." That same year he wrote: "When I look back to the great past, and forward to the greater future, and trace the little footprints growing larger as they grow nearer until today they mark the pathway of a man in his pilgrimage. When we look forward over the untrodden fields of the great beyond where we must go, fields covered with clouds…strewn with thorns and we must go alone. No, not all alone."[23]

Hiram Talbert Holt

Holed up inside Fort Morgan with little in the way of hostile military engagement occurring, Talbert Holt was anxious to face the enemy. He also expressed concern that the war would end before he had the opportunity to fight. A few weeks after arriving at his post, the Alabamian boasted to his wife, Carrie, "Our company has been placed in the Casemates, where there will be no danger to us and while we can kill hundreds of the enemy at a shot." Hearing of Union naval activity off the coast of South Carolina in November 1861, he hoped that the Yankee fleet would "give us a call before long, as we

[22] Guerrant diary, 12 February, 25 March, 24 August 1863. Guerrant expressed thankfulness to God other times as well. See ibid., 28 February, 21 November 1862; 18 May, 19 June 1864.

[23] Ibid., 7 October 1864; and appendix of vol. 26. In his entry for 3 October, Guerrant mentions the massacre of black troops that occurred immediately after the Battle of Saltville. He wrote, "Scouts were sent, and went all over the field, and the continued ring of the rifle, sung the death knell of many a poor negro who was unfortunate enough not to be killed yesterday. Our men took no negro prisoners. Great numbers of them were killed yesterday and today." See ibid., 3 October 1864.

are spoiling very fast for a fight." The daily drudgery of military camp life and boredom stoked Holt's desire for combat. In November 1862 he wrote: "Carrie you may think that I am satisfied here at least better than if I were north, but it is a mistake. I am not winning glory here as they are, and not faring any better and I feel exactly like a caged bird that is always flapping its wings in vain to free itself. I never was so restless in all my life as I have been here for some weeks. I do wish with all my soul that the Yankees would try this place."[24]

The anxiety Holt experienced when it was rumored in July 1861 that his regiment would be sent to Virginia belied his bravado. Although he had declared in an earlier letter that he looked to God for protection during his military service, Holt expressed a lack of faith when he wrote Carrie about their impending move: "We will shortly leave for Virginia [and] there I expect to end my career! I shall perchance, never see my loved Carrie more on earth! And though my hands tremble and tears fall like rain drops while I write it, yet I feel it is so!… I must say farewell, you will get this with my trunk when I am no more!" Caught up in the prospect of what seemed his certain and soon-to-be demise, Talbert encouraged Carrie to remarry and offered instructions on how to raise their child. Holt no doubt spent much time in prayer over this matter and eventually placed his trust in God for the preservation of his own life, for a few days later he remarked, "Carrie I [am] more calm now. I lean more confidingly upon the Great I Am and trust him to help and bless you."[25]

The rumored deployment to Virginia did not occur, but in 1862 Holt participated in some minor military operations that enabled him to experience some of war's reality. In January the Union ships

---

[24] Talbert Holt to Carrie Holt, 25 April, 22 October, 7, 20 November 1861; 20 September, 20 November 1862 (typescript), Robert Partin Papers, Draughon Library, Auburn University, Alabama.

[25] Talbert Holt to Carrie Holt, 25 April, 17, 22 July 1861, Partin Papers. He undoubtedly drew comfort from describing God in such a manner. "And God said unto Moses, I AM THAT I AM: and he said, Thus shalt thou say unto the children of Israel, I AM hath sent me unto you" (Exod 3:14 KJV).

blockading Mobile ran aground a blockade-runner. When the Yankees attempted to capture it, nearby Confederates engaged the Federals and repulsed them, but not before the Yankees attached a hawser to the ship and towed it out to sea. Days later, Holt and others happened upon the body of a Union soldier killed in that engagement, an experience he described in his next letter home: "We found a dead man this morning supposed to be a Yankee, it was the most *awful sight I ever saw*."[26]

On 3 March, the 2nd Alabama was ordered to reinforce Fort Pillow, located on the banks of the Mississippi River in Tennessee. There the garrison endured a seventeen-day bombardment from Union mortar boats. During the shelling Holt scribbled a note to Carrie in which he requested her prayers: "Carrie let us pray for each other always. God *will* hear *us*." He survived the bombardment and credited God with answering their prayers and sparing his life. Later he described to his wife the horrifying experience of combat: "I must confess I have got enough of it. It was more dreadful than you can imagine…. Yesterday a shell struck a fellow and literally tore him into fragments, you could find pieces of him scattered all around." Holt's regiment soon returned to Mobile, but his limited exposure to combat had taken its toll. In a June 1862 letter, he made it clear that he had grown weary of war: "Maybe the time will come once more when some will be permitted to see home again but many poor soldiers will sink to their graves unnumbered uncoffined and unknown and even unwept. I feel sad all the while seeing so much of this."[27]

Although early on his faith had wavered, Holt grew to trust God as the war dragged on. In May 1862 rumors spread among members of his regiment that they were moving to Corinth, Mississippi, where two contending armies faced each other. Evidently Holt had prayed

---

[26] *War of the Rebellion*, 6:498–99; Talbert Holt to Carrie Holt, 25 January 1862, Partin Papers.

[27] *War of the Rebellion*, 7:915; Talbert Holt to Carrie Holt, 26, 29 April and 2 June 1862, Partin Papers. Holt also expressed his thankfulness to God for sparing him in Talbert Holt to Carrie Holt, 1–2 May 1862; and to Carrie Holt, no date, all in Partin Papers.

that they would not be sent, for in a letter to Carrie he wrote, "I have found out we remain at Mobile. Good, don't you say so?... *Truly God provides for those, who ask his aid.*" In April 1863, Holt's regiment (now the 38th Alabama Infantry), was sent to Tullahoma, Tennessee, to reinforce General Bragg's Army of Tennessee. Realizing that his wife was distraught over this, Holt wrote her, "Carrie no doubt you are uneasy, but you ought not to be, the power governs me hear that did in Mobile. Let us put our entire trust in him and all shall be well."[28]

Holt was comforted by his faith as well. He wrote Carrie before he departed for Tullahoma, "my body may get killed! If so it will suffer but a little while, thank God they can't kill the Soul...if I get killed, I shall go to a better world than this." Talbert was thankful for God's protection in the fighting near Tullahoma in the summer of 1863: "I feel too thankful to object to...any thing. Oh! I feel so grateful to you, my people all, my God! I have so much to be thankful for, that I was spared through the awful scenes which I have past, while others better were taken to their long home." Having participated in the Tullahoma campaign and General Bragg's retreat from Middle Tennessee, Holt wrote home: "Let us be grateful to God that He has protected us from all harm. True I have suffered since the middle of June more than I thought man or beast could endure, and while I have seen both fall and die, I am still spared & well.... Yet I feel even more faith now in the declaration of the inspired writer than ever before, 'That all things work well together for those who serve the Lord'.... Let us this day renew our vows & increase our devotions to Him."[29]

Felix Pierre Poché

Felix Poché saw his faith in God grow as a result of the battles in which he fought. After entering the army in July 1863 as a member of the staff of Brigadier General J. J. A. Alfred Mouton, Poché saw few major engagements. He did, however, participate in the Red River

---

[28] Talbert Holt to Carrie Holt, 7 May 1862; 23 April 1863, both in Partin Papers.

[29] Talbert Holt to Carrie Holt, 22 July 1861; 25 November 1862; 13 April, 1 September 1863; to Carrie Holt, no date; to Harriet and Drucilla Holt, 19 July 1863; and to L. L. Dewitt, 19 December 1863, all in ibid.

campaign that began in March 1864. On 14 March, the Confederates attempted to halt the Union advance at a point on Bayou De Glaize where the Rebels expected them to cross. "Being anxious to see the fight," Poché volunteered to serve as aide-de-camp to Brigadier General William R. Scurry, who commanded a brigade of Texans. Realizing that he could be killed during the fight, Poché "spent a few minutes in prayer asking God to forgive me my sins, and commending my soul to His mercy and to prayers to our good Mother, Mary.... I could not but ask him to preserve me for...[my] two loved ones." The Yankees, however, skirted the waiting Rebels and moved toward their ultimate objective by another route.[30]

Poché received his baptism of fire on 8 April 1864, when he participated in Lieutenant General Richard Taylor's successful effort to halt the Union advance up the Red River at Mansfield, Louisiana. After the battle, Poché visited the hospitals near Mansfield in search of a wounded friend. He was greatly moved by what he saw: "What a pitiful sight were those hospitals crowded with the wounded, the dying and the dead, friends and enemies side by side, some calling for help, others groaning in pain so pitifully that I left with a heavy heart." General Taylor pursued the retreating Federals and caught up with them at Pleasant Hill on 9 April, where the Yankees turned and dealt the Rebels a resounding defeat. Although Poché did not participate in the engagement, he walked over the battlefield afterwards and observed the appalling carnage: "We saw great numbers of dead, dying, and wounded. The field presented a very dismal and sorry spectacle with its dead the greater number of whom were mutilated, some without heads, the faces of other[s] completely mangled." Affected greatly by what he had experienced over the past few days, Poché attended Mass at his first opportunity and "received

[30] John D. Winters, *The Civil War in Louisiana* (Baton Rouge: Louisiana State University Press, 1963) 328; Edwin C. Bearss, ed., *A Louisiana Confederate: Diary of Felix Pierre Poché*, trans. Eugenie Watson Somdal (Natchitoches LA: Louisiana Studies Institute, Northwestern State University, 1972) 94; Patricia L. Faust, ed. *Historical Times Illustrated Encyclopedia of the Civil War* (New York: Harper & Row, Publishers, 1986) 663.

Holy Communion which I offered to God in thanksgiving for his special protection on the battlefield of Mansfield."[31]

Poché's experiences on and near the battlefield led him to rely more on God. On his way back to his command after a short furlough in late April 1864, he stopped by Grand Côteau and visited the priests at the college. "Being enroute to my Brigade, and the field of military operations and feeling that in these times of danger, one should do everything possible to be in God's good Graces, I approached the sacraments of confession and communion, and prayed God that he would preserve me." Poché arrived back in camp in time to take part in the small engagement near Mansura on 16 May. Although the battle was more maneuvering than fighting, the 18th Louisiana regiment, with which Poché was temporarily serving, endured a prolonged bombardment before withdrawing. He also participated in a small but fierce engagement at Yellow Bayou on 18 May, where the Confederates caught up to retreating Federals forces near the Atchafalaya River. Having survived all of these engagements, Poché was convinced that God was protecting him and that he would survive the war to be reunited with his loved ones. In a July 1864 diary entry he showed his great confidence: "I feel encouraged by the voice of God that I seem to hear in my heart assuring me that he will not permit this separation of those whom he had joined together...that soon he will bring me back happy and joyous to the side of my beloved."[32]

The three men in this study who experienced conversions during the war also grew in faith. These soldiers had attended church regularly before the war, but their faith was of a nominal character. Their wartime experiences triggered deep personal conversions and served further to strengthen the quality of their faith. Like the others in this study, these three endured horrific battles and the threat of death during their military service. They placed their trust in God for protection; and as the war continued, their faith in him increased considerably.

---

[31] *War of the Rebellion*, 34 (1): 564–69; Bearss, *Louisiana Confederate*, 108, 111, 114.

[32] Bearss, *Louisiana Confederate*, 119, 121–22, 151, 161, 137.

Alexander Tedford Barclay

Although Ted Barclay did not profess faith in Christ until April 1862, he and his family had long attended the Presbyterian church in Lexington, Virginia. There he undoubtedly received biblical instruction in the ways of the Lord and learned of his providence. On 22 July 1861, the day after First Manassas, Barclay hurriedly scribbled this remark in a letter home: "I write this morning to let you know that I am by the oversight of an all merciful God spared and untouched through a battle that was so destructive to others." His regiment, the 4th Virginia Infantry, had been in the thick of the fight and stood with Brigadier General Thomas J. Jackson on Henry House Hill, where "Stonewall" acquired his nickname. Barclay was greatly moved by the experience of the battle and in a letter home he described in detail the wounds of his friends who had fallen.[33]

Early in the war his thoughts turned increasingly to death. In 1862 Barclay made a profession of faith in Christ. After the Battle of Kernstown in March he wrote to his sister, "The voice of a Mother and Sister, the early death of a brother, [and] two bloody battlefields all warn me of the shortness and uncertainty of life." Two weeks later, Barclay informed those at home that he had professed Christ: "I have had a conversation with Hugh White on the subject of religion and trust that I have found the way to heaven. I am willing to trust my self in the arms of my Saviour." Hugh White was a private (and later captain) in Barclay's company and the son of Reverend William S. White, Barclay's home church pastor.[34]

The vicious fighting in which he participated and the carnage he witnessed served to increase Barclay's dependence upon faith. He

---

[33] Charles W. Turner, ed., *Ted Barclay, Liberty Hall Volunteers: Letters from the Stonewall Brigade, 1861–1864* (Rockbridge VA: Rockbridge Publishing Company, 1992) 23, 25.

[34] Oren F. Morton, *A History of Rockbridge County, Virginia* (Staunton VA: The McClure Company, 1920) 422; Robert F. Hunter, *Lexington Presbyterian Church, 1789–1989* (Lexington VA: News-Gazette, 1991) 62, 81; Lexington (Virginia) *Gazette*, 15 May 1874; A. T. Barclay, "The Liberty Hall Volunteers From Lexington to Manassas," *Washington and Lee University, Historical Papers* 6 (1904): 131; Turner, *Letters from the Stonewall Brigade*, 60, 62.

was, in particular, affected by the Battle of Chancellorsville in May 1863. On 3 May the Stonewall Brigade participated in an assault against well-entrenched Federals that bogged down in dense underbrush. As the hapless Rebels struggled to free themselves from their entanglement, the Yankees cut them to pieces with musketry and canister until the survivors withdrew. During the action that day, the gallant 4th Virginia suffered 48 percent casualties. After it had ended, Barclay described what he considered "the most terrible battle of the war." He wrote, "We marched slowly down the road, all the time under the fire of several batteries of the enemy.... A piece of shell struck my knapsack, but was too spent to hurt me.... Men were falling thick and fast all around me." After the battle, Barclay's regiment marched across the battlefield, which he depicted in another letter home: "The Yankee dead and wounded lay thickly over the field. Many had not yet had their wounds dressed and lay groaning on the wet ground.... Others could hardly be recognized as human bodies. Mangled and torn...they seemed to have suffered agonies before death released them." Barclay's letters suggest that after Chancellorsville his thoughts turned more to religion. In particular, his references to religion in his letters home increased noticeably.[35]

By mid-1863, Barclay was exhibiting characteristics of a maturing faith. In June 1863, as the Army of Northern Virginia moved north toward Pennsylvania, he hastily sent a letter to his sister: "I think before you hear from me again we will in all probability have had a battle. Fear not for my safety. God can protect me amidst the storm of battle as well as at home, and if I shall fall I trust that I will go to a better world and is that not gain?" Barclay endured intense fighting at the Battle of Gettysburg in early July 1863. Major General Edward Johnson, who had taken command of Stonewall Jackson's old division, led the attempt to take Culp's Hill, southeast of the town. Barclay described the action on the morning

---

[35] *War of the Rebellion*, 25(1): 1013–1018; James I. Robertson, Jr., *The Stonewall Brigade* (Baton Rouge: Louisiana State University Press, 1963) 185–89, 189n, 190; Turner, *Letters from the Stonewall Brigade*, 78–79, 82, and passim.

of 3 July: "Three or four times did he throw our gallant band against powerful breastworks and Yankees without number each time mowing them down.... I escaped by being in the rear of the regiment to prevent men from going off the field unnecessarily."[36]

Surviving yet another desperate engagement, the thankful Virginian credited God with sparing his life. Just five days after the pivotal battle, Barclay wrote: "We have pulled through trying scenes. Through all of which, by the mercy of God, I have been spared whilst others have been cut down.... Truly I feel thankful that I am spared." Again, God had demonstrated faithfulness and Barclay responded by trusting in him further: "My dear sister, how differently I feel now exposed to death and dangers with God as my protector. I care not what may be the privations and danger knowing that God can bring me through them all." After a small skirmish near the Rapidan River in February 1864, Barclay again articulated his strong faith, from which he derived immense comfort:

> I have just had another manifestation of His mercy towards me in being safely spared through the battle of another day. Though it was not a severe fight, it requires only one ball to end our lives and many a one passed harmlessly by. That is the time it is to feel how sweet it is to be a Christian. When the balls are flying thick around you and dealing death all around, to commit yourself into His care, that He has power to hurl by harmless the missiles of death.[37]

During the Battle of Spotsylvania in May 1864, many men of the renowned Stonewall Brigade, including Lieutenant Barclay, were captured. He was sent north to the dreaded Union prison at Fort Delaware, located on an island in the Delaware River. There he remained resolute in his faith. He wrote home soon after arriving, "Remember I have the same good God to watch over me and protect me here as on the battle field, and I still look to him for comfort and

---

[36] Turner, *Letters from the Stonewall Brigade*, 86, 90; *War of the Rebellion*, 27(2): 446–48.

[37] Turner, *Letters from the Stonewall Brigade*, 90–91, 125, 144; W. G. Bean, *The Liberty Hall Volunteers: Stonewall's College Boys* (Charlottesville: University of Virginia Press, 1964) 149.

consolation. I know that you remember me in your prayers to the Throne of Grace, so am willing to trust all things to His keeping."[38]

Robert Augustus Moore

During winter quarters at Fredericksburg, Virginia, in February 1863, Robert Moore made a profession of faith in Christ. Just seven months later he was killed during the Battle of Chickamauga. Although he made few references to religion in his brief diary, what little he did say suggests that he, like Barclay, became firm in his faith in God during the war.[39]

Moore was eager to meet the enemy on the field of battle. When his regiment, the 17th Mississippi Infantry, received marching orders to Virginia in June 1861, Moore boasted, "All seem anxious to go and I dare say will do some execution should they meet Lincoln's cohorts on Via. soil or if need be on that of any other state." His regiment arrived in time to participate in the first Battle of Manassas on 21 July 1861. Moore's regiment, however, was not heavily engaged and suffered only slight losses. The first battle in which it was heavily engaged was in October 1861 at Ball's Bluff, where a handful of Confederate regiments opposed the Union crossing of the Potomac River. The Confederates launched an attack while the Federals were in the open and vulnerable with their backs to the river. The commander of the 17th Mississippi, Colonel Winfield S. Featherston, ordered his men "to charge and drive the enemy into the river or drive them into eternity"—an order they obeyed. After the battle, the Rebels camped near the battlefield, which was subject to desultory Yankee artillery fire. Moore admitted: "Some of our boys were very badly scared. We all slept in an old barn when we were not on post. These are times that try a souldier and have found several of them inclined to play off."[40]

---

[38] Robertson, *The Stonewall Brigade*, 149, 221–26; Bean, *Liberty Hall Volunteers*, 189; *War of the Rebellion*, 36(1): 1072–73; Faust, *Encyclopedia of the Civil War*, 272.

[39] James W. Silver, ed., *A Life for the Confederacy: As Recorded in the Pocket Diaries of Pvt. Robert A. Moore* (Jackson TN: McCowat-Mercer Press, 1959) 136.

[40] Ibid., 26, 28, 36, 44, 44n, 70, 72–73; *War of the Rebellion*, 2:537–39, 5:357–60; Hewett et al., *Supplement to the OR*, 33:430.

Moore would endure many other trying times that tested and strengthened his faith. After desperate fighting in the Peach Orchard and Wheatfield at Gettysburg on 2 July, Moore was grateful to God that he survived: "Our loss was heavy, in the Regt. 223 killed and wounded, in our Co., 29. Several of them were my dear friends.... Miss. has lost many of her best and bravest sons. How thankful should all be to God who have escaped. OH! the horrors of war." Although Moore made no overt statements that reflected a growing faith, his writings suggest that his commitment to the Lord was strong and that he derived immense comfort from that relationship. In mid-July 1863 he wrote, "How very sweet it is to commune with God. What a dear friend is Jesus to those who live in constant prayer with him." In September 1863, just days before his death, Moore wrote what appears to be his last religious statement on record: "Oh that all would praise the Lord for his goodness and for His wonderful works to the children of men."[41]

Giles Buckner Cooke

War also strengthened the faith of Giles Cooke, who made his profession in June 1861. Although he served as a staff officer during the war, Cooke was often close to the fighting. Thoughts of death crowded his mind early in the war, particularly, after the Battle of Shiloh in April 1862. As an assistant adjutant general on General Braxton Bragg's staff, he compiled the numbers of killed, wounded and missing in Bragg's corps. Cooke was deeply moved by the carnage at Shiloh and feared that he too might soon be killed. Union forces were approaching the Confederates at Corinth in May and another major battle appeared imminent. During this time, Cooke prayed urgently to the "Most High that rules the Universe" to watch over him and "save my soul from death for Jesus sake Amen." Realizing that he was weak, he "prayed fervently to God, my Heavenly Father, to strengthen my faith and spare my life to live to glorify His holy name." His supplications to the Lord encouraged

---

[41] Silver, *A Life for the Confederacy*, 153, 157, 164.

and comforted him. Cooke wrote after offering one such prayer that he "felt much relieved."[42]

Giles Cooke's early experiences with battle clearly strengthened his faith. After he was transferred to the staff of Brigadier General Sam Jones in mid-1862, Cooke exhibited considerably less anxiety about the possibility of death and even made clear his willingness to yield to the will of God. Although he spent much of his time traveling on inspection trips, Cooke was occasionally in harm's way. When Confederate general John Echols was bracing for an attack by Union cavalry in December 1863, Cooke, who was serving temporarily as an aide to Echols, wrote that he "commended my own soul…to my Heavenly Father." In April 1864 Cooke was again transferred and joined the staff of General P. G. T. Beauregard in time to take part in the following month's second Battle of Drewry's Bluff. Acting as an aide to Major General W. H. C. Whiting, whose command played a minor part in the action, Cooke nevertheless witnessed heavy skirmishing. That evening he noted in his diary, "Have been mercifully spared through the dangers of the day, and all through the goodness and mercy of my Heavenly Father, to whom, I do from my heart give most hearty thanks." A few days later the Confederates assaulted the Union lines at Bermuda Hundred. Cooke witnessed the attack first hand and wrote:

> I could not help being very much affected at some of the sights I saw.… My heart is full of thankfulness to my Heavenly Father, when I reflect upon the many dangers that I have thus far passed safely through. I only hope and pray that it may be the will of Him who ruleth all things that I may be spared even to the end of this cruel war and then may I so live as to redeem in some measure my past sinful life and atone to some extent for [my] sins.[43]

---

[42] Cooke diary, 2 June 1861; 17, 19, 30 April, 3–5, 8, 15, 17–21, 25–26, 28–29 May, 2, 4, 7–8 June, 13 July, 27 August, 3, 9 September 1862; 9 August 1863; 5 June, 23 October 1864.

[43] Ibid., 18 December 1863; 16, 20 May, 6 July 1864; 6 February, 31 March 1865; Compiled Service Records, General and Staff Officers, National Archives, Washington DC; *War of the Rebellion*, 36(2): 197–204, 256–60.

Concern for loved ones at home was another source of anxiety for many of the Christian soldiers in this study. Unable to care for their families, these men, especially those who had wives and children, turned to God and prayed fervently that the Lord would shield them from suffering. Indeed, the concern for loved ones engendered nearly as much prayer and reflection as did the soldiers' anxiety about the possibility of their own death. As was the case when their own lives were spared, the Lord's faithfulness in protecting their families generated feelings of gratefulness and served to strengthen the supplicants' faith.

William Nelson Pendleton

During the war, Reverend William Pendleton often worried about his family back home in Lexington, Virginia. Mustered into the Rockbridge Artillery in early May 1861, he wrote home a few days later from Harpers Ferry, expressing concern for the family's well-being. As a devout, mature Christian he entrusted his family to the Lord's "Supreme Protection." Evidently, early letters from home indicated that all was well, for which Pendleton was grateful to God. Having received a letter from his wife in July 1861, he wrote, "I am thankful for your merciful preservation and I pray God to continue to shield you and all I love." He was likewise thankful for the Lord's protection of his son, Sandie, who served on the staff of Brigadier General Thomas J. Jackson. After the Battle of First Manassas in July 1861, Pendleton wrote his wife, "I am thankful to our Heavenly Father that he has been pleased to preserve you and my dear son." He was troubled when he received no letters from home, but he maintained his faith that God was watching over his family. In April 1862, he wrote from Louisa Court House, Virginia, "I have not heard for a long time, but trust you all to the gracious keeping of God. His peace is much with me."[44]

The state of affairs at home served to increase Pendleton's solicitude about his loved ones. In August 1862, the vestry of Grace

---

[44] William Pendleton to Anzolette Pendleton, 30 May, 12, 24 July 1861, Pendleton Papers; Lee, *Memoirs of Pendleton*, 174, 177, 180.

Church wrote Pendleton asking that he either return as rector at once or resign his position. They reported that since his departure the church had had difficulty procuring substitute ministers and had held only irregular services. Furthermore they said, Virginia Military Institute was in full operation with many students and a large number of refugees had arrived in Lexington. A permanent rector was needed to minister to them. After much reflection, Pendleton reluctantly resigned as rector. The vestry then requested that his family vacate the rectory. Concerned that his family would have no place to live during his absence, a distressed Pendleton had to find his family a new home. The new rector, however, intervened and agreed to rent the house to the Pendletons. The situation served to remind Pendleton that while serving in the army, the care he could provide his family was limited.[45]

Union general David Hunter's mid-1864 raid into the upper Shenandoah Valley was perhaps the event that generated the most anxiety for Pendleton. This was nevertheless a time when his faith in God was strengthened. Learning that the Yankees were advancing on Lexington, a disturbed Pendleton wrote his wife, Anzolette, in May 1864: "But committing you all, as well as myself to God's covenant goodness, I am strongly hopeful." He realized that he had no alternative but to entrust his family to the Lord's keeping. Two weeks later, and with still no word from his family, he reaffirmed his belief that his heavenly father was able to protect them from harm: "Language cannot express the concern I have felt for you all since it became known that the Yankees were likely to reach Staunton and

[45] Grace Episcopal Church, Lexington, Virginia, Vestry Minutes, 1840–1913, 4 August, 31 December 1862; and 15 July 1863, Robert E. Lee Memorial Church, Lexington, Virginia; Grace Episcopal Church Vestry to William Pendleton, 4 August 1862; Anzolette Pendleton to William Pendleton, 8 August 1862; William Pendleton to Anzolette Pendleton, 22 December 1862; to Grace Episcopal Church Vestry, 24 December 1862; T. H. Williamson to William Pendleton, 15 January 1863; all in Pendleton Papers; George M. Brooke, Jr., *General Lee's Church* (Lexington VA: News-Gazette, 1984) 18–19; W. G. Bean, *Stonewall's Man: Sandie Pendleton* (Chapel Hill: University of North Carolina, 1959) 146–48.

Lexington. My trust is strong in the overruling care of the Almighty that He will not permit you all to be cruelly injured."[46]

Pendleton's apprehension, it seems, was not unwarranted. During the battle for Lexington, Mrs. Pendleton and her daughters endured many trying circumstances, including a Union bombardment. She wrote afterwards, "The wretches shelled the town for hours. Shells fell everywhere in the town.... [O]ne fell in the garden here...[and] several small bullets were found in the upper porch." After the small Rebel force defending Lexington withdrew, the Yankees poured into the defenseless town. They pillaged several private dwellings, including Parson Pendleton's. His daughter wrote, "They were as insolent as possible and cursed and swore, vowed they would have anything and everything they wanted." They demanded food and searched all parts of the house, confiscating those items they considered contraband. "All day they threatened to burn this house," his daughter Rose wrote. Indeed, Union soldiers torched several homes and buildings in Lexington, including Virginia Military Institute. Mrs. Pendleton was immensely grateful that the brief occupation had not been worse: "God be praised for delivering us from our cruel foes so far!"[47]

After the Yankees departed Lexington, but before he heard directly from his family, General Pendleton again wrote home. Although concerned, he again expressed firm faith in God: "I have been all the while as deeply anxious about you all as my trust in our all-faithful Divine Father and Saviour admitted." Having learned that his family had endured Yankee occupation, Pendleton wrote his wife: "I am indeed thankful that you were so providentially guarded from injury. He who hears and answers prayers has not been unmindful of the petitions constantly urged in your behalf.... That you are not rendered uncertain about subsistence from day to day is to me a

---

[46] Lee, *Memoirs of Pendleton*, 337, 340.

[47] Charles W. Turner, ed., "General David Hunter's Sack of Lexington, Virginia, June 10–14, 1864: An Account by Rose Page Pendleton" in *The Virginia Magazine of History and Biography* 83 (April 1975): 176–83; Robert J. Driver, Jr., *Lexington and Rockbridge County in the Civil War* (Lynchburg VA: H. E. Howard Publishing, 1989) 57–78; *War of the Rebellion*, 37(1): 96–97; Lee, *Memoirs of Pendleton*, 349.

matter of deep thankfulness.... On the whole I am very grateful to God that you are in proportion so well provided for."[48]

Alfred Tyler Fielder

Alfred Fielder, like Pendleton, expressed apprehension for his family during the war. Thoughts of his loved ones frequently crowded his mind, particularly early in the war when he had time on his hands. On guard duty at Columbus, Kentucky, in September 1861, the Tennessean's thoughts turned to his family: "Thought much of home and the dear ones I had left behind and devoutly asked Gods protection and blessings over them and in their behalf. I found my mind much drawn out in prayer during the night." He furthermore was grateful to God when he learned they were doing well. On hearing a report from a friend who had visited Fielder's farm and said that all was well, Fielder recorded in his diary that he was "devoutly thankful to God."[49]

At times, however, Fielder was uneasy about the well-being of his loved ones. After the fall of Forts Henry and Donelson in February 1862, his concern for family and home in West Tennessee was evident: "For the last two or three days my mind has much run out in prayer for myself and family...my mind [was] much upon home my family and all my earthly possessions being between me and Lincolns army." Although Dyer County, where Friendship lay, was not subjected to any long-term Federal occupation, it did experience raids and foraging expeditions by both sides during the war. After the Army of Mississippi evacuated Corinth, Mississippi, in May 1862, Fielder visited his brother in nearby Grenada. There he attended church with his brother's family and was moved to think about those back home: "I felt my heart much drawn out after my wife and family and friends who are now exposed to the enemy. Oh! that God may throw the arms of his protection around them and protect them from insult and abuse." When he heard in July 1862 that his family had been "unmolested" by the Yankees, Fielder

[48] Lee, *Memoirs of Pendleton*, 342, 350.
[49] Franklin, *Fielder Diaries*, 5, 7–9, 13, 30, 32, 35, 41, 51, 59, 62–63, 65, 91, 94, 105, 121, 133, 135, 172, 193.

acknowledged God's faithfulness: "I thank God, for in his care I commit myself, my wife and family and all that I possess."[50]

Fielder's belief that God would shield his family during the war never wavered. Indeed, as the war progressed, he grew more resolute in that faith and expressed a willingness to trust in God further. Resting under a tree near Tupelo, Mississippi, in July 1862, he again turned his thoughts toward his loved ones: "Thought much of home...my mind was much drawn in prayer for my self and family...my trust is still firmly fixed in God." As the war drew to a close his increased faith in the Lord's providential protection was even more evident. He wrote in January 1865 before returning to his command following a brief furlough home: "This is the day I am to start for the army of Tennessee. My trust is firm in God and into his hands I commit my family as into the hands of a faithful and trusty friend.... Although we parted in tears I trust we will meet again."[51]

William Lewis Nugent

Married to Nellie just months before he began military service to the Confederacy, William Nugent considered the absence from his young wife a severe trial. Responding in March 1862 to a letter in which she expressed how she longed for his return, he admitted that he too missed her: "Oh! Nellie, you don't know how sad and lonely I am without you." He never became inured to her absence; indeed, his desire to reunite with her grew stronger during the war. In April 1864 he wrote that "our separation haunts me at every leisure moment." Moreover, Nugent was clearly concerned for Nellie, for he prayed daily for her protection and often closed his letters with sentiments such as: "May He who 'tempers the wind to the shorn lamb' have you in his holy keeping is the daily prayer of your devoted husband." Like Pendleton and Fielder, when Nugent learned that all was well at home, he credited and thanked God for the glad circumstances. He wrote in June 1862: "To know that you are alive

---

[50] Ibid., 35, 41, 59, 63; *History of Tennessee from the Earliest Time to the Present; Together With an Historical and a Biographical Sketch of Gibson, Obion, Dyer, Weakley and Lake Counties* (Nashville: Goodspeed Publishing Company, 1887) 847.

[51] Franklin, *Fielder Diaries*, 62, 121, 214.

and comparatively well…induces a large outpouring of heartfelt gratitude to God for his unspeakable goodness and mercy."[52]

There were times when Nugent grew uneasy about Nellie's well-being, but he maintained firm faith that God would continue to protect her. In the spring of 1862 Nellie was expecting their first child. Although concerned about the delivery and her delicate health, Nugent felt "assured…that God will answer my prayers and bring you safely thru'…all your troubles. The feeling is impressed strongly upon my mind at everytime I kneel before the throne of Grace." After the birth, Nugent desired to return home and share the responsibilities of child-rearing that fell heavily on Nellie, but knew he could not. He instead relied on the Lord to strengthen her, and he encouraged her to rely on God as well. He admitted, "the thought is a painful one that I am not privileged to be with you and bear the heavy responsibilities and great anxiety in reference to our darling baby…. Trust in God and fear not. I feel, when I pray, for you as I do every day, that a good Providence will watch over and protect you and your little babe from all harm and danger." The birth of their second child in the fall of 1863 was difficult and it appeared that the child might not survive. In a letter home soon after hearing the news, Nugent placed his trust in the "Giver of all good" and gave voice to a steadfast faith: "If God, my darling, in his infinite mercy, see fit to take our babe away from us, we must bow with resignation to his afflicting hand and draw therefrom lessons of fortitude and usefulness."[53]

Nugent also worried about the military activity near their home in Greenville, Mississippi. The river town suffered from frequent Union raids and occasional naval bombardment. Indeed, shots fired by Union gunboats in January 1863 claimed the life of Nellie's father, Abram F. Smith, who reportedly was riding on a levee when he was struck. Such news made Nugent anxious. In late 1863 he

---

[52] Cash and Howorth, *My Dear Nellie*, 42, 45, 47, 55, 58, 61, 63, 74, 81, 171–72, and passim.

[53] Ibid., 64, 83, 143, 145-147. In a subsequent letter, Nugent learned that the child was doing well and would survive, for which he was thankful to God.

requested and received a leave of absence in order to move his family inland, out of harm's way. In August 1864 a Union force raided the town and burned almost every building and private dwelling, including the Smith's home. But Nugent's faith did not falter. He encouraged Nellie to "be in good heart and trust in Providence…. The good Lord will not forsake us."[54]

Although he made no explicit statements that his faith had grown during the conflict, the "Sober-sided Methodist" likely enjoyed a stronger trust in God late in the war. He, like Pendleton and Fielder, had expressed concern about many matters over which he had little control; he nevertheless placed his trust in the "Giver of all good." Furthermore, he acknowledged the Lord's faithfulness when his prayers were answered and his faith never wavered. One of Nugent's letters to Nellie in the last few weeks of the war demonstrates the resoluteness of his faith: "Were I not comforted continually by a firm belief that the promises of the bible are true, I would often feel miserable on your account. As it is, I live on, work on, think on sustained by an unfaltering trust that he who numbers the hairs of our heads will surely care for my wife and my little child."[55]

The Christian neophytes also were concerned about their loved ones back home. They initially were not only more anxious about the state of affairs at home than the mature Christians in this study, but also exhibited less ability to call upon faith's resources to quell that anxiety. Like their mature brethren, however, these three men eventually found recourse in the Lord, asking God to watch over their families and placing their trust in the mercy of divine

[54] Bern Keating, *A History of Washington County, Mississippi* (Greenville MS: self published, 1976) 36–43; Cash and Howorth, *My Dear Nellie*, 96, 105n, 110; Compiled Service Records, 28th Mississippi Cavalry, National Archives, Washington DC; Notes on Greenville, no date, Susie Trigg papers, William Alexander Percy Memorial Library, Greenville, Mississippi. Greenville's close proximity to the Mississippi River posed other threats as well. In late 1862 a Union steamer put off several prisoners infected with smallpox near Greenville. Nugent was distressed about the potential spread of the disease and wrote a letter of complaint to the commanding general at Grenada. See *War of the Rebellion*, Series Two, 5:803.

[55] Cash and Howorth, *My Dear Nellie*, 143, 231.

providence. When these soldiers learned that all was well at home, they credited and thanked God for the good news. Their faith and confidence grew in proportion to the experience of God's care and provision for themselves and their families.

Hiram Talbert Holt

With little military activity occurring at Fort Morgan, Talbert Holt frequently found himself thinking of loved ones back home. Less than two years before he was mustered into Confederate service, he and Carrie were married. Their first child, a daughter, was born in March 1861, just days before he departed for Mobile. Holt longed to be with his young family. A few weeks after arriving at Fort Morgan, suffering the pangs of homesickness, he wrote: "Carrie when I am not on duty I spend my time in looking far away over the blue waters towards my old dear home…and ponder and think of you."[56]

In addition to being homesick, Holt was immensely anxious about his family's welfare. Indeed, early on he exhibited little faith and feared the worst when her letters were slow to arrive. In mid-April 1861, he wrote, "Carrie I am puzzled to know the reason that I dont get more letters from you…. I feel like something has happened to you…. Probably I may be writing to a dead wife." Even brief periods without hearing from home caused Holt to worry: "There has no letters come from any of you for the last 7 or 8 days. I am getting very uneasy about you for I believe you would have answered my many letters if there was not something rong." When Carrie did write him, he often perceived her news in the worst possible light. Having learned in her recent letter that their baby was ill, a distressed Holt wrote, "Carrie you don't know how sad and lonely I feel this morning. I see nothing but my sick or dead baby and your tear-washed face…. I know *almost* after what you have written, that she is dead!" Holt prayed fervently for his wife and child, but struggled to believe that God would care for them. In one early letter he wrote, "Carrie for God's sake write to me and conceal *nothing*. I am

---

[56] Compiled Service Records, 38th Alabama Infantry; Holt manuscript, 7, 13; and Talbert Holt to Carrie Holt, 25 April, 12 May 1861; and passim, Partin Papers.

prepared to receive the worst. I try to place my reliance upon the God of the Just, who I feel will not desert me."[57]

Holt's precarious financial situation aggravated his worry over his family. Before the war, he had split his time between teaching school and operating a small farm in a struggle to earn a living. He did little better in the army and often was forced to borrow money from his comrades to pay for postage. Moreover, he had very little money to send home to Carrie. To make matters worse, in the spring of 1862 Clarke County was deluged by heavy rainfall that destroyed many crops. Things got so bad that neighboring counties donated food to Clarke County families. After a visit home in September 1861, Holt returned to camp greatly concerned for the welfare of his family. He was determined, however, to provide for them and began selling various items to his fellow soldiers to make a few extra dollars to send home. In his letters to Carrie he requested that she send him items in demand: hats, gray cloth, soap, and even hogs. Indeed, Holt became an enterprising young man always on the lookout for a quick profit. In November 1862 he even instructed Carrie to keep an eye out for deserters and "catch all you can; it pays to catch them."[58]

Holt's anxiety over his loved ones eventually drew him closer to the Lord. Two months after his daughter's recovery from illness, he revealed a stronger faith: "The soul that can lean upon God, has a prop both sure and steadfast, one that will never forsake him." Furthermore, as each letter from home confirmed that all was well and that his concerns were unwarranted, Holt became more grateful and acknowledged the Lord's faithfulness. In April 1862 he wrote,

---

[57] Talbert Holt to Carrie Holt, 13 April, 5, 23 May, 20 June, 12 July, 1, 3 November, 29 December 1861; 22 May, 2, 23 June, 22, 30 August, 22, 24 September 1862; 10 March 1863, Partin Papers.

[58] Talbert Holt to Carrie Holt, 11 April, 5 May, 22 September 1861; 10, 23 June, 6, 12 July, 22, 30 August, 6, 20, 24 September, 25 November 1862; 17–18 February 1864, ibid.; Helen M. Akens, "Clarke County, 1860–1865" (M.A. thesis, University of Alabama, 1956) 80–81. The lack of money for postage may also be the reason for the intermittent letters from Carrie. See Talbert Holt to Carrie Holt, 13 April, 5 May, 3 November 1861, Partin Papers. For a complete description of Holt's enterprising activities, see Robert Partin, "'The Money Matters' of a Confederate Soldier," *Alabama Historical Quarterly* 25 (Spring–Summer 1963): 49–69.

"How unthankful we creatures are, other poor soldiers have returned to their homes and found their families dying or dead! God has been good to me. I have always found you well in every way.... Yes Carrie trust God for his mercies." Months later, when Carrie reported that she was ill, Holt's response was much different than his earlier comments: "Carrie I was pained to hear...that you was sick.... I was pained to know it...but I ask God to take care of you for me, I believe he will do it. The lone Soldier's midnight wakings, tears, sighs, and prayers will be heard and you will get well!" Holt would still endure anxious moments as the war dragged on, but his faith had grown significantly.[59]

As with Pendleton, the extent to which Holt's faith had grown is also evident in his response to the news of a loved one's death. Upon learning that his second daughter had died, an infant whom he had never seen, Holt wrote Carrie: "I hope you have borne your loss with Christian fortitude, and that like good old Job, you have exclaimed 'The Lord giveth and the Lord taketh away, thrice blessed be the name of our Lord.'"[60]

Felix Pierre Poché

Felix Poché was another young Christian whose faith was tested by absence from loved ones. The Lafourche district was abandoned by the Confederates in mid-1863, but Poché found it difficult to leave his wife and young daughter behind. Soon after joining the commissary department of Brigadier General J. J. A. Alfred Mouton's brigade in July 1863, a troubled Poché placed the protection of his family in God's hands: "I hope however, that God, seeing that I am unable to assist the two dear beings that he has given to my care, and placed under my protection, will guide them safely through their troubles, and soon allow me to be solaced in hearing good news from [them]." Poché continued to plead that God would act on behalf of his family and derived considerable comfort from these special times of prayer. In January 1864, after attending Mass and offering "most

[59] Talbert Holt to Carrie Holt, 22, 27 July 1861; 4 January, 29 April, 6, 20 September 1862; 1 September 1863; and to Carrie Holt, n.d., all in Partin Papers.
[60] Talbert Holt to Carrie Holt, 29 January 1864; and Holt manuscript, 13, ibid.

fervent prayers" for his family, Poché noted that he "enjoyed several moments of perfect happiness which could only be surpassed in this world by the presence of my precious Sélima."[61]

Upon learning that all was well at home, Poché credited God and expressed his gratefulness that the Lord had sheltered his family. By early 1864 it was evident that Poché's trust in God was growing. Although, like Holt, he grew more concerned about his loved ones when he had not heard from them, his strengthened faith was a source of encouragement during these times. In January 1864 he wrote: "The complete lack of news of those two, so dear to their exiled husband and father is the most bitter sacrifice I have had to make for my country up to now. But animated by the hope of the supreme happiness which God has in store for me when he reunites me with that dear Sélima I bear up under it…with more patience than I thought possible."[62]

In July 1864, Poché obtained a medical furlough and retired to the Catholic college at Grand Côteau to convalesce. While at the college, he attended Mass almost daily and even began assisting in the services. It was there that he made his most forceful statements about faith: "What supreme happiness could I enjoy in this delightful sojourn…I feel encouraged by the voice of God that I seem to hear in my heart assuring me that he will not permit this separation of those whom he had joined together for their mutual happiness to last for too long a time, that soon he will bring me back happy and joyous to the side of my beloved." Several weeks later, after morning Mass, he noted in his diary: "I received Holy Communion, which I offered in a very special way to God, for the Benediction of soon being reunited with my beloved Sélima, and it seems as if God speaks to me, and promises me the realization of this sincere wish."[63]

---

[61] Bearss, *Louisiana Confederate*, 3–9, 13–15, 64, 70–71, 73, 76–77, 85, 117, 132, 139; Christopher G. Peña, *Touched by War: Battles Fought in the Lafourche District* (Thibodaux LA: C. G. P. Press, 1998) 400–403. The Lafourche district constituted the region southwest of New Orleans. See ibid., 3–4.

[62] Bearss, *Louisiana Confederate*, 30, 54, 78, 96–97.

[63] Ibid., 137, 147–48.

Poché's prayers were, indeed, answered. In October 1864 Sélima joined him at his aunt's home in Ascension Parish, just north of St. James. When she arrived, Poché expressed his appreciation: "I thank God to be granted my most ardent prayers at last.... I thank God and his good mother for the wonderful happiness that I experienced in this moment which will always be the most memorable and the happiest moment of my life.... I can never sufficiently thank him who took me by the hand and led me to the side of the one whom he gave to me as my companion on this earth."[64]

During their time together, Felix and Sélima worshipped together by reading Mass each Sunday morning. Poché's service to the Confederacy, however, was not over. In December 1864 he agreed to take command of a "little expedition" to capture some Yankee pickets near a mill on the Blind River in St. James Parish. The squad carried out its mission successfully, and Poché set out soon afterwards to obtain a permanent command of partisan rangers to carry out operations near his home. Such a command would not only allow him to operate in a locality with which he was familiar, but also would permit him to visit Sélima regularly. In March 1865, he was appointed captain of a company of partisans and was ordered to harass the Federals near the Mississippi River in southern Louisiana. His command carried out one or two small operations, but Poché was weary of war and was mostly interested in reuniting permanently with his family. In February 1865, after partaking of Holy Communion that he offered to God for a speedy reunion with his wife, he noted in his diary that he was "prostrated at the altar of my Saviour, addressing the most sincere prayers of an afflicted heart. I left inspired with courage, as an inner voice, sweet and full of goodness, spoke to me and told me that our prayers will soon be granted."[65]

---

[64] Ibid., 176–79, 182, 313.

[65] Ibid., 197, 214, 229–30; Unfiled Papers and Slips Belonging to Confederate Compiled Service Records, National Archives, Washington DC. Although the Confederate Congress repealed the Ranger Act in February 1864, many ranger companies continued to operate. See Daniel E. Sutherland, "Guerrilla Warfare, Democracy, and the Fate of the Confederacy," *Journal of Southern History* 68 (May

Edward Owings Guerrant

Edward Guerrant was, like Poché and Holt, a spiritual neophyte whose faith was tested by absence from his family. He was unmarried, however, and the concern he expressed about his family was much less intense than that of the soldiers in this study who had wives and children. But separation from his family did depress Guerrant. En route to his command in early 1862, he was thinking of home: "How my heart aches...with the galling thought that I may never witness them again! O my father, my little sisters, brothers, my relatives and friends—You nor I never knew the depth of the affection I cherished for you."[66]

Homesickness was the larger cause for Guerrant's frequent reminiscing about home and loved ones. Before the war he had grown devotedly attached to his family. His mother had died in 1850 and Guerrant, the oldest child, was expected to help his father care for the other five children in the family. His extraordinary affection for his siblings was evident not only in his wartime diary but in circumstances following the war as well: he became the guardian for his sisters and provided for them financially. Absence from family was a trial for Guerrant and one to which he never became inured. Wearied by war, Guerrant wrote in mid-1863: "And more than all this is the continual soul-harrowing isolation of myself from all I love. Though I never mention this grief it is ever present with me."[67]

Guerrant also occasionally made clear his concern for family back home in Kentucky, which he characterized as the "land of bondage." Indeed, there was reason to be concerned about his family. In the summer of 1862 he learned that the "Lincolnites" were

---

2002): 290–91. For a definition of partisan rangers and the distinction between them and guerrillas, see Stephen V. Ash, *When the Yankees Came: Conflict and Chaos in the Occupied South, 1861–1865* (Chapel Hill: University of North Carolina Press, 1995) 47–49.

[66] Guerrant diary, 3 February 1862.

[67] Ibid., 25 July 1863; and passim; Edward Guerrant to unnamed correspondent, 3 June 1862, Edward O. Guerrant Papers, Southern Historical Collection, University of North Carolina, Chapel Hill; McAllister and Guerrant, *Edward O. Guerrant,* 7–9, 59–60.

arresting both "old and young" Kentuckians who expressed Southern sympathies. During this time both his father, Henry, and his brother, Richard, were arrested. Although his father was soon released, his brother was sent to Camp Chase near Columbus, Ohio. Guerrant participated enthusiastically in General Braxton Bragg's campaign in the fall of 1862 to free Kentucky of this "oppression." Kentuckians, however, did not rise up as expected, and a disillusioned Guerrant returned to southwestern Virginia with his command.[68]

Although making no explicit statements that his trust in the Lord grew because of the concern for family, Guerrant nevertheless prayed frequently for his loved ones and entrusted them to God's keeping. Furthermore, it was common for Guerrant to turn to God in times of adversity. During the disappointing retreat from Kentucky after the Battle of Perryville, a despondent Guerrant drew nearer to the Lord: "'In God is our trust'…Still we will cling closer the Hand that afflicts us. 'He doeth all things well.'" As in other times of adversity, Guerrant likely turned to God when cast down because of separation from his family and concern for their welfare. That confident faith no doubt inspired him to remark in September 1863: "I have a firm, unshaken hope, it will all be well yet, and that I will again return in peace and joy to my long left home!"[69]

The three soldiers who converted during the war were, like Guerrant, younger than the other soldiers in this study and unmarried. While they expressed concern for their loved ones on occasion, on the whole they exhibited far less anxiety about their families back home than did the married Christian soldiers. When

[68] Guerrant diary, 24, 31 March, 30 April, 11 May, 4, 26 July, 10, 17 August, 7 September–30 October 1862; J. Gray McAllister and Grace Owings Guerrant, *Edward O. Guerrant: Apostle to the Southern Highlanders* (Richmond: Richmond Press, 1950) 42; Faust, *Encyclopedia of the Civil War*, 109. In June 1862 Union general Jere T. Boyle became the commander of Kentucky. He aggressively identified Confederate sympathizers and ordered them to take an oath of allegiance to the Union. Those refusing were arrested and transported out of the state. See E. Merton Coulter, *The Civil War and Readjustment in Kentucky* (1926; reprint, Gloucester MA: Peter Smith, 1966) 151.

[69] Guerrant diary, 30 April, 1 May, 17 August, 10–11, 26 October, 20, 30 November 1862; 28 February, 30 April, 5, 15 September 1863.

circumstances affecting their families aroused concern, however, these men turned to God and there found solace.

Robert Augustus Moore

Holly Springs, Mississippi, the hometown of Robert Moore, was subject to more than sixty raids by both sides over the course of the war and was Union general Ulysses S. Grant's headquarters for a time during his first campaign to capture Vicksburg. By late 1862 the Federals had stockpiled supplies in many of the private dwellings in Holly Springs to support the overland effort through north Mississippi to Vicksburg. On 20 December, however, Major General Earl Van Dorn and a small force of Confederates raided the town and destroyed over a million dollars' worth of supplies. In the process the Rebels burned several houses and other buildings. Despite these dramatic events, expressions of concern for his family are absent from Moore's diary. Indeed, the only reference to this action is his brief description of Van Dorn's successful raid: "Very cheering news from the West. Gen. Van Dorn has made a dash on the enemy's rear at H. S. Gen. Grant is reported falling back."[70]

The situation at home apparently was stable enough to allay Moore's fears. Although absent himself, his father, Austin, and mother, Elizabeth, were alive and well and able to look after the family's affairs. Robert undoubtedly derived comfort from this and expected little disruption of the plantation routine. While on furlough in March 1863, Moore noted in his diary, "Arrived at H. S....I can see but little change. Everything looks very near as it did two years ago." He did, however, have strong feelings for his family, and his faith surely comforted him during their separation. When his furlough had expired and he had departed for his command, Moore wrote, "Left home, relative and friends this morning and know not

---

[70] Silver, *A Life for the Confederacy*, 126; Ruth Watkins, "Reconstruction in Marshall County," in Franklin L. Riley, ed., *Publications of the Mississippi Historical Society* 12 (1912): 157–58; J. G. Deupree, "The Capture of Holly Springs, Mississippi, Dec. 20, 1862," in ibid., 4 (1901): 50–57; Faust, *Encyclopedia of the Civil War*, 781.

when I shall meet them again. Were it not for hope how dark would look the future."[71]

Alexander Tedford Barclay

Ted Barclay, an unmarried seventeen-year-old volunteer, seldom expressed any solicitude for his family back in Lexington, Virginia. He did get homesick, however, particularly at the outset of the war. Mustered into the 4th Virginia Infantry on 10 June 1861, Barclay wrote five letters home before the end of the month. He often enjoyed reminiscing about his loved ones at home. In a letter to his sister in August 1861, he even imagined what the family was doing at that moment: "It is about dinner time.... Ma is at the old safe getting the dinner; you, good-for-nothing girl, are sitting by your workstand pretending to sew.... but what was my own dinner consisting of bread and water." His devotion to his family and his desire to hear from them did not diminish during the war.[72]

Although he missed his family immensely, Barclay expressed concern for them only rarely. In mid-1863 his mother wrote Ted that she was having a difficult time at home and asked him to leave the army and return to Lexington. Although his concern for his family was evident, Barclay decided to remain with his regiment and entrust his family to the Lord's keeping. In August 1863 he wrote, "I know that you are troubled more than usual. God help you sustain yourself under them all.... God can shelter us in the storm of battle as well as at home.... God bless you is the prayer of your son." Union general David Hunter's June 1864 raid on Lexington, which deeply distressed Pendleton, generated some concern for Barclay as well. In August 1864 he wrote his sister from Fort Delaware, "I am greatly relieved at hearing of the welfare of you all; I feared it might be

---

[71] Silver, *A Life for the Confederacy*, 140–41; *Biographical and Historical Memoirs of Mississippi*, 2 vols. (Chicago: Goodspeed Publishing Company, 1891) 2:464. Both Austin E. Moore and Elizabeth Moore were listed in the 1870 census for Marshall County. See Ninth Census, 1870, Manuscript Returns of Inhabitants, Marshall County, Mississippi, 618, and Ninth Census, 1870, Manuscript Returns of Productions of Agriculture, Marshall County, Mississippi, 15.

[72] Turner, *Letters from the Stonewall Brigade*, 11–20, 31; Compiled Service Records, 4th Virginia Infantry.

otherwise." This, however, was the only reference Barclay made to Hunter's raid.[73]

Why Barclay did not exhibit more concern about his family during his absence is unclear. The reasons may be, in part, his youthfulness and marital status. Furthermore, it is possible that his firm faith was responsible; after placing matters in the Lord's hands, he did not dwell on the negative possibilities further. Clearly, his letters indicate that God's protection during battle increased his faith significantly. At Fort Delaware in July 1864, he expressed his firm faith: "I hope you do not allow yourself any uneasiness on my account. Remember I have the same good God to watch over me and protect me here as on the battle field, and I still look to him for comfort and consolation."[74]

Giles Buckner Cooke

Giles "Buck" Cooke, like Moore and Barclay, seldom exhibited anxiety about loved ones in his correspondence during the war. He, too, was unmarried but immensely devoted to his parents and siblings, and regularly corresponded with them over the course of the war. Cooke often had opportunities to visit with his father during the war. His father, John K. Cooke, served as a captain in the commissary department of the Army of Northern Virginia and when nearby often dropped in to visit Buck. Cooke therefore experienced little homesickness and thoughts of his family are noticeably absent from his early diary entries. As war weariness set in, however, his thoughts turned increasingly to his loved ones. While serving in April 1864 with General P. G. T. Beauregard in the Confederate Department of South Carolina, Georgia and Florida, he prayed for God to grant a "speedy, lasting and honorable peace. Oh! how I long for the time when I can return to the bosom of my family." Just days later, he

---

[73] Turner, *Letters from the Stonewall Brigade*, 100–101, 150. It should be noted, however, that Barclay was captured during the Spotsylvania campaign in May 1864 and was en route to Fort Delaware when Hunter's raid took place. There are no extant letters soon after the raid. His next letter was written on 21 July 1864 and does not address the subject. See ibid., 148.

[74] Ibid., 149.

noted in his diary that he had taken a ride on his horse "to indulge in interesting thoughts about the dear ones at home."[75]

Cooke prayed faithfully each morning and evening during the war. Although the specific content of most of his prayers is unknown, he likely included supplications for the Lord's mercy on his family back home. When he learned all was well at home, he thanked God and acknowledged the Lord's faithfulness in the good news. Sick and bed-ridden in December 1864, Cooke nevertheless gave thanks to God: "Though in bed did not forget to offer up a prayer in the morning to the Throne of Grace for the many mercies bestowed upon me and all those near and dear to me.... Particularly was I struck with a feeling of thankfulness for the Divine mercy."[76]

While serving as a member of General Robert E. Lee's staff late in the war Cooke did experience anxiety about his family's fate—as well as his own. In early April 1865 the Army of Northern Virginia evacuated Petersburg, Virginia, and retreated westward. Cooke exhibited grave concern for the welfare of his uncle's family, which resided in the town. He stopped by his uncle's home to say farewell and later wrote in his diary: "My heart ached—in contemplating what might be done by these [Yankee] demons." During the evacuation, Cooke also stopped by and visited momentarily with his mother and sisters, who evidently were residing near Petersburg. His concern for them was apparent and upon his departure he committed his family to the "care and protection of Almighty God." During the retreat, he was ordered to superintend the army's wagon train and participated in the engagement at Sayler's Creek on 6 April, where he suffered a leg wound. Uncertain about his fate as the Federals closed in, Cooke again turned to God and offered his final wartime prayer on 8 April: "Great God—make me strong—prepare me for whatever fate awaits

---

[75] Giles B. Cooke questionnaire, 1, Giles B. Cooke folder, Virginia Military Institute; Compiled Service Records, General and Staff Officers; Cooke diary, 13 October, 15, 29 November 1863; 30 January, 8, 17 April, 24 May, 9, 15–16, 23–24 September 1864; and passim.

[76] Cooke diary, 23 September 1862; 5 December 1864; and passim.

me, and do then—Almighty Father—watch over and protect while life shall last those who are near and dear to my heart."[77]

Although the nine men in this study may have experienced trials during the antebellum period, those former tribulations paled by comparison with the ordeals they endured during four years of civil war. The horrors of war, the possibility of their own deaths and the prolonged separation from loved ones tested the faith of all these Christian soldiers, regardless of their spiritual maturity. The three who were mature Christians when the war began relied on their strong faith to persevere. When battle appeared imminent they showed no fear but sought refuge in the arms of God. When they perceived the Lord's faithfulness in the sparing of their lives, these Christians made clear their deep gratitude and expressed their willingness to trust God further. They furthermore entrusted their families' safekeeping to the Lord. Unable to provide for them, these mature Christians turned the matter over to their God, and again found that trust well placed. Their faith in the Lord grew despite the circumstances of warfare that engulfed their lives. In the words of Alfred Fielder, God became a "faithful and trusty friend."[78]

The three spiritual neophytes saw their faith strengthened as well. Although these soldiers served mostly on the periphery of the war, they were deeply affected by the limited action in which they participated. Initially, their faith was given little expression. When battle seemed imminent or when it appeared that their regiment would move to the front, however, each man relied on God for his protection and credited the Lord with sparing his life. Consequently, their faith grew stronger over time. Their faith was strengthened by the perception that God had been faithful in watching over their families. Each of the three exhibited great concern for his loved ones. When the Lord again proved faithful to their family needs, these Southern soldiers of the cross acknowledged and thanked God; and His faithfulness served to increase their trust in him. Indeed, the faith of these men late in the war resembled that of their mature brethren.

---

[77] Ibid., 2, 4–6, 8 April 1865.
[78] Franklin, *Fielder Diaries*, 214.

The three soldiers who experienced wartime conversions also found their faith significantly transformed by the war. Affected by the uncertainty of life inherent in war, each of these men professed faith in Christ and became devout men of God. Like the others in this study, they entrusted themselves to God and expressed their profound appreciation for the Lord's faithfulness. Unlike the other Christians in this study, these three men seldom exhibited anxiety about their loved ones back home. On the occasions when they did, they entrusted their families to God's keeping. These Christian men, like the others in this study, experienced a strengthening of their faith in God.

Chapter 4

EYES ON THE UNSEEN WORLD
SPIRITUAL-MINDEDNESS AND NEARNESS TO GOD

> While we look not at the things which are seen, but at the things which are not seen: for the things which are seen are temporal; but the things which are not seen are eternal.—2 Corinthians 4:18 (KJV)

Adversity not only engenders from Christians supplications for divine assistance, it also draws them nearer to God and causes them to focus more on spiritual matters. Such was the case for the nine Christian soldiers in this study. Although steadfastness and strengthened faith were evidence of their increased devotion to God, these Christian soldiers also exhibited a growing interest in the matters of the "unseen world." They turned their thoughts increasingly to eternal matters and their everlasting home beyond this life. The prospect of heaven offered not only a refuge from the ubiquitous hardships, privations and death found in war, but also a place to reunite with loved ones who had passed on. These men furthermore evinced a genuine concern for the spiritual welfare of others. They noted with approbation the religious fervor they observed among an increasing number of their comrades-in-arms as the war dragged on, and expressed a desire to see soldiers as well as family and friends saved. For most, an ecumenical religious spirit prevailed, as petty denominational differences commanded far less attention than before the war. These men attended services not to adhere to a particular religious doctrine but to worship their heavenly father.

As these men drew nearer to God, their relationship with him was greatly strengthened. Their own shortcomings or sins became more evident to them and they demonstrated a deeper sense of personal humility. They expressed their desire to become more devout, enjoyed a comforting peace and joy, and exhibited a genuine thankfulness for the Lord's evident mercies and blessings.

The mature Christians in this study undoubtedly possessed a certain degree of spiritual-mindedness in the antebellum period. Two of the three (Pendleton and Fielder) had been spiritual leaders in their churches, while the other (Nugent) was an ardent Christian who consistently offered spiritual advice to his wife. During the war, however, these men concentrated even more on matters of the spirit.

William Nelson Pendleton

Unique among the subjects of this book, William Pendleton was an ordained minister of the Gospel during the antebellum period. As such, his outlook on human existence was already religious. As a soldier he did not forget his long-standing commitment to Christ. In this "double capacity of soldier and minister of Christ," he demonstrated genuine concern for the spiritual welfare of the men in his unit as well as those in others. He preached regularly to the troops and led his own men in Bible study and prayer. His concern for the souls of his fellow-soldiers did not abate during the war. Writing from near Fredericksburg in May 1863, he expressed his desire to continue God's work among them: "[God] will enable me, I trust, to do some good to the country, and promote His glory in the upholding of His cause and in the salvation of souls." Pendleton even sought to further the cause of Christ through the unfortunate death of his son, Sandie. Following the younger Pendleton's death in 1864, Parson Pendleton began preparing a biographical sketch of Sandie, including a description of his religious character, with the intention of publishing it: "[It] might be of interest and benefit to a number of young men, especially in the army."[1]

During the war, Pendleton's thoughts turned increasingly to eternal matters. He was immensely comforted by thoughts of heaven as a place where loved ones who had been separated through death could be reunited. In February 1862 he wrote one of his daughters, "[S]hould it be ordained by the High and Holy One that either of us must bid adieu to the earth and its beloved, each survivor amongst us may amid the desolation and anguish rejoice in tribulation and anticipate the day of a blessed reunion." Although Reverend Pendleton had lost a daughter to illness before the war, he was particularly distressed over the death of Sandie. He derived considerable encouragement, however, from his certainty that his son was in his Master's care: "The sadness we all feel...although natural, ought not to be indulged.... We are almost as sure of his being...in heaven as we are that so blessed an abode has been prepared for God's servants. And this assurance, rightly cherished, may well authorize the most cheerful state of heart we can cultivate." Furthermore, his letters suggest that he reflected often on this subject, for he wrote frequently about his son: "The sweet blue heavens speak of where the beloved of our hearts is now rejoicing; the lovely landscape, with its varied beauties, tells of scenes far more exquisite in which his ransomed spirit from henceforth delights, and where we may hope to join him in sacred joy."[2]

Pendleton also found thoughts of an eternal home free from earthly trials immensely comforting. In a letter of condolence to William Garnett in July 1863 about his son who was killed during General George Pickett's charge at Gettysburg, he wrote that he had

---

[1] William Pendleton to unnamed correspondent, 25 October 1864, William Nelson Pendleton Papers, Southern Historical Collection, University of North Carolina, Chapel Hill; Susan P. Lee, *Memoirs of William Nelson Pendleton, D.D.* (Philadelphia: J. B. Lippincott Company, 1893) 142–43, 171, 180, 184, 189, 191, 236, 272, 302, 336–37, 344, 359, 374.

[2] William Pendleton to unnamed daughter, 25 February 1862, Pendleton Papers; Lee, *Memoirs of Pendleton*, 370–78, 385.

"received admission into a home where pain ceases, because sin cannot enter."[3]

Although he had attended the religious services of other faiths occasionally before the war, Pendleton was a faithful member of the Episcopal Church. During the war, however, he occasionally attended religious services administered by a clergyman of another denomination. Although convenience may have also been a motivation, it is evident that his focus had become more interdenominational. As a minister, Pendleton could have easily held his own services or worshipped privately if he found none suitable. But his desire for formal worship overcame any negative opinions he may have held about the other denominations. Indeed, he was deeply gratified—and perhaps surprised—by the eloquence of one Baptist gentleman: "[He] spoke extremely well, and made a most appropriate and fervent prayer." Furthermore, Pendleton often performed sacraments or ordinances for persons of other Christian faiths. Near Fredericksburg in May 1863, the parson-general baptized by immersion a fellow officer whose family were Baptists.[4]

As he became more spritiual-minded and drew nearer to God, Parson Pendleton became a more devout Christian. Indeed, his growing sense of closeness to God served to enhance the perception of his own shortcomings or sins and produced in the parson-soldier a genuine and deepening spirit of humility. Writing from Fredericksburg, Virginia, in November 1862, he remarked, "He sees that I desire in all sincerity to be a faithful soldier of the Cross.... And He graciously accepts, I trust, my unworthy services, whatever

---

[3] William Pendleton to William Garnett, 9 July 1863, file G-392, Eleanor S. Brockenbrough Library, Museum of the Confederacy, Richmond, Virginia.

[4] William Pendleton to Anzolette Pendleton, 23 February 1862, Pendleton Papers; Lee, *Memoirs of Pendleton*, 160, 256, 272, 313. Drew Gilpin Faust maintains that the war produced a strong ecumenical spirit among Protestants. See Drew Gilpin Faust, "The Civil War Soldier and the Art of Dying," *Journal of Southern History* 67 (February 2001): 8–9. See also G. Clinton Prim, "Southern Methodism in the Confederacy," *Methodist History* 23 (July 1985): 241–42.

error, whatever sin be chargeable against me in this as in other portions of my life."[5]

Pendleton's increasing desire to be close to God allowed him to thank and praise God in the midst of hardship. After the death of his son, he wrote: "May the Infinite mercy commemorated this day fill our hearts with peaceful gratitude amid the trials in which the season finds us! Surely we are blessed with abundant privileges still, though it has pleased God to lay His hand upon our joys." His birthday in 1864 prompted similar reflections: "I am to-day fifty-five years old, and the remembrance brings up the past with its privileges and its sins, its joys and its sorrows, and points to the future with its trials and mercies, its uncertainty and end. The most amazing fact that strikes me in the retrospect is that so much favor has been granted to one so unworthy."[6]

Alfred Tyler Fielder

Alfred Fielder, a pious lay-leader in his Friendship, Tennessee, home-church, also became more spiritual-minded during the war. Indeed, his wartime experiences reinforced his beliefs about the transitory nature of life on earth. When some of his comrades became preoccupied with drawing and hoarding supplies in 1861, he commented about their fixation on earthly possessions: "Every day experience teaches me the truth of what the wise man said all is vanity and vexation of spirit and that this world is all a fleeting show for mans illusion given…. There's nothing true but heaven." Other comments also suggest his thoughts turned increasingly to the spiritual realm as the conflict wore on. Convalescing from the wounds suffered in the summer of 1864 near Atlanta, Fielder wrote: "After I had committed myself in well being to God last night I commenced thinking on the love of God to man and my heart was melted down in thankfulness and God [descended] to pour his love

---

[5] Lee, *Memoirs of Pendleton*, 236.
[6] Ibid., 381–82.

into my soul—I felt that this world was not my perpetual home but I looked forward with pleasing anticipation to a home in heaven."[7]

During the war, Fielder expressed concern for the souls of his comrades as well as for the piety of the army. He was disappointed by the irreligiousness of the troops early on and, in particular, in their lack of reverence for the Sabbath. At Columbus, Kentucky, in December 1861, he noted, "I am sorry to say the Sabbath is but little regarded in the army[.] May God have mercy upon our rulers and our men and help them to learn righteousness." After another Sunday without services, Fielder remarked, "The day past away as usual without any public worship in Camp that I heard of. I awfully fear that religion and the worship of God is on the retro[grade]."[8]

Religious enthusiasm in the Army of Tennessee did increase as time progressed. The discouraging retreat from Kentucky in the fall of 1862 and the bloody stalemate at Murfreesboro at year's end triggered a wave of religious fervor that swept the army during its winter quarters near Tullahoma, Tennessee. Fielder noted with approbation the outbreak of revival meetings. He expressed his hope that religious interest would continue and that the men would derive some spiritual benefit from the meetings. After one prayer meeting he remarked, "I pray God that [the meetings] may be to his glory and our good." Fielder attended the services faithfully and often noted in his diary how many came forward as mourners. The meetings continued with much ardor until the summer of 1863, when the army commenced a new campaign.[9]

---

[7] Ann York Franklin, ed., *The Civil War Diaries of Capt. Alfred Tyler Fielder, 12th Tennessee Regiment Infantry, Company B, 1861–1865* (Louisville KY: self published, 1996) 21, 194.

[8] Ibid., 21–22. Fielder also thought that soldiers should be pious in order to win favor with God. In a December 1861 diary entry he quoted Proverbs 14:34, "rightiousness exalth [*sic*] a nation but sin is a reproach to any people." See ibid., 22. For more on the providential significance of a righteous army, see Gardiner H. Shattuck, Jr., *A Shield and Hiding Place: The Religious Life of the Civil War Armies* (Macon GA: Mercer University Press, 1987) 106.

[9] Franklin, *Fielder Diaries*, 102–24, 148, 164. For a description of the revivals that swept the Army of Tennessee, see Shattuck, *Shield and Hiding Place*, 100; and Larry J. Daniel, *Soldiering in the Army of Tennessee* (Chapel Hill: University of North Carolina

During the winter of 1863–64 at Dalton, Georgia, the Army of Tennessee experienced an even more intense outbreak of revivals. The wounds Fielder suffered at Missionary Ridge in November 1863, and a journey home in early 1864, prevented him from participating in most of these meetings. He would certainly have been encouraged by the soldiers' enthusiasm at Dalton; even late in the war he continued to express his hope that the cause of Christ was being advanced in the army. Attending a service held by his chaplain on 30 April 1865, just days after General Joseph E. Johnston surrendered the Army of Tennessee, Fielder remarked, "I trust its fruits will be seen in eternity—I felt that my abiding home would be in heaven."[10]

Before the war, Fielder was a devout Methodist and strictly adhered to the tenets of his faith. Indeed, he and his mother even donated property for the construction of a Methodist church near his home in 1859. Yet by 1863 Fielder was regularly attending services held by ministers of other faiths. In January he not only listened to a sermon by Episcopalian clergyman, Dr. Charles Quintard, but also partook of the sacrament of the Lord's Supper administered in that service. After another Episcopalian service, he noted its formality but minimized it: "The discourse was well arranged but every thing about their worship is too formal for me but I suppose it is just as one has been raised." It appears, however, that during this time Fielder continued to harbor some denominational tendencies, for when a Christian association was organized in his regiment in April 1863, he refused to join because he feared it might embrace doctrine contrary to that of the Methodist Church. Less than two months later, however, he reconsidered and admitted in his diary, "[To]night the Christian Association met and quite a number joined it, myself among the number." He seldom missed the meetings and at one even read an essay on prayer he had written. Fielder's primary desire was

---

Press, 1991) 116–17. For a description of revivals in all armies, both Union and Confederate, see Steven E. Woodworth, *While God Is Marching On: The Religious World of Civil War Soldiers* (Lawrence: University Press of Kansas, 2001) 193–255.
   [10] Franklin, *Fielder Diaries*, 180, 230.

to hear the Gospel preached regardless of the setting or the denomination of the officiating minister, a desire he retained for the remainder of the war. On one Sabbath near Augusta, Georgia, in 1865 he was privileged to attend a Methodist service in morning, an Episcopal church in the afternoon, and still another Methodist church that evening.[11]

Like Pendleton, Fielder thought increasingly of heaven during the war. Depressed over his prolonged separation from his family, he found hope in an eternal home free from trials and adversity. He wrote in his diary in June 1862, "I [feel] that this world was not my perpetual home but I was enabled to look by faith beyond the vail that skirts time from eternity where there will be no wars, no sickness, no pain, no death but...triumph o'er sorrow and death." Furthermore, he found comfort in the promise that heaven was a place where loved ones would one day be reunited. Following worship one Sunday in March 1863, he wrote:

> I felt that this earth was not my home but that by and by my spirit would be dislodged from this tenament of clay and go to dwell in my fathers house above, made without hands, eternal in the heavens.... I thought of loved ones and from whom I have so long been sepperated...perhaps we never should be permited to enjoy those privaliges again in this world but by faith I looked forward to the day when we shall meet again where...peace and joy shall for ever reign without a rival.

Upon receiving word that his mother had passed away, Fielder wrote in March 1864: "Thank God she had long been a faithful follower of the Lord Jesus Christ and...I expect to overtake her by and by in the kingdom of heaven where we shall never more be seperated, but where we shall spend a long eternity together."[12]

---

[11] Susanna W. Fielder and Alfred T. Fielder to A. W. Swift and Others, 10 February 1859, Deed Book L, 1858–59, 350, Register of Deeds Office, Dyer County, Tennessee; Franklin, *Fielder Diaries*, 103–104, 106, 114, 121, 137, 219, and passim. Fielder's chaplain for much of the war was a Baptist. See Franklin, *Fielder Diaries*, 95; and John W. Brinsfield et al., eds., *Faith in the Fight: Civil War Chaplains* (Mechanicsburg PA: Stackpole Books, 2003) 213.
[12] Franklin, *Fielder Diaries*, 55–56, 110–11, 137, 168, 194.

Fielder's nearness to God generated in him a desire to become more devout. Like Pendleton, he considered himself unworthy and sought to become a better Christian. He noted in September 1861: "Thought much of home and dear ones I had left behind...I found my mind much drawn out in prayer during the night and hope the morning found me a better more devoted man." Fielder's desire to improve his spiritual condition did not abate during the war. At Chattanooga, Tennessee, in July 1863, he climbed Lookout Mountain to commune with God and remarked: "My mind was actively engaged almost all the time I was there thinking of the great power and wisdom of him that spoke all things into existance...and in comparison of which how weak, feeble and insignificant...[is] man—I trust that what I have this day seen may bring about reflections that will make me a better man." Overcome with emotion after hearing the conversion testimonies and observing the baptism of several soldiers on a Sabbath day in September 1863, Fielder commented: "I can say of a truth that I have this day been enabled to rejoyce with that joy inexpressible and full of glory—This world is not my home but I look by faith to heaven as my home.... Lord help me to live more religious[ly] in the future than I have done in the passed is my prayer for Jesus sake."[13]

Fielder also manifested a heightened sense of God's presence. Following the Army of Mississippi's retreat from Corinth in May 1862, his regiment was quartered near Holly Springs, Mississippi. During this time he was able to attend church and did so on his first Sunday in town. He described in his diary the emotions he experienced during the service: "[W]hen the congregation commenced taking thier seats I took mine and looked around and my God the feelings that came upon me were indescribable.... [A] reverential awe overshadowed me and I truly felt that God was in this place." He continued to experience these feelings throughout the conflict. After attending preaching in camp near Tullahoma, Tennessee, in May 1863, he commented in his diary: "Thank God I

---

[13] Ibid., 8, 59, 100, 105, 108, 111, 121, 130, 137, 168.

felt his presents with me to day. I felt the consolations of his gracious spirit."[14]

Fielder furthermore derived immense comfort from his strengthened relationship with God. During one worship meeting in June 1863, he was moved by the stream of mourners who responded to the preacher's message: "We had a good meeting. I was enabled to feel that God was still my father and friend and in my soul there was a peace the world can neither give nor take away." Like Pendleton, he focused on God's blessings in the midst of adversity. In May 1863, he wrote: "God has blessed me much of late though I have been the subject of some bodily affliction, yet he has blessed my soul and I have been enabled to look by faith beyond the Jordon of death to a better and happier home." Even one of Fielder's lesser activities denotes his increased attention to spiritual matters. Near Tullahoma in May 1863 he noted that he had sent his wife "two crosses...which I made from shell taken from Stones River."[15]

William Lewis Nugent

Like Fielder, William Nugent was a devout member of the Methodist Church in the antebellum period. Although he made no explicit comments during the war indicating his concern for the spiritual welfare of his fellow soldiers, he did desire that they conduct themselves with moral uprightness. The day after arriving in the camp of the 28th Mississippi Cavalry, he related to Nellie a first impression of his comrades: "The men evince a disposition to be good soldiers. Very little cursing is heard and no drunkenness.... I am in hopes they will continue to behave as well; but who can predict ahead the behavior of soldiers." Nugent was to be disappointed in those hopes. The ubiquitous temptations in camp proved too much for many of the men. Writing in June 1863 from central Mississippi, Nugent informed his wife: "I find it almost impossible to *enjoy* religion surrounded by everything that is evil."[16]

---

[14] Ibid., 55–56, 111, 117.

[15] Ibid., 111, 119, 121.

[16] William M. Cash and Lucy Somerville Howorth, eds., *My Dear Nellie: The Civil War Letters of William L. Nugent to Eleanor Smith Nugent* (Jackson: University

In the summer of 1864 Nugent's unit was transferred to the Army of Tennessee and sent east to help defend Atlanta. The army had experienced a wave of revivalism the previous spring that had resulted in thousands of soldiers making professions of faith in Christ. Nugent welcomed his new assignment: "I have...been greatly pleased since I came to the Army of Tenn. There is a better moral tone exhibited here than I have ever seen among soldiers. Thousands have been converted and are happy Christians.... [T]he army is fast becoming literally a God-fearing soldiery."[17]

The 28th Cavalry spent the first two years of the war in Mississippi defending it against Union incursions. Constantly on the move during that time, Nugent seldom had an opportunity to attend formal religious services. In a letter to Nellie in March 1864, he lamented, "It is the Holy Sabbath day—Alas in the army how little regarded." Although it is unclear whether the "sober-sided Methodist" would have attended services of another denomination if the opportunity arose, his comments suggest that he may have placed the worship of the "Giver of all Good" above denominational differences. Overwhelmed with emotion while passing an Episcopal church near Vicksburg in March 1862, Nugent described it simply as a "House of God" and lamented, "When shall I again be privileged to go up to the Church to worship?"[18]

Nugent, like Fielder and Pendleton, turned his thoughts increasingly to heaven during the war. Deeply affected by what he saw and experienced, he longed to escape the trials inherent in an earthly existence. He wrote in November 1863: "Of one thing we must be convinced, that this world is one of trouble and continued

---

Press of Mississippi, 1977) 51–53, 89, 113, 233. Like Fielder, Nugent believed that an army of Christian soldiers would trigger God's intervention in the conflict. See ibid., 233. Although Nugent observed little religious interest among the men in his cavalry regiment, the armies in Mississippi, particularly the troops defending Vicksburg, experienced revivals in 1863. See G. Clinton Prim, "Revivals in the Armies of Mississippi During the Civil War," *Journal of Mississippi History* 44 (August 1982): 227–29.

[17] Cash and Howorth, *My Dear Nellie*, 179–80; Stewart Sifakis, *Compendium of the Confederate Armies: Mississippi* (New York: Facts On File, 1995) 54.

[18] Cash and Howorth, *My Dear Nellie*, 24, 56–57, 166, 230.

privation and that there is and can be no rest except in Heaven."
Thoughts of an eternal home comforted him: "While here we have
no continuing pleasures; but when the days of this life are past we
have an eternity of bliss beyond the grave." Nugent also found solace
in his conception of heaven as a place where loved ones would be
reunited. Writing in December 1863, he closed his letter: "May God
Almighty in his abundant mercy throw the protecting aegis of his
Providence around you and our babe and have you in his everlasting
keeping until we are gathered together in his upper and better
mansion not made with hands." How meaningful heaven had become
to Nugent is best illustrated in a November 1864 letter to Nellie, in
which he included a few verses of what he described as "the most
beautiful poem I have seen in a twelve-month":

> And I wondered why spirits should cling
> To their clay with a struggle and sigh
> When life's purple Autumn is better than Spring
> And the soul flies away like a sparrow to sing
> In a climate where leaves never die.[19]

As his concentration on matters of the unseen world increased,
Nugent—like the other mature Christians in this study—grew more
humble in spirit. This humility resulted in part from recognizing that
his fate was out of his hands. He concluded that it was upon God
alone he must rely for his protection and that of his loved ones.
Pondering whether he would become a prisoner of war like the
Yankee prisoners he had observed in Jackson, Mississippi, in May
1862, he wrote: "There is no telling; but my faith in the watchful care
of a beneficent Providence of the least of whose mercies I am
altogether unworthy, precludes the possibility of such a thought."
Nugent furthermore recognized that he had been ungrateful in the
past. Writing from Okolona, Mississippi, in November 1863, he
remarked: "The constant trouble with which we have been afflicted
for the last year or so has made me a much soberer man than I ever

---

[19] Ibid., 143, 153, 221.

was…. God has blessed and mercifully preserved me so far, and how ungrateful have I been." Nugent's humility is also evident in a letter to Nellie late in the war: "I have no doubt, when the war is over, we will both grow wiser and better. Humility is a crowning virtue when properly exercised…. We must not think of ourselves more than we ought! But then we must think soberly."[20]

Nugent's closer relationship with God also provided him with joy and peace. Sadness over his and Nellie's prolonged separation prompted this assertion in January 1864: "Oh! What a blessing it is to possess an elastic nature…when sustained by the favoring smile of Divine Providence…. [It] points, as an inducement to patience, to the 'mansion not made with hands' beyond the surging billows of life's troubled sea. To that mansion may we all so live as happily to terminate our pilgrimage."[21]

The Christian neophytes likewise drew nearer to God during the war. Although the recent converts may have exhibited some traits of spiritual-mindedness in the antebellum period, they grew more attentive to matters of the spirit during the four-year struggle.

Edward Owings Guerrant

On the eve of the Civil War, Edward Guerrant had decided to heed God's calling and become a minister of the Gospel. His first year at seminary, however, was interrupted by illness and the outbreak of war. Guerrant enthusiastically volunteered to serve in the Confederate army but never forgot completely his "higher and holier calling." Indeed, the interruption of studies and war weariness caused him to contemplate returning to that calling: "I serve my country now at a great sacrifice to myself. Not only my life is at her disposal but my happiness—my usefulness—my destiny!"[22]

---

[20] Ibid., 76, 148, 205. Nugent made a similar statement in May 1862: "I can, I feel, humbly trust you in the hands of Providence, being satisfied that all things will work together for good." See ibid., 66.

[21] Ibid., 156.

[22] Edward O. Guerrant diary, 22 January, 6, 19 April 1860; and 17 December 1862, Edward O. Guerrant Papers, Southern Historical Collection, University of North Carolina, Chapel Hill; J. Gray McAllister and Grace Owings Guerrant,

Continued military operations served only to intensify these sentiments. In the spring of 1863 General Humphrey Marshall's command again invaded Kentucky to gather supplies and show the colors. During its retreat back into southwestern Virginia, Guerrant once more seriously considered resigning his post and leaving the army. He noted in his diary in April: "My duty to Him who governs the armies of Earth and Heaven calls me to another and nobler field—where laurels are won which are stainless with human blood, and fade not through eternity:—emblems of those who are *saved* and not who are *slain*.... [W]ith a full conviction of that higher duty, I now turn away to more peaceful paths--to follow my destiny." Guerrant sought the counsel of General Marshall about resigning and traveling to Europe to study for his profession. He eventually decided to remain with his command and continue in his position as assistant adjutant general, but the sense that he had a higher calling did not abate: "I feel within me a power yet undeveloped; a destiny to reveal; something I am not and yet should be. I feel as if I had buried my talent in a napkin."[23]

Although he stayed in the army, Guerrant turned his thoughts more frequently to what he called "life's true object." Reflecting on the brevity of life, he transcribed this verse in his diary: "This is the bud of being; the dim dawn, the twilight of our day, the vestibule.... Yet man, here buries all his thoughts." His thinking on this subject continued and in the fall of 1863 he wrote, "Men generally live in some fond delusion. A romance is life to them! Riches, honors, fame, pleasure, etc., spread their seductive charms over life's stern features, and mar its great realities." His increased concentration on the other world is also evident in his response to a minor event during a church service in 1865. While listening to the sermon, Guerrant was distracted by a young girl who, in an attempt to draw attention to her new shoes, tapped them against the pew. Afterwards, a disapproving Guerrant remarked in his diary, "Alas, 'how vain are all things here

---

Edward O. Guerrant: Apostle to the Southern Highlanders (Richmond: Richmond Press, 1950) 24–25.
    [23] Guerrant diary, 11 March–21 April, 26 September 1863.

below'! How vain the human heart! 'Vanity of vanity, all is vanity!'...Her *soul* was in her *shoes*. It was her *treasure* and her *heart* was there also!"[24]

Guerrant also expressed concern for the spiritual welfare of others. During the army's retreat from Kentucky in October 1862, they observed a drunken civilian galloping past them on the road. When General Marshall asked where he was going, the man replied "To hell!" Overhearing the man's reply, Guerrant wrote, "Oh! Did he know the import of his answer?! It may be too true! 'To Hell!' How many are going that road! It is crowded! 'The gates of hell are open *night* and day. Smooth the descent and easy is the way." Guerrant also took a personal interest in the well-being of his eighteen-year-old assistant, whom he characterized as one "liable to be led astray." He placed his protective wing around the young man and attempted to steer him "from bad company." Guerrant even wrote him while away on furlough and noted in his diary: "[I] gave him some good advice—hope he may observe it."[25]

Like the mature Christians, Guerrant thought often of eternal matters during the war. Incensed by the soldiers' lack of reverence for the Sabbath, he commented in the spring of 1862, "The Sabbath.! *War* and *Hell* have *no Sabbaths!* Dreadful thought!...In Heaven there are no weeks. But *one* day. That is Sabbath day—and Sabbath is Eternity.... Rest and joy and peace—eternally!" The deaths of friends and loved ones also led to thoughts of heaven. Residing temporarily with friends near Bristol, Tennessee, in July 1863, Guerrant learned that a neighbor's child had died recently. Touched by the news, he remarked how fortunate the child was: "[It had] gone back to its Father in Heaven. A happy child! Better be raised there—in its upper home, by its Heavenly Father than here, in sin and suffering.... It seems to me that such a birth and life were infinitely blessed. To be

---

[24] Ibid., 21 January 1863; 19 February 1865; and the appendix of vol. 19.
[25] Ibid., 12, 24 November 1863.

born & *raised* in *heaven!* To never shed a tear, to never feel a pain, to never see a grave, Ah! Delightful land!"[26]

The hazards of military duties also spurred Guerrant to thoughts of a better place. Preparing to move to Vicksburg to help defend the river citadel, he found the thoughts of an eternal home far from the horrors of war immensely comforting: "Into his hands I commend my soul…. [A]nd at last He may bring me to that land where the bugle's shriek and the cannon's boom disturb not the eternal rest of the soul—and the 'crown of my rejoicing' and the palms of victory have no stain of the *blood of brothers* upon them."[27]

As with the others in this study, Guerrant's "home beyond the clouds" became a place to reunite with departed loved ones. In May 1864 the legendary general John Hunt Morgan, with whom Guerrant was now serving, carried out another raid into Kentucky. His troops penetrated far into the state and engaged the Federals at Mt. Sterling, near Guerrant's hometown of Sharpsburg. Following the engagement, Guerrant stopped by his home for a quick visit. Discovering that his younger brother, Marshall, had recently died, a distraught Guerrant expressed certainty that his brother was in heaven: "He died peacefully and happily in the strong assurance of a better world above, hoping and believing in the salvation of the cross…. May God grant I meet him in a *better* land!…The better half in Heaven; for mother and Mary and Martha and Henry and Marshall are there. How soon may I be! O may we all be!"[28]

It had been Guerrant's custom before the war to attend churches of different denominations, a practice he continued throughout the conflict. Although he harbored some denominational tendencies early in the war, Guerrant came to believe that worshiping his "Maker" was more important than refusing to worship with others because of denominational differences. On occasion, however, he was extremely critical of the ministers or their sermons. After one Baptist

---

[26] Ibid., 6 April 1862; 3 February, 19 July 1863; and 26 April 1864; William C. Davis and Meredith L. Swentor, eds., *Bluegrass Confederate: The Headquarters Diary of Edward O. Guerrant* (Baton Rouge: Louisiana State University Press, 1999) 64.

[27] Guerrant diary, appendix of vol. 15.

[28] Ibid., 21 May, 8 June 1864.

service, he described the preacher as a "very pious, zealous minister—rather illiterate, and not overly intelligent—with some knack at declamation." He was, in particular, critical of the majestic edifices and unemotional services common to the more liturgical Christian faiths. While in Richmond in May 1863 he attended an Episcopal service that he later described as "rather philosophical in its character.... The house was far more grand than the *sermon*: and *the organ sang* much better than the *congregation*." En route to Vicksburg in June 1863 with General Marshall and his staff, Guerrant attended a Catholic church in Mobile, Alabama. He described his first experience at Mass:

> The building within was a grand piece of architecture—and the ceremonies of the church were as grand pieces of impious mockery. I wonder in amazement that with the Bible before them sensible people could be gulled into the belief of such a wicked imposition upon Christianity.... I never saw any of all this in the Bible. 'By the *traditions of men* they have made the Word of God of none effect.'[29]

By the fall of 1863, however, Guerrant seemed to be more accepting of the other Christian denominations. While on medical furlough in August 1863 near Bristol, Tennessee, he attended a Methodist service. The minister, he said, preached "a very good sermon" and was "well educated and fluent." Later that month, Guerrant attended a Baptist service held in a "little, log church." He recorded in his diary that it was "refreshing to worship God in the simplicity of the ancient time, away from the airs of elegance and fashion.... Here in the wilderness—'God's first temple,' in an humble log church and schoolhouse, I'd rather be, than in the most elegant church in the land!"[30]

Awareness of the hazards of military duty drove Guerrant closer to God early in the war. His nearness to God humbled him and produced in him a desire to become a better Christian. On his birthday in February 1862, just weeks after joining the army,

[29] Ibid., 25 December 1856; 13 February, 10 July 1859; 23, 30 March, 22 June 1862; 3 May, 7 June, 26 July, 9, 23, 30 August 1863; and in the appendix of vol. 15.
[30] Ibid., 9, 23 August 1863.

Guerrant wrote, "To Him I owe every energy of my body and every emotion of my soul.... O may another birthday—if it finds me living on Earth find me a better and worthier man and Christian!" A few days later his thoughts turned to the past, and again he demonstrated increasing humility: "In this review of my past life I must sorrowfully confess the innumerable instances of omissions of duty to my fellow men, but more especially to my Father in Heaven. I reflect continually upon the entire unworthiness of men generally and myself particularly—of the manifold blessings of Providence we enjoy from day to day.... I read more in my Bible today than usual." Believing in May 1863 that he was to be sent to Vicksburg, Mississippi, a reflective Guerrant noted in his diary: "Into his hands I commend my soul—with a full confession of a multitude of sins committed against Him—while I enjoyed life, and its manifold blessings by His favor. I pray he may not visit upon me the punishment due my wickedness." Guerrant sought to ameliorate his sinful condition. His comments in early 1865 make clear his desire to become more Christlike. He wrote, "Lord! *Show* me *myself*. Lord! Show me *Thyself*."[31]

His thoughts turning increasingly to religious matters, Guerrant readily acknowledged God's blessings and expressed thankfulness. The first anniversary of his enlistment prompted ruminations on his service to country and gratefulness for his position on Marshall's staff. In January 1863 Guerrant wrote: "Unexpected to me—the God of my destiny has been, as in times past, pleased to repay my humble endeavors with honors perhaps more than I deserve. But I acknowledge my indebtedness to Him for it all, and feel that I am no more worthy of His or men's consideration."[32]

Guerrant furthermore was able to see God's blessings in the midst of tragedy. Writing to the father of a friend who had been killed in battle, Guerrant encouraged him to yield to the "will of God, who *gave* and hath *taken away*, you can *rejoice* that you *had* such

---

[31] Ibid., 28 February, 9 March 1862; (last will and testament inserted after 31 May 1863 entry); 4 February 1865.
[32] Ibid., 30 January 1863.

a son to offer, and *lament* the necessity that demanded so great a sacrifice." Of the fighting that was occurring near Chattanooga in 1863 he wrote: "I thank God that He permitted my eyes to behold the light of another day, while so many are closing them forever! *Life* itself is a blessing and *health* another superadded. How unthankful are we all. How unthankful am I?!" The Christian soldier also made efforts to express appreciation for even the smallest of blessings. Foraging in East Tennessee in February 1863, Guerrant remarked: "*I thank God when I see a haystack*, or corn crib. The very sight is reviving to one now. I shall never forget to prize them hereafter, nor cease to be grateful for these common blessings of life."[33]

Guerrant also grew more appreciative of the natural handiwork that he readily attributed to God's creative initiatives. While encamped during the Confederate invasion of Kentucky in the fall of 1862, Guerrant remarked: "The night was surpassingly beautiful. Glorious sight of Gods sky!" In November 1864, he noted that he loved to hear the singing of the katydids, "simply because God learned it to them."[34]

Further evidence of Guerrant's spiritual-mindedness was his increasing references to the Bible. Indeed, he often made biblical allusions when describing events in his diary. His command preparing to join General Braxton Bragg's invasion of Kentucky in the fall of 1862, Guerrant remarked: "On to Kentucky! Now at last we are about to undertake our pilgrimage to the 'promised land', though a long and arduous journey through the 'wilderness'. May Moses' God be with us." When Kentuckians failed to rise up and join the Confederates, Guerrant commented: "We came to rescue them from worse than Egyptian bondage but they 'would not', and we go whence we came." Learning in November 1863 that Rebels had burned Danville, Kentucky, a jubilant Guerrant remarked, "A meaner abolition nest never shared the fate of Sodom and Gomorrah!"[35]

---

[33] Ibid., 16 February, 8, 24 August 1863. He furthermore gave God credit for his talent in ibid., 21 June 1862; and in the appendix of vol. 19.

[34] Ibid., 5 October 1862; 11 November 1864.

[35] Ibid., 13 October 1862; 23 October, 9 November 1863; Davis and Swentor, *Bluegrass Confederate*, 142.

Felix Pierre Poché

Religious matters became more important during the war for Felix Poché as well. His desire to attend Mass and worship God increased significantly as the war dragged on. Concerning matters beyond his own control, Poche learned to trust in the Lord. As a result, his relationship with God grew stronger. From the Catholic college at Grand Côteau in July 1864, he wrote about his prolonged separation from Sélima: "I feel encouraged by the voice of God that I seem to hear in my heart assuring me that he will not permit this separation of those whom he had joined together."[36]

Unlike some of the Protestant Christians discussed above, Poché exhibited no ecumenical spirit during the war. A devout Roman Catholic, he was uncompromising in regard to the tenets of the Church, for he believed that it was the one true Church. Unable to attend Mass for several weeks in early 1864, he seized the opportunity when his brigade was near Monroe, Louisiana, and visited a Catholic church. In his diary, he described his emotions during the service and expressed his firm embrace of Catholic dogma: "I experienced sweet sensations at the sight of the minister of God at the foot of the altar renewing the Sacrifice of the Saviour on the Cross…I [took] part in the holy Sacrifice in receiving the body of the Divine Saviour in the Holy Eucharist. It is in these moments of happiness and of rapture of divine joy that the Christian feels in the bottom of his heart the truth of the Catholic Church." Furthermore, Poché applauded priests who reaffirmed the doctrine of the Church in their sermons. He described one service he attended in August 1863: "Old Father Foltier made again a very impressive and eloquent sermon on 'Confession.' The subject is one upon which the Catholic Church is universally attacked, and which needs a great tact to defend. And this Father Foltier did in a handsome manner." Poché's beliefs, however, did not keep him from fraternizing with those of

---

[36] Edwin C. Bearss, ed., *A Louisiana Confederate: Diary of Felix Pierre Poché*, trans. Eugenie Watson Somdal (Natchitoches LA: Louisiana Studies Institute, Northwestern State University, 1972) 137. See chapters 2 and 3 for more on Poché's church attendance and his faith in God.

other faiths. In March 1864 he wrote, "This morning I crossed the River and assisted at mass. I brought two Methodist ministers with me who behaved very well."[37]

References to heaven are noticeably absent from Poché's diary. Catholic beliefs about life after death may have been responsible for his lack of reflection on eternal matters. Unlike evangelical Protestants, who believe that the soul of a Christian joins Christ in Paradise immediately after death, Catholics maintained that upon a person's death the soul can end up in either heaven, hell, purgatory or limbo. The souls of those who have sinned and require atonement (almost everyone) go to purgatory to be tormented and purified before moving on to heaven. Poché's writings suggest that he believed strongly in the doctrine of purgatory; he prayed for the release from torment of the soul of an old friend who had died. It is likely that he did not hope for immediate bliss in the life after death as did the Protestant Christians in this study.[38]

Poché's wartime comments suggest strongly that he drew closer to God. Indeed, late in the war he remarked that he could sense God's presence while he worshipped. At the college in Grand Côteau in July 1864, Poché attended Mass and "received holy communion, which I offered in a very special way to God, for the benediction of soon being reunited with my beloved Sélima, and it seems as if God speaks to me, and promises me the realization of this sincere wish." He continued to experience these feelings throughout the war. After one service in February 1865, Poché wrote: "Prostrated at the altar of my Saviour, addressing the most sincere prayers of an afflicted heart, I left inspired with courage, as an inner voice, sweet and full of

---

[37] Ibid., 18, 51–53, 70–71, 100; J. Paul Williams, *What Americans Believe and How They Worship* (New York: Harper & Brothers, Publishers, 1952) 16–17; Roderick Strange, *The Catholic Faith* (New York/Oxford: Oxford University Press, 1986) 51–53.

[38] Williams, *What Americans Believe*, 32–33; Strange, *The Catholic Faith*, 163–64. By praying for someone who had died, Poché not only demonstrated his belief in purgatory but also his concern for the spiritual welfare of his friend. See Bearss, *Louisiana Confederate*, 142.

goodness, spoke to me and told me that our prayers will soon be granted."[39]

Poché experienced joy and peace from participating in religious services. Having attended Mass at a Catholic church in Monroe, he again offered fervent prayers for his loved ones, after which he wrote: "I enjoyed several moments of perfect happiness which could only be surpassed in this world by the presence of my precious Sélima."[40]

Hiram Talbert Holt

Although he spent the first two years of his military service at Fort Morgan where he saw limited fighting, Talbert Holt nonetheless experienced numerous trials during the war that caused him to draw nearer to God. Homesickness, anxiety for his loved ones back home in Choctaw Corner, Alabama, the hazards of army life and the death of his child all contributed to Holt's increasing attention to eternal matters. Ruminating on his first year in the army and their prolonged separation, Holt encouraged his wife Carrie in January 1862 to "lean upon God.... Remember that the joys that come from earth are transitory, leaving always stings behind, but let us get our happiness from Heaven, the fount of all joy, this will never part to leave a sting."[41]

The death of a brother furthermore served to remind Holt of the evanescence of an earthly existence. In November 1862 near Strasburg, Virginia, Talbert's older brother, John, was killed in a skirmish with the Yankees. Upon hearing the news, Holt exhorted Carrie: "Oh! if I had not warned him to turn from his sins, how would I now feel! Take a lesson Carrie, for you have sisters at home and a brother mid the snows of Tennessee to warn and oh! may you not neglect it." In one of his last letters home, written just before his death in February 1864, Holt evinced his increasing concentration on matters of the unseen world. In this letter to his sister Drucilla he

---

[39] Bearss, *Louisiana Confederate*, 147–48, 214.
[40] Ibid., 76–77.
[41] Talbert Holt to Carrie Holt, 4 January 1862 (typescript); and Holt manuscript, 7, both in Robert Partin Papers, Draughon Library, Auburn University, Alabama. See chapter 3 for more on Holt's homesickness and concern for his loved ones.

wrote: "There is something about us besides flesh and blood...there is a part not intended for this state of existence but for a home beyond the clouds. Most people care for their bodies as if it was the principle thing to care for. Be not one of them—which is the more valuable, the jewel or the casket holding the jewel.... [I hope] you may attain the object for which you were created."[42]

Talbert Holt found thoughts of heaven comforting. He was consoled by the belief that if he were to die in the war he could expect a glorious reunion with his loved ones. Writing in June 1861 he encouraged Carrie: "If [I] should chance to die away from you, it will do you good to know how devotedly you [are] loved and remembered through all the storms of life...with the fond assurance that we shall meet in that upper world to part no more!"[43]

The death of loved ones also led to thoughts of heaven. Learning that his brother-in-law had been killed in Virginia, he wrote Carrie in June 1862: "Great God of Heaven saw fit to transplant him from this world of sin and trouble, to a nobler, a better, purer sphere of existence, where there are no mad wars of passions, turmoils and wars, where all is peace, where Heaven is forever jubilant with the happy songs of released ones from this terrestial sphere." In early 1864, Talbert and Carrie endured another and even more grievous loss—their infant daughter died. Soon after receiving the news, Holt wrote his wife and consoled her: "Instead of weeping o'er her departure from earth let us look upward to Heaven and rejoice that we will forever have in that blest abode 'an angel baby'.... Yes we will now forever have a baby in Heaven, thank God!"[44]

His exposure to danger also produced hope in an eternal home. During the bombardment of Fort Pillow in April 1862, Holt was troubled not only by the possibility of his death but also by thoughts that he might never see his loved ones again. He expressed assurance,

---

[42] Estate of John Holt, Record Book L, 1861–1865, 383, Probate Office, Clarke County, Alabama; Talbert Holt to Carrie Holt, 13 December 1862; and to Drucilla Holt, 14 February 1864, Partin Papers.

[43] Talbert Holt to Carrie Holt, 19 June 1861, Partin Papers.

[44] Talbert Holt to Carrie Holt, 16 June 1862; 29 January 1864, ibid.

however, that although an earthly reunion might not occur, "I know that in Heaven we shall see each other and rejoice in an everlasting day of peace." Furthermore, he saw heaven as a place where war would never trespass. As his regiment prepared to reinforce General Bragg's army at Tullahoma in April 1863, Holt drew comfort from his faith: "If I get killed, I shall go to a better world than this.... If I die Carrie I hope we will meet again in fairer scenes than these! Where there will be no more warring! no more bloodshed, no hatred or confusion."[45]

Holt also exhibited concern for the spiritual welfare of his fellow soldiers. Writing from Fort Pillow in April 1862, he told Carrie: "Remember me in your prayers. Alas! Too few pray, thousands of poor soldiers are daily dying and I am afraid few prayers are offered for their souls salvation!" Holt was delighted when his comrades exhibited an interest in spiritual matters. In April 1863 the 38th Alabama was assigned to the Army of Tennessee and reported to Tullahoma. There the regiment participated in the religious revivals occurring in that army. Holt informed Carrie, "There is a good deal of religious feeling manifested in our Regiment. Durden Daniel, Pa Martin and the notorious Alf Keel...are under conviction and have gone to praying in earnest. Oh! if it were possible to have Pa preach to them a week what a glorious change would be wrought." In late 1863 he wrote to his father-in-law and home church pastor, L. L. Dewitt, and expressed concern for the young men in his regiment who were members of the church in Choctaw Corner. He requested of the elder Dewitt, "The next time you have preaching...appoint some brother or brothers to write letters to these young members, inquiring the state of their religion, encouraging them to hold fast to the faith, and the good works, wherin they started, and such other things as you may deem needful."[46]

---

[45] Talbert Holt to Carrie Holt, 26 April 1862; and 13 April 1863, ibid.
[46] Talbert Holt to Carrie Holt, 29 April 1862; 17 March, 15 June 1863; and to L. L. Dewitt, 19 December 1863, all in ibid.; Stewart Sifakis, *Compendium of Confederate Armies: Alabama* (New York: Facts on File, 1992) 108.

As he focused more on spiritual matters, Holt grew into a more mature and humble Christian. At the outset of the war, however, he was hot-tempered—especially about letters from home. Writing to Carrie in April 1861, Holt caustically remarked, "No letter has come to hand yet. I intend to write to you all hereafter only as you write to me." Apparently Holt's disposition was well known to those close to him, for early in the war his brother, John, warned him to guard his temper and avoid quarreling with officers. Holt was aware of his temperament and even teased Carrie about it. In an 1862 letter to her he quipped, "I know my temper better than you do, but I suppose you think you know enough about it."[47]

Furthermore, Holt was pretentious and self-righteous early in the war. Although he expressed displeasure with Carrie's sometimes infrequent letter-writing, Holt remarked that he was certain she still loved him: "I believe you have seen *somethings* in me to admire." He also was proud of the impression he made on his comrades. In November 1861 he informed Carrie that his captain had said that "I was the best man he ever saw in his life and commented upon my stability of character when surrounded by vice." Holt's increasing closeness to God, however, humbled him. In July 1863 he wrote with application to himself: "When I view man in his vileness, his insignificance, what a miserable, low, degraded, abject creature is he, but vile as he is [God still loves him]." Holt also demonstrated remorse for the wrongs he had committed in the past. Writing from Mobile, he lamented, "I very often and naturally travel over my departed days, and bring up my spent life, and in doing so, I find a great deal to regret, a great deal to amend." In an 1863 letter to his sisters, he wrote that he would "weep my eye balls out [if it] could bring back some harsh words spoken in momments of anger…. oh! what would I give to recall all the little unpleasantries that have

---

[47] Talbert Holt to Carrie Holt, 19 April 1861; 11 February 1862; and John Holt to Talbert Holt, 29 April 1861, all in Partin Papers. Several of his other letters also indicate that he had a temper. See Talbert Holt to Carrie Holt, 19 June, 12 July 1861; and 11 February, 23 May 1862, ibid.

passed between us here!...I hope you will take warning from me and act wisely, you have doubtless already much to regret."[48]

Holt's strengthened relationship with God also produced feelings of gratefulness in the Confederate soldier. Carrie wrote in 1863 that she was preparing to send him several articles of clothing she had sewn, but added that they were not very "nice and pretty." Holt replied, "I have not yet seen them but I care not a fig about them being nice and pretty. I feel too thankful to object to any kind or any thing. Oh! I feel so grateful to you, my people all, my God! I have so much to be thankful for.... [L]et us praise Him all our life." Holt admonished his wife to do likewise: "Carrie, you may think you *all* are seeing hard times, but let me tell you. If any people under the canopy of Heaven have cause to thank God for his mercies, you form part of that people."[49]

Holt expressed appreciation for even the smallest blessings from God. Writing Carrie from Mobile in January 1863, he mused: "God has shown us his taste, do you know how? Well, every time you look at the nice pencilled flowers you see a portion of God's taste, things set for our example and the author which needs our constant contemplation." Camped in a "beautiful" forest near Wartrace, Tennessee, he wrote in May 1863: "I could listen to the chirp of the birds. See the tricks of the squirrel, and expand my mind and soul in viewing the beauty bounty, and beneficence of...my Creator."[50]

Holt, like Guerrant, made frequent references to the Bible in his wartime correspondence. Thinking of his love for Carrie and how he wished to be with her, Holt wrote: "Well might father Adam weep and mourn till a comforter was given him [in] the form of Eve and methinks I can behold him run to embrace her when his eyes were first blessed with the sight." Holt also made biblical allusions in admonitions to his wife: "Carrie, continue firm and unchangeable in what is right, keep up good cheerful spirits. God will bear you

[48] Talbert Holt to Carrie Holt, 1 November, 2, 29 December 1861; 19 January 1863; and to Harriet and Drucilla Holt, 19 July 1863, all in ibid.
[49] Talbert Holt to Carrie Holt, undated (most likely mid-1863); and 20 November 1863, ibid.
[50] Talbert Holt to Carrie Holt, 23 January, 28 May 1863, ibid.

through the deep waters, if you like Peter of old will trust in him." In January 1864, Talbert and Carrie's infant-daughter died. Upon hearing the news, he encouraged his wife to bear the loss "with Christian fortitude," and expressed the hope "that like good old Job, you have exclaimed 'The Lord giveth and the Lord taketh away, thrice blessed be the name of our Lord.'"[51]

Those soldiers studied in this book who converted during the war—Giles Cooke, Robert Moore and Ted Barclay—saw their relationship with God significantly strengthened as the conflict wore on. Although each of these men had attended church regularly in the antebellum period, they were not Christians as defined by their own denominations. After undergoing emotional wartime conversion experiences, they not only grew more devout but also more spiritual-minded in pursuit of their relationship with God.

Giles Buckner Cooke

Following his profession of faith in June 1861, eternal matters soon dominated the thoughts of Giles Cooke. In April 1862 he noted in his diary, "Have been very much exercised as to the means and way of effecting the most good in this sin-stricken world.... May God enlighten me as to my duty." Believing that he had been called to the ministry, Cooke decided to become a clergyman after the war. Writing to a friend back home in May 1862, he remarked, "If God should spare my life I intend to quit the army and enter some more humble sphere of life, wherein I may be able to do some good for the cause of Christ on Earth. My heart has finally found its own true love." During the war Cooke never wavered in his commitment to become a minister of the Gospel; and throughout the conflict he frequently spoke and corresponded with clergymen of all denominations about his decision.[52]

---

[51] Talbert Holt to Carrie Holt, 3 November 1861; 13 December 1862; 20 June, 18 December 1863; and 29 January 1864, ibid.

[52] Giles Buckner Cooke diary, 28, 30 April, 17, 22 May, 18 June, 8 July, 3, 5 August, 11 September 1862; 22 March, 5 April, 14 May, 20 June, 6, 14 July, 22 August, 23 December 1863; 10 January, 7, 17 February, 19 April, 10, 16 July, 18, 20, 23 September, 18 December 1864; in Giles Buckner Cooke Papers, Virginia Historical Society, Richmond.

Cooke, however, did not wait until the postwar era to begin ministering to others. Learning in August 1862 that a fellow officer's child had died, Cooke consoled him and talked with him "about his immortal soul." He was genuinely troubled over his friend's bereavement and found it difficult to sleep for thinking of him. Visiting friends in Virginia in March 1865, Cooke encountered a doctor who "broached the subject of religion *to me*. I talked with him for some time.... I hope our conversation will result in good—and I pray God, it may eventuate in bringing the doctor to a saving knowledge of the merits of the atoning blood of our blessed Savior." The next day he followed up on their conversation and sent the doctor a friendly note with a copy of a hymn. Throughout the conflict Cooke offered encouraging words to those in need and counseled those who were not saved. He believed, however, that he failed miserably in his duty to God. In September 1863, he wrote: "Oh! if I could only feel at all times, wherever I may be whatever I may be doing, that I was doing my whole duty to my Heavenly Father...then could my fears be quieted, but when I examine my heart and behold, how derelict I am in the performance of all my duties in thought and in deed and how unworthy I am in the sight of the Holy and Everlasting God, I am filled with fear and trembling."[53]

During the war Cooke expressed a growing concern for the spiritual welfare of others. He prayed earnestly that friends and loved ones who were not Christians would come to know Christ, and he was delighted when those close to him made professions of faith. Upon learning that two of his close lady-friends had experienced conversions, Cooke exclaimed, "Oh! with what joy was my heart filled." He was particularly concerned about the spiritual state of his parents and prayed fervently for the "Lord [to] have mercy upon them and bring them to Thee." He also hoped that the trials of war would turn others to God. Observing in August 1863 the destruction caused by a Union raid in Wytheville, Virginia, he commented in his

---

[53] Ibid., 2, 4, 25 May, 23 June, 13 July, 21–22, 24, 26 August, 14 September, 9 October 1862; 13 September, 28 October, 30 December 1863; 4 January, 29 February, 4 June 1864; and 14–15 March 1865.

diary: "I trust that these sufferers by their late misfortunes may be...impressed with the solemn importance of seeking the Lord while He may be found." Upon hearing of the death of someone he knew, Cooke often remarked: "I trust that he was prepared for death."[54]

Cooke's thoughts turned increasingly to heaven during the war. There, he believed, he would be reunited with friends and loved ones. Having been transferred in February 1864 from the staff of General Sam Jones in southwestern Virginia to General W. M Gardner's staff in Florida, Cooke was heavyhearted about leaving friends behind in Virginia. He was comforted, however, by the hope that they would meet again on that "bright and happy day...when we shall all be reunited in heaven above where we shall be happy forever-more." Cooke also found thoughts of heaven consoling when loved ones departed this life. When his aunt Betsy died in early 1865, Cooke wrote that she had been taken to her heavenly home where she was "better off...she is spared the grief...[of] these terrible times" and resides now in that "happy land above—where—with those we love—we will never be parted any more."[55]

Perhaps more than any other soldier in this study, Cooke possessed a genuine ecumenical spirit. A devout Episcopalian, he routinely attended religious services of other denominations. Although his travels as an inspector general meant that he often had to attend whatever services were convenient, he seemed to enjoy all of the sermons he heard and endeavored to learn from each experience. After one emotional Presbyterian service, he remarked, "I felt like being able to glorify my God all the days of my life." Cooke's only desire was to worship, and he never made disparaging remarks about the services he attended. At one Methodist church in August 1863 he even participated in the Lord's Supper. In February 1864, Cooke heard a sermon on the need for spiritual unity among all

[54] Ibid., 21, 25 May, 11, 13, 16 July, 27 August, 5 October 1862; 19 January, 20 August 1863; 27 February 1865; and passim.

[55] Ibid., 17 May 1862; 14 April 1863; 21, 29 February 1864; 13–14 February, 8 April 1865; Compiled Service Records, General and Staff Officers, National Archives, Washington DC.

Christians, which the pastor maintained would "bring about a happy state of things in this wicked world." Afterward, he noted in his diary that it was "an excellent sermon."[56]

Cooke's profession of faith and increasing concentration on spiritual matters led to an increased desire to embrace humility and to ameliorate his "wicked" condition. In October 1862 he noted in his diary: "Oh...may my wicked [soul] become purged of all impure feelings and may I live a better man." His feeling of unworthiness was especially strong when he partook of the Holy Communion or Lord's Supper. After taking communion in a February 1864 service, Cooke wrote: "With fear and trembling did I eat of the bread and drink of the wine symbolical of the body and blood of our most blessed Lord and Saviour. I trust that the impurities of my poor sinful heart were in a measure washed away by the prayers.... My effort is to do right. May the Lord help me for as myself I can do nothing." As the war went on, his growing character of humility showed no sign of decrease. On Christmas day in 1864 he wrote: "Approached the communion table to-day with feelings of utter unworthiness to partake of the blessed body and blood of Christ."[57]

Cooke also evinced an attitude of greater thankfulness during the war, even for the smallest of blessings. As he was traveling back to his command from furlough, Cooke's possessions were stolen from the hotel where he was staying. Although the thief made off with $75, Cooke expressed his thanks that the amount stolen was not more. Cooke experienced a great sense of joy and peace as he drew nearer to God. Following a June 1864 service, he wrote: "Felt happier and better to day than I have for some time though I have had much to distress me."[58]

---

[56] Cooke diary, 18 September 1862; 9 August 1863; 28 February 1864; and passim.

[57] Ibid., 26 October 1862; 3 January, 7 February, 6, 27 March, 4 September, 25 December 1864; and passim.

[58] Ibid., 20 April, 19, 24 June, 4, 10 August, 7, 10, 17 September, 19 October 1862; 21 January 1863; and 5 June, 5 December 1864.

Robert Augustus Moore

Robert Moore professed faith in Christ in February 1863, just seven months before his death. During his brief tenure as a Christian, he too began to focus more on spiritual matters. Indeed, just days after his conversion he expressed delight with the success of the revivals occurring at Fredericksburg, Virginia. Following one prayer meeting in March 1863, he commented in his diary: "Have had a very good meeting to-night. Had nearly an hundred mourners." A few days later he reported: "The meeting in this place still continues. Much good is being done." As his command prepared to join the Army of Tennessee near Chattanooga in September 1863, Moore expressed his desire "that all would praise the Lord for his goodness and for His wonderful works to the children of men."[59]

Moore's diary also suggests that he may have become more interdenominational in his religious outlook. A Methodist, Moore had attended the preaching of other denominations before his conversion, including a Quaker meeting near Leesburg, Virginia, where he heard two women preach. Although he may have had some interest in such services, he appears to have attended them out of habit or because there was little else to do. After he became a Christian, however, he began attending meetings of all sorts with the sincere purpose of worshiping his heavenly father. Just days after his conversion, he noted in his diary: "Have been blessed with the privilege of meeting once more in the Lord's Sanctuary to worship." His command still encamped at Fredericksburg in May 1863, Moore again documented the importance he placed on worship: "Have been blessed with the privilege of worshiping in a house dedicated to the Lord."[60]

Moore said little in his brief diary about drawing closer to God, but undoubtedly he did so. His entries suggest that he regularly communed with God, deriving peace and joy from a strengthened relationship with the Lord. Moore wrote in 1863: "All seems bright

---

[59] James W. Silver, ed., *A Life for the Confederacy: As Recorded in the Pocket Diaries of Pvt. Robert A. Moore* (Jackson TN: McCowat-Mercer Press, 1959) 137–38, 164.

[60] Ibid., 56, 102, 138, 146–47.

to me. I hope to walk so as to never bring reproach on the cause of Christ."[61]

Alexander Tedford Barclay

In April 1862 Ted Barclay made a profession of faith in Christ, and soon after his outlook on an earthly existence underwent a transformation. Writing home in August 1863, he admitted: "Since I have changed my course in life, everything is interesting. I don't feel as I used to; I trust that I have now learned to view life in a different light, not intended to be spent in a gay and reckless manner but for higher and nobler purposes." Barclay indicated the increasing importance he gave to spiritual matters when, in the late spring of 1863, he expressed the desire to join his home church back in Lexington, Virginia. Although his membership meant little in a formal sense while he was in the army, Barclay considered it important and went out of his way to find a Presbyterian chaplain to examine him and forward a recommendation of admission to his church. Barclay impatiently wrote his sister in May 1863, "Has my certificate of membership arrived in Lexington yet?" Upon receiving his certificate, the church session promptly voted to admit him.[62]

As the days of war dragged on, Barclay placed even more importance on eternal matters. In March 1864 he informed his sister that although the confidence of the troops in the Army of Northern Virginia was exceptionally high, other issues should also command their attention: "Whilst our temporal affairs are thus bright and prosperous, how is it with our spiritual lives? Do we continue to grow in the Grace of God, are we found continually pressing forward to the work of our higher calling—I trust we are."[63]

Barclay also demonstrated a concern for the spiritual welfare of others and wanted to see good done among the men. When his

---

[61] Ibid., 136, 157.

[62] Charles W. Turner, ed., *Ted Barclay, Liberty Hall Volunteers: Letters from the Stonewall Brigade, 1861–1864* (Rockbridge VA: Rockbridge Publishing Company, 1992) 62, 85, 100; Presbyterian Church, Lexington, Virginia, Session Minutes, 1775–1920, 27 June 1863, Presbyterian Church, Lexington, Virginia.

[63] Turner, *Letters from the Stonewall Brigade*, 131, 135.

bunkmate was struggling with the death of his father, Barclay commented: "May his affliction be sanctified to the good of his immortal soul." In September 1863 he reported to his sister that he had been attending religious services in camp and expressed great satisfaction with what the meetings had accomplished. He was particularly impressed by the preacher: "We have had Rev. Grasty preaching to us for a few days…. He is a very powerful man, always had an immense congregation and I think has been the instrument of doing some good here." In March 1864, Barclay was happy to learn that the memoirs of his former captain, who was not only the son of his home church pastor but also the man who had led Barclay to Christ, were to be published posthumously: "Hope it will soon get to the army, for the life of such a Christian must be a benefit to those who read it."[64]

Barclay also hoped to advance Christ's cause through his own efforts. He wrote in May 1864 that he had "just finished conducting the company prayer meeting…. Oh, that I could conduct it in such a manner as to impress upon some of our numbers to leave the ranks of sin and fly to God." The expectation of military operations also caused Barclay to express urgent concern for his comrades. In May 1864, just before the Federals opened their spring campaign, he wrote: "Some must certainly fall this summer. Oh, that all were prepared…. Their souls would be safe and it matters little what would become of this earthly tabernacle…. May God impress it on their minds, if we can do nothing more can we at least pray for them."[65]

The importance Barclay placed on eternal matters is also evident in his ecumenical outlook. A Presbyterian, Barclay not only attended religious services of other denominations but also joined the interdenominational Christian Association in his brigade and even served a stint as president.[66]

---

[64] Ibid., 104, 106, 129, 136.
[65] Ibid., 144.
[66] Ibid., 98, 136; *Constitution, By-Laws and Catalogue of Christian Association of The Stonewall Brigade* (Richmond: William H. Clemmitt Printing, 1864), Richard

As his relationship with God grew stronger, Barclay expressed the desire to become a better Christian. On his eighteenth birthday, which occurred just weeks after his profession of faith, he wrote: "This is Thanksgiving Day and have I not cause to give thanks that my birthday finds me as I hope, awakened from my sins and looking forward to a blessed eternity. I hope I may spend this year to better advantage than I have my others." As with the others in this study, Barclay also reflected a growing sense of personal humility as the years of warfare continued. In March 1864, he wrote: "Have I as one of God's soldiers upon earth kept my courage and arms efficient? Will I be able to stand the review of souls on the last day? I feel that I have not done my whole duty towards myself and my fellow men. May God enable me to lead a more consistent and upright life."[67]

Barclay derived immense peace and joy from his relationship with God. In February 1864 he wrote: "The life of a Christian must be dear to anyone, but how doubly dear it is to a soldier. How sweet it is to feel that I am a Christian when all is dark and gloomy around me. The light that emanates from the Cross of Christ drives away this gloom and makes my heart so light and happy."[68]

The hardships and horrors of civil war drove the nine soldier-Christians studied in this book closer to God. The men who entered the war as Christians increased their religious activities, such as prayer, Bible study and worship. Each one grew to rely more on God. Those who were not Christians when the war began underwent emotion-laden conversions, and like the others, became more devout. As their relationship with God was strengthened, these nine men focused increasingly on higher and nobler matters. Two of them (Guerrant and Cooke) pledged to enter the ministry after the war. Most of the men manifested concern about the salvation of others and were gladdened by the spiritual revivals occurring in the Confederate armies. And all but Poché exhibited a more ecumenical

---

Harwell and Marjorie Lyle, eds., *Confederate Imprints* (New Haven CT: Research Publications, 1974) microfilm, 7.

[67] Turner, *Letters from the Stonewall Brigade*, 67–68, 131.

[68] Ibid., 124.

outlook. They each found immense hope and comfort in thoughts of a heavenly home where hardship would not exist and where they would be reunited with loved ones.

Furthermore, their nearness to God changed these men. All expressed feelings of unworthiness and a desire to become better Christians. They also recognized God's blessings more readily, even in the midst of tragedy. Some became more sensitive to God's presence, especially during times of worship. Although their experiences varied in many respects, all the Christian soldiers in this study became increasingly focused on matters of the unseen world.

Chapter 5

YIELDING TO GOD
CONFEDERATE DEFEAT AND
POSTWAR SERVICE

Feed the flock of God which is among you, taking the oversight thereof, not by constraint, but willingly; not for filthy lucre, but of a ready mind; Neither as being lords over God's heritage, but being ensamples to the flock."—1 Peter 5:2–3 (KJV)

A common religious trait among Southern Christians in the nineteenth century was a belief in providence. The nine soldier-Christians who are the subjects of this study believed when the war began God favored the South and that their cause would triumph. They prayed earnestly for the Lord to grant them victories and thanked God for the military successes enjoyed. Although early military reversals caused concern, these men maintained their belief that God was in control of events and would intervene on their cause's behalf at a time of God's own choosing—a belief some held even late in the war. The ultimate defeat of the Confederacy, however, ended all hopes of divine intervention. The Confederate-Christians were forced to reconcile their faith with the reality of the South's surrender. They did so by resigning themselves to the belief that God, in his infinite wisdom, had a reason for their defeat, and they accepted it as part of his divine plan. These men took great comfort from Bible verses such as Hebrews 12:6: "For whom the Lord loveth he chasteneth" and believed that the Confederate loss was God's chastisement, a disciplining that in reality was preparing them for something far greater than they had imagined.[1]

Furthermore, several of the men in this study concluded that the Lord refused to intervene on behalf of the South because of their unrighteousness. Although thousands of soldiers professed Christ during the revivals that swept the Confederate armies, these men maintained that many Southerners had turned away from God. Indeed, they believed that many had placed their trust in Confederate leaders and even idolized them. Such a people, they insisted, did not deserve God's favor.

The Christian soldiers in this study who survived the war maintained their religious fervor in the postwar period. Although they made fewer religious references in their writings, all became the Lord's servants in the postwar South. Some assumed or resumed vocational positions in the ministry, while others became office-bearers in their home churches. As times of adversity visited them as the years passed, these Christians relied on the lessons they had learned during the war in order to persevere through faith.

The three men whose faith was mature at the outset of hostilities returned home with an increased desire to serve God. William Pendleton and Alfred Fielder resumed their leadership roles in their churches; and William Nugent, who had held no leadership position during the antebellum period, became a highly respected Methodist lay-leader in postwar Mississippi.

William Nelson Pendleton

William Pendleton believed firmly in the providence of God. In 1864, after learning his son Sandie had been wounded, Pendleton wrote: "Oh, how it extracts the bitterness from affliction to know that

---

[1] Lewis O. Saum, *The Popular Mood of Pre-Civil War America* (Westport CT: Greenwood Press, 1980) 3–17. Simply put, the doctrine of providence is the belief that a sovereign God controls all things. According to Lewis Saum, the belief in providence was the most pervasive religious theme in antebellum America. Therefore, most Americans during this era interpreted trials as part of God's plan and resigned themselves to his will. Their belief in providence allowed the soldiers in this study to accept the deaths of their comrades and the defeat of the South as the inscrutable will of an all-wise heavenly father. See ibid., 3–20, 87–88.

it is ordered by our Almighty Father as part of His boundless plan of righteousness and love!... Shall we not, therefore, submissively bow under His dealings." Pendleton adhered to the belief that God favored the South while maintaining that the Lord punished not only individuals for their sins, but nations as well. He wrote in 1861: "For ourselves and for our country we must turn to him with full purpose of heart, relying on his great covenant of grace." Early military setbacks reinforced his belief that firm trust in the Lord was necessary to secure divine blessings. After the fall of Fort Donelson in February 1862, Pendleton wrote his daughter: "There is so much sadness in the country under the danger which threatens us since the loss of Fort Donelson.... God has for us, I trust, something better in store, but we must all look up to Him and rely upon his promise to his servants." He feared, however, that "the godlessness of so many amongst us, [may be] provoking the wrath of heaven."[2]

The Confederate defeats at Vicksburg and Gettysburg in the summer of 1863 led Pendleton to question whether God truly sanctioned the Southern cause. Writing from Culpeper Court House in late July 1863, a reflective Pendleton commented: "It is undoubtedly a time to try our faith and fortitude. But God has not vacated His throne, nor will He, except for wise purposes, permit iniquity to triumph ultimately. And if, for such purposes, although impenetrable by us, He see[s] fit to allow our enemies to triumph, we can, I hope submit to Him even therein, as did our Saviour under the hand of his enemies—'Not my will, but thine, be done.'" Convinced of the likelihood of Confederate defeat, Pendleton in May 1864 expressed his belief that God might have some larger plan for the

---

[2] Susan P. Lee, *Memoirs of William Nelson Pendleton, D.D.* (Philadelphia: J. B. Lippincott Company, 1893) 370–71; William Pendleton to Anzolette Pendleton, 3 December 1861; 23 February 1862, all in William Nelson Pendleton Papers, Southern Historical Collection, University of North Carolina, Chapel Hill. See also Eugene D. Genovese, *A Consuming Fire: The Fall of the Confederacy in the Mind of the White Christian South* (Athens: University of Georgia Press, 1998) 45; and W. G. Bean, *Stonewall's Man: Sandie Pendleton* (Chapel Hill: University of North Carolina Press, 1959) 174. For Pendleton's comments about God's sanctioning of the Confederate cause, see chapter 2.

Southern people: "The Lord may not see fit to deliver us as we pray, but if not...He will make it ultimately work for good to all who love Him, and among them ourselves, if such be our hearts."[3]

As the end of the conflict drew near, Pendleton—no longer anticipating an earthly victory—sought a spiritual one. In January 1865 he wrote: "We cannot expect to retain our earthly blessings, and may well find our chief happiness in those which are spiritual and unfailing." Soon after the war he concluded that God's chastisement did indeed have a purpose: "It may be one reason why Supreme wisdom has allowed us to be so overwhelmed, that we must cease to be such comparative idolaters in our estimate of Virginia and our character and privileges as freemen—that we must be content to live without a country, having our hearts engrossed with that better land where no sin enters, and where peace and charity prevail forever."[4]

General Pendleton surrendered with the Army of Northern Virginia at Appomattox Court House on 9 April 1865. He returned home to Lexington, Virginia, on Good Friday, 14 April. His first Sunday at home found Pendleton in attendance at Grace Episcopal Church, where he baptized his grandson, the child of his own beloved and slain son, Sandie. Reverend George H. Norton, who had

---

[3] Lee, *Memoirs of Pendleton*, 299, 336, 380. For an explanation of Southern Christians' attempts to reconcile defeat and God's will, see Gardiner H. Shattuck, Jr., *A Shield and Hiding Place: The Religious Life of the Civil War Armies* (Macon GA: Mercer University Press, 1987) 40, 100, 102, 108–109, 113; Steven E. Woodworth, *While God Is Marching On: The Religious World of Civil War Soldiers* (Lawrence: University Press of Kansas, 2001) 270–86; Daniel W. Stowell, *Rebuilding Zion: The Religious Reconstruction of the South, 1863–1877* (New York/Oxford: Oxford University Press, 1998) 5, 33–44; Daniel Stowell, "Stonewall Jackson and the Providence of God," in Randall M. Miller, Harry S. Stout, and Charles Reagan Wilson, eds., *Religion and the American Civil War* (New York/Oxford: Oxford University Press, 1998) 197–202; Genovese, *A Consuming Fire*, passim; Charles Reagan Wilson, "Introduction," in Miller, Stout, and Wilson, eds., *Religion and the American Civil War*, 10; and Paul Harvey, "'Yankee Faith' and Southern Redemption," in ibid., 175.

[4] Lee, *Memoirs of Pendleton*, 384–85; William Pendleton to unnamed daughter, 12 June 1865, Pendleton Papers. For more on the Confederate Christian soldiers' resignation to military defeat and subsequent quest for spiritual victory, see Shattuck, *Shield and Hiding Place*, 102–109.

taken over as rector of Grace Church in 1863, resigned soon after Pendleton arrived in Lexington. The vestrymen asked General Pendleton to serve temporarily as rector of the church until a successor to Norton could be found. They could not offer him a regular salary, but did agree to pay an unspecified amount based on contributions from the congregation: "This" they said, "is all we can promise." Pendleton and his family were, however, allowed to remain in the rectory.[5]

Conditions in postwar Lexington were difficult, and Pendleton spent much of his time tending the garden in order to feed his family. Although he produced plenty of vegetables and had an abundance of flour, meat was difficult to procure. During this time Confederate soldiers en route home often happened by and requested food, which the Pendletons generously provided. Making an already difficult situation harder, they refused to trade with the Northern carpetbaggers who had swarmed to Southern cities such as Lexington. In June 1865 Pendleton informed his daughter that "Yankee adventurers are appearing among us with money to cheat our people out of their little remaining coin." In the years following the war, Pendleton slowly began to recover the wealth he had lost; in 1870 he claimed a real estate value of $5,000.[6]

The Pendletons remained defiant toward their "oppressors" in the immediate postwar period. Although he had indicated his resignation to the will of God when the Confederacy's defeat appeared imminent, Pendleton remained politically unreconstructed. In June 1865 he wrote to one of the United States commissioners

---

[5] Compiled Service Records, General and Staff Officers, National Archives, Washington DC; Bean, *Stonewall's Man*, 226–27; Lee, *Memoirs of Pendleton*, 408; Anzolette Pendleton to unnamed sister, 26 May 1865, Pendleton Papers; George M. Brooke, Jr., *General Lee's Church* (Lexington VA: News-Gazette, 1984) 19; Grace Episcopal Church, Lexington, Virginia, Vestry Minutes, 1840–1913, 22 April 1865, Robert E. Lee Memorial Church, Lexington, Virginia. The vestry minutes show that Pendleton was paid a mere $115 in 1865. See ibid., 28 September 1870.

[6] Anzolette Pendleton to unnamed sister, 26 May 1865; William Pendleton to Mr. Turner, 13 May 1865; and to unnamed daughter, 12 June 1865, all in Pendleton Papers; Lee, *Memoirs of Pendleton*, 408–409, 411; Ninth Census, 1870, Manuscript Returns of Inhabitants, Rockbridge County, Virginia, 460.

looking into adjusting the terms of the Appomattox surrender: "For myself I cannot, without falsifying my convictions, apply for executive 'clemency.' Because wholly conscious of having but the most virtuous intentions in my share of the late defensive struggle…I cannot do or say anything which signifies that I condemn myself therefor…. [M]y convictions remain wholly unchanged respecting the rights of the States, and the great wrongs inflicted on Virginia and her Southern sisters." Writing to his daughter that same month, he remarked:

> At one swoop they have robbed the South of two thousand millions of dollars worth of property vested in labor…. Thousands, ay, tens of thousands, of our noblest population have been shot down by…Yankee wretches invading our homes under the impulse of Northern envy and malice…. Grant and his officers know well enough that instead of surrendering we should have fought to the death and have destroyed many of them in spite of odds against us.

Pendleton's anger over the South's defeat and consequent imposition of Northern dominance ran deep. He expressed regret over some of the Confederacy's tactical mistakes during the war. For instance, he had an on-going dispute with Confederate general James Longstreet about his delay in launching the attack on the Union left at Gettysburg on 2 July 1863, which may have cost the Confederates the battle.[7]

Pendleton also exhibited unrepentant contempt for the war's victors. During religious services, he omitted the prayer for the president of the United States found in the Episcopal Prayer Book.

---

[7] Lee, *Memoirs of Pendleton*, 412, 419–20; William Pendleton to unnamed daughter, 12 June 1865; to James Longstreet, no date (most likely April 1875); 6 December 1875; and James Longstreet to William Pendleton, 4, 19 April 1875, all in Pendleton Papers. Pendleton and Longstreet often traded barbs in the argument. In one letter, Longstreet commented that "you flatter yourself in presuming that your 'evidence comes in conflict with' my interests or reputation," and added that no one "will believe one word that you have written about myself, and precious little that you have written about them." Longstreet remarked that "school boys may be mislead by you" but only temporarily. See James Longstreet to William Pendleton, 19 April 1875, ibid.

Alerted to this "treasonable" behavior, Federal authorities in Lexington visited Grace Church on a Sunday in July 1865 and arrested him at the conclusion of the service. They furthermore closed the church and placed Pendleton under house arrest. Undaunted, he held services each Sunday at the rectory and even administered the Holy Communion. Grace Church reopened in January 1866 after Reverend Pendleton had taken the oath of allegiance and agreed to pray for the president. Federal troops remained in Lexington until early 1866.[8]

The year 1866 also found Pendleton re-entering the full-time ministry. In April, the vestrymen of Grace Church—headed by Robert E. Lee, the new president of Washington College—asked Pendleton to assume the duties of permanent rector. They provided him with a modest annual stipend of $800. His first order of business was repairing and enlarging the church's "defaced and damaged" edifice and collecting funds to retire an old parish debt, no easy task for a congregation "crippled in means." To raise money, Pendleton wrote letters to Northern clergymen and visited Northern cities to solicit funds.[9]

Larger attendance at Sunday services, due to increasing student enrollment at both the Virginia Military Institute and Washington College, prompted the Grace Church vestrymen in 1870 to discard plans to enlarge the existing church. They instead planned a new edifice as a memorial to their beloved fellow vestryman, the recently deceased Robert E. Lee. Pendleton undertook a new fund-raising campaign that included a tour of several Southern cities where he addressed the audiences with his "Personal Recollections of General Lee." He planned his travels wisely and for maximum profit. To a pastor in North Carolina, he wrote, "I would be unwilling to deliver it [the speech] for less than a hundred dollars for my object; and should much prefer $200." His separation from his family during this

[8] Lee, *Memoirs of Pendleton*, 422–24, 428; Brooke, *General Lee's Church*, 19.
[9] Grace Episcopal Church, Lexington, Virginia, Vestry Minutes, 16 April 1866; William Pendleton to Rev. Horatio Potter, 1 June 1868, Pendleton Papers; Brooke, *General Lee's Church*, 22, 24; Lee, *Memoirs of Pendleton*, 445–49.

time troubled him immensely, but Pendleton relied on lessons learned during the war: "Committing you also to God's goodness," he wrote, "I am as peaceful as possible."[10]

The construction of the new edifice also offered Pendleton the opportunity to continue nurturing the spirit of ecumenism he had developed during the war. Once the old sanctuary was demolished, the congregation of Grace Church had no building in which to hold services. Out of "fraternal kindness," other churches in town offered their buildings to the Episcopalians. Pendleton seized the opportunity and held regular services in the Methodist church. Furthermore, the vestry used that church for its meetings; and the Episcopalians even contributed to the repairs of the Methodist church during this time. When the basement of the new building was completed, they resumed services at Grace Church.[11]

During the postwar period, Pendleton proved untiring in his ministerial endeavors. Twice a week he held services at VMI, and in conjunction with other ministers conducted morning prayers at Washington College. He also provided religious instruction to those young men interested in Episcopal confirmation, and in 1869 confirmed sixty-six students. Parson Pendleton also provided room and board (and undoubtedly moral guidance) in his own home to several college students. Furthermore, he seldom turned down an opportunity to preach, particularly in nearby congregations who were without ministers. Pendleton's fund-raising travels also provided

---

[10] Grace Episcopal Church, Lexington, Virginia, Vestry Minutes, 6 July, 28 September 1870; "Historical Sketch of R. E. Lee Memorial Church, Lexington, Virginia," 1, Washington and Lee Miscellaneous Collection, Leyburn Library, Washington and Lee University, Lexington, Virginia; Lee, *Memoirs of Pendleton*, 455–62; Brooke, *General Lee's Church*, 26; William Pendleton to Rev. Richard S. Mason, 15 March 1873, Battle Family Papers, Southern Historical Collection, University of North Carolina, Chapel Hill; William Pendleton to Anzolette Pendleton, 31 October 1870, Pendleton Papers. Robert E. Lee died in October 1870. Pendleton also served as president of the Robert E. Lee Memorial Association, which sought funding for a monument to the Confederate chieftain. It was to be placed in Lexington, Lee's final resting place. See Lee, *Memoirs of Pendleton*, 453.

[11] Grace Episcopal Church, Lexington, Virginia, Vestry Minutes, 7 October 1872; 14, 21 April 1873; 15 April 1874; 29, 31 March, 8 June 1875; and 17 April 1876.

opportunities to preach the Gospel. Following a service in Louisville, Kentucky, in 1870, he wrote Anzolette: "It was God's blessing in answer to prayer and a sincere purpose to honor Him and do good." Also, the former soldier regularly took advantage of opportunities to share privately an encouraging word with others. On his morning and evening walks Pendleton often engaged in cordial conversation with those he met along the way. Following one such incident, his daughter questioned the wisdom of his being seen with a man of known evil repute. Pendleton replied: "'Poor fellow, he can't hurt me, and I may do him some good.'"[12]

In the postwar period, the Episcopal Church emphasized the necessity of assimilating former slaves into society and providing educational and religious instruction to them. Pendleton considered the issue a vital one and acted to incorporate a freedman Sunday school at Grace Church. The endeavor bore fruit and by 1878 the Sunday school claimed ten African-American teachers and sixty pupils. Despite these efforts, however, Pendleton continued to believe that blacks were inferior and that the institution of slavery had been ordained by God. In a letter to a Northern clergyman in 1880, he wrote: "The Allwise Sovereign *in His revealed Word Sanctions Slavery*. And whosoever denounces it as in its very nature sinful, just in so far dishonors the Bible."[13]

In part to augment his meager income, Pendleton opened a boarding school for young boys in 1871. The boys were housed and taught in the attic of the rectory. Although his widowed daughter provided most of the instruction, Pendleton oversaw the administration of the school and took part in the teaching. The boys

---

[12] Lee, *Memoirs of Pendleton*, 430, 447, 458, 460–61, 482; Robert E. Lee to Board of Trustees, June 1866, Trustees' Papers, Leyburn Library, Washington and Lee University, Lexington, Virginia. In addition to his own family, the 1870 census listed nine Washington College students in Pendleton's household. See Ninth Census, 1870, Manuscript Returns of Inhabitants, Rockbridge County, Virginia, 460.

[13] William W. Manross, *A History of the American Episcopal Church* (New York: Morehouse-Gorham Company, 1950) 326; Brooke, *General Lee's Church*, 20; William Pendleton to Rev. A. T. Irving, 27 January 1880; and to unnamed daughter, 12 June 1865, both in Pendleton Papers.

received instruction in the "principles of piety and virtue, according to the Bible and Prayer Book," as well as in the recognized classical branches of learning and knowledge. During his fund-raising travels, Pendleton attempted to recruit boys for the school. The enterprise was very successful and the school operated for ten years.[14]

Despite increased age and failing health, Pendleton labored on in his ministry. By 1870, he was more than sixty years-old. To the vestry's suggestion that he retire, the old general retorted: "His authority virtually placed me here, and until He more clearly orders my withdrawal, I cannot be at liberty to do so." In 1872, the vestry authorized Pendleton to take an overseas trip to rest and renew his strength. On the steamer, he was asked to preach, which he gladly did. Soon after his return to Lexington, he requested an associate pastor to assist him in his duties. Reluctantly, the vestry agreed and asked Reverend George Nelson to join the staff at Grace Church. Nelson, however, found it difficult to work with the contentious Pendleton and resigned in less than a year.[15]

Parson Pendleton pressed on without a full-time assistant and continued to preach despite his poor health. In an 1882 letter to his sister, he reported suffering from episodes of "suspended consciousness" and remarked that "I am quite uncomfortably deaf, so as to miss a chief part of conversation where I am and to risk not regulating aright the pitch of my own voice in desk or pulpit." Yet he continued preaching, literally up to the day of his death. On Sunday, 14 January 1883, he preached his last sermon. He died the following day, after preparing a service for the following Sunday. He never saw

[14] Circular, "Home School for Young Boys," 1 January 1871, Pendleton Papers; Lee, *Memoirs of Pendleton*, 460; Brooke, *General Lee's Church*, 19. Pendleton's salary was often a source of contention between him and the vestry. See Grace Episcopal Church, Lexington, Virginia, Vestry Minutes, 8 April 1867; 28 September 1870.

[15] William Pendleton to Anzolette Pendleton, 4 August 1872; to Grace Church Vestry, 28 May 1877; and Rev. George W. Nelson to William Pendleton, 1 February 1876, all in Pendleton Papers; Grace Episcopal Church, Lexington, Virginia, Vestry Minutes, 23 September 1876.

the completed edifice of Grace Church, which his efforts were instrumental in bringing to completion.[16]

Alfred Tyler Fielder

Alfred Fielder also believed strongly in the providence of God. Indeed, at the outset of the war, he expressed the belief that God's blessing was indispensable to victory. The confederate-Christian, however, feared that the iniquitous behavior of Southern soldiers would instead incite the wrath of God. In December 1861, he wrote: "I am sorry to say the Sabbath is but little regarded in the army. May God have mercy upon our rulers and our men and help them to learn righteousness...'righteousness exalth [*sic*] a nation but sin is a reproach to any people.'" Fielder also asserted that Southerners, in order to secure victory in the struggle against the North, must demonstrate firm faith and practice unflinching obedience to the Lord: "Our cause is just and will prevail. God is a Just God and if we will but trust him as we ought he will bring us off conquerors. Lord help us as a nation to humble ourselves under Thy mighty hand."[17]

Essential to Fielder's acceptance of the South's defeat was his resignation to the will of God. Although initially he held the firm belief that God favored the Confederate cause, military setbacks cast doubt on that conviction. Following the retreat from Corinth in May 1862, he wrote: "I still put my trust in God and try to feel resigned to his will." Later in the war, however, Fielder realized that God's will might be contrary to his own; yet he expressed his willingness to yield to God's wisdom. Expecting a major engagement in September 1863, he wrote: "May God give us the victory and as bloodless a one as possible, nevertheless not my will but Thine be done."[18]

There is little direct evidence about Fielder's activities after the war. He discontinued his diary shortly after arriving home and no

---

[16] Lee, *Memoirs of Pendleton*, 480–81, 483.

[17] Ann York Franklin, ed., *The Civil War Diaries of Capt. Alfred Tyler Fielder, 12th Tennessee Regiment Infantry, Company B, 1861–1865* (Louisville KY: self published, 1996) 22, 127–28. See also Shattuck, *Shield and Hiding Place*, 106.

[18] Franklin, *Fielder Diaries*, 53, 139, 153. Many Christian soldiers concluded that defeat was consistent with the will of God. See Shattuck, *Shield and Hiding Place*, 40, 109.

postwar correspondence exists. A few obscure sources provide the few details about his life in the postwar years.

Fielder was paroled on 1 May 1865, at Greensboro, North Carolina. He reached his home in Friendship, Tennessee, on 26 May. After his arrival, he commented in his diary, "I felt in my heart to thank God I was at home once more where if permited to remain undisturbed I expect to spend my days let them be many or few."[19]

Once home, Fielder resumed his religious routine. His first Sunday back he attended both morning and evening services and hoped that he had spent the day "profitably." He returned to his duties as a trustee of Mt. Zion Methodist Church and played an integral part in its operation. During this time, the former soldier placed immense importance on furthering "the cause of Christ." In 1868 Fielder and others chartered a new Methodist church in Friendship. Whether he became an active member of Friendship Church is uncertain. It is clear, however, that he continued his affiliation with Mt. Zion, for in 1889 he gave a half acre to the church for a cemetery and he is listed as a trustee in the deed. He furthermore served as a lay-delegate to the Dyersburg District Conference during the late 1880s and early 1890s.[20]

Fielder worked hard to get his farm back into shape and evidently was successful. According to the 1870 census, the farm's agricultural productivity nearly equaled prewar levels. Fielder eventually increased his total farm acreage by one third and doubled the value of his real estate. Of course, the loss of twelve slaves considerably reduced the value of his personal property. Fielder also operated one of the two cotton gins in the vicinity.[21]

---

[19] Compiled Service Records, 12th Tennessee Infantry, National Archives, Washington DC; Franklin, *Fielder Diaries*, 235.

[20] Franklin, *Fielder Diaries*, 235–36; Pearl Dunagon, Elizabeth Kirby, and Virginia Kirby, *The History of Friendship Methodist Church*, (n.p., n.d.) 1, Friendship Methodist Church, Friendship, Tennessee; *The History of the Mt. Zion Methodist Church* (n.p., n.d.) 1, Mary Alice Badget personal paper, Friendship, Tennessee; Dyersburg District Conference Journal, 1884–1898, 24 May 1889; 29 May 1891; 24 May 1892, McIver's Grant Public Library, Dyersburg, Tennessee.

[21] Franklin, *Fielder Diaries*, 235–36; Ninth Census, 1870, Manuscript Returns of Productions of Agriculture, Dyer County, Tennessee, 7; Ninth Census, 1870,

Fielder also resumed his role as an influential member of the community. He was elected delegate to the Tennessee Constitutional Convention of 1870, representing Dyer and Lauderdale counties. He played only a minor role in the convention, but vehemently opposed African-American suffrage. Fielder also returned to the Tennessee General Assembly for four years during the 1880s. He died 1 August 1893, and was buried in the Mt. Zion church cemetery he helped establish.[22]

William Lewis Nugent

Early victories seemed to confirm for William Nugent that God supported the South. Following the Battle of Manassas in July 1861, he wrote Nellie: "If God be for us, as I firmly and conscientiously believe he is—who can prevail over us." Early defeats aroused some concern, but Nugent maintained his belief that the Lord sanctioned the Confederate cause and operated according to his own timetable. In May 1862 when the Confederate army withdrew from Corinth, Mississippi, he wrote: "If in the Providence of God, abolitionism be put down, the design will be accomplished in some way or other. 'God moves in a mysterious way, His wonders to perform'—and we

---

Manuscript Returns of Inhabitants, Dyer County, Tennessee, 181; *History of Tennessee from the Earliest Time to the Present; Together With an Historical and a Biographical Sketch of Lauderdale, Tipton, Haywood and Crockett Counties* (Nashville: Goodspeed Publishing Company, 1887) 832.

[22] At the Constitutional Convention, Fielder served on the committee responsible for defining the duties of the executive department. Most debate at the convention centered on African-American enfranchisement. The ex-Confederate contingent opposed black suffrage, while Republicans favored it. After much wrangling and many rejected resolutions, a majority of delegates approved a new constitution that upheld African-American suffrage. To placate ex-Confederates, a poll tax qualification was added. A handful of Republican delegates, most of whom were from East Tennessee, refused to sign the document. See Nashville *Republican Banner*, 9, 13–14, 28 January 1870; George W. Stanbery, "The Tennessee Constitutional Convention of 1870" (M.A. thesis, University of Tennessee, 1940) 31, 59–62, 79, 83; Stanley J. Folmsbee, Robert E. Corlew, and Enoch L. Mitchell, *History of Tennessee*, 2 vols. (New York: Lewis Historical Publishing Company, 1960) 2:130–32; Robert M. McBride and Dan M. Robison, *Biographical Directory of the Tennessee General Assembly*, 2 vols. (Nashville: Tennessee State Library and Archives and the Tennessee Historical Commission, 1979) 2:1031–32; Franklin, *Fielder Diaries*, 248.

may expect a deliverance from all our present woes in a way we little dream of."[23]

As the war continued, Nugent grew increasingly convinced that divine intervention would be necessary to secure a Southern victory. To win that intervention, he believed that Southerners must turn from iniquity and rely wholly on the Lord for all things. In April 1862 he told Nellie: "I feel when I pray that a merciful Providence is over us and that all things will work together for good if we are only righteous." Encouraged by the revivalism in the Army of Tennessee at Dalton, Georgia, during the winter of 1863–64, he wrote: "the army is fast becoming literally a God-fearing soldiery. This I regard as a very favorable omen and as strongly indicative of our success." In the end, however, Nugent admitted that Southerners had "left undone those things essential to secure that intervention."[24]

By late 1863, Nugent had concluded that military setbacks were evidence of God's chastisement, for his belief in providence meant that the Lord either directed or allowed the defeats. After the fall of Atlanta he admitted, "the hand of God is laid heavy on us just now." Nugent never doubted that his heavenly father still loved the Southern people; therefore, he concluded that the Lord was chastening them for a greater purpose: "We should learn that life, beset though it be, by so many sorrows and afflictions was given us for the wise purpose of preparing for Eternity, and that all its real joys are purchased by an humble submission to God's will." This was a belief he also applied to the other trials he and Nellie had experienced during the war. In January 1865, he wrote: "Sorrows have come and gone; days of trial, nights of ceaseless vigil…. [B]y

---

[23] William M. Cash and Lucy Somerville Howorth, eds., *My Dear Nellie: The Civil War Letters of William L. Nugent to Eleanor Smith Nugent* (Jackson: University Press of Mississippi, 1977) 43, 80, 128. Nugent maintained late in the war his belief that God was on the South's side. See ibid., 180. Early Confederate victories inspired many "God is with us" sermons on the Southern home front. For more on this and Southern Christians' belief that God would intervene at the appropriate time, see Genovese, *A Consuming Fire*, 38, 45; Stowell, *Rebuilding Zion*, 37; Woodworth, *While God Is Marching On*, 277–85.

[24] Cash and Howorth, *My Dear Nellie*, 63, 180, 233.

ways, we little dream of, he is gently leading us to fix our affections upon the things which make for our Eternal good and guide our wind-shaken, tempest-tossed barks to the Haven of Rest."[25]

After the war, Nugent returned home to Greenville, Mississippi, and to his beloved Nellie. The river town had been destroyed during the four-year struggle. He joined the remaining inhabitants in rebuilding it at a location north of the original site. The war had also taken its toll on his frail wife, and in January 1866, she died. Nugent remarried in 1867 but suffered another tragic loss when his second wife died the following year. He married a third time in 1870. Soon after the war, Nugent and his longtime friend, William G. Yerger, entered into a successful law partnership in Greenville. Nugent also owned two plantations in nearby Bolivar County.[26]

Unlike Pendleton and Fielder, Nugent held no leadership post in his home church before the war. In the postwar years, however, he became an office-bearer in the Methodist Church. Although there are no extant records from his home church, details about Nugent's service can be pieced together from Methodist conference records. In 1868 and 1871 Nugent attended the Greenville District Quarterly Conference as a steward of Lake Lee Church. Others in the congregation evidently thought highly of him, for the stewards were expected to exhibit "solid piety...[and] know and love the Methodist doctrine and discipline." He also attended the Mississippi Annual

---

[25] Ibid., 87, 111, 143, 210, 230. Historian Lewis Saum asserts that antebellum Americans ordinarily interpreted trials as God's chastisement. See Saum, *Popular Mood of Pre-Civil War America*, 17–20.

[26] Cash and Howorth, *My Dear Nellie*, 30n, 204, 237–38; Bern Keating, *A History of Washington County, Mississippi* (Greenville MS: self published, 1976) 45; *Biographical and Historical Memoirs of Mississippi*, 2 vols. (Chicago: Goodspeed Publishing Company, 1891) 2:516; Lucy Somerville Howorth, interview by William M. Cash, 18 May 1976 (audio tape), Lucy Somerville Howorth and William Cash Papers, Capps Archives and Museum, Delta State University, Cleveland, Mississippi; Recollections of Lucy Somerville Howorth, 13 January 1971 (audio tape), Lucy Somerville Howorth Papers, Capps Archives and Museum, Delta State University, Cleveland, Mississippi.

Conference in Jackson in 1869 where he served as a member of the Joint Board of Finance.[27]

Seeking professional opportunities, Nugent moved to Jackson in 1872. There he formed a law partnership with William and J. R. Yerger. Nugent was a bright and gifted attorney. Indeed, a chief justice of the Mississippi Supreme Court judged him to be "in the front rank of the eminent lawyers of Mississippi." Evidently other attorneys held him in high regard as well, electing him president of the Mississippi Bar Association in 1887. Nugent was conscientious in his work, believing that God wanted Christians to be "examples of diligence in business…[and to remain] unspotted."[28]

Although he had no desire to hold political office, Nugent played a role in the efforts of conservative Democrats to undo the policies of radical Republicans who controlled the government of Mississippi during Reconstruction. The most pressing political issue for him was taxes. During the six years of Republican administration, state taxes increased 1,400 percent. Although most of increase was to pay for expanded facilities and programs that benefited all Mississippians, the state's increasing reliance on ad valorem property taxes enraged land-owning whites. Opponents of high taxes organized in each county and in January 1875 sent delegates to Jackson for a Taxpayers' Convention. Nugent served as a delegate from Hinds County and presided over the first day's business and the election of W. S. Featherston, a former Confederate general, as president. He also was a member of the committee responsible for

---

[27] Greenville District Quarterly Conference Minutes, 1867–1881, 20 November 1868, First United Methodist Church, Greenville, Mississippi; Nell Thomas, *This Is Our Story…This Is Our Song: First United Methodist Church, Greenville, Mississippi, 1844–1994* (Greenville MS: Burford Brothers Printing, 1994) app.; *Minutes of the Fifty-Fourth Session of the Mississippi Annual Conference, Methodist Episcopal Church South… December 8–15, 1869* (Jackson: Clarion Steam Printing, 1870) 4; *The Doctrines and Discipline of the Methodist Episcopal Church* (New York: Nelson & Phillips Publishing, 1876) 126.

[28] Cash and Howorth, *My Dear Nellie*, 239; Charles B. D. D. Galloway, *Colonel William L. Nugent* (n.p., n.d.) 13, 18, Mississippi Department of Archives and History, Jackson; Dunbar Rowland, *Courts, Judges, and Lawyers of Mississippi 1798–1935* (Jackson: Hederman Brothers Printing, 1935) 358.

conferring with the governor and the legislature about the convention's recommendations for revising the state's tax laws.[29]

Nugent participated in the conservatives' attempt to recapture the state government in 1875 and remove Mississippi's carpetbagger governor, Adelbert Ames. During this time Nugent was an active member of the Democratic Party and addressed several Democratic clubs. He also spoke to African-American groups in an attempt to lure votes away from the Republicans. The Democrats' campaigning, along with rampant voter intimidation, produced an overwhelming conservative majority in the legislature. Governor Ames resigned the following year under the threat of impeachment.[30]

In Jackson, Nugent continued as a leader in the Methodist Church. Soon after his arrival, he joined that city's First Methodist Church and served the congregation as both a steward and a trustee. He also helped in the effort to enlarge the church edifice: he contributed financially and served as a member of the committee overseeing construction. He was furthermore elected Sunday school superintendent, a position he held for twenty-two years. Nugent's appointment as superintendent testifies to his piety and faithfulness, for such appointments required approval by the Quarterly Conference. He carried out his Sunday school duties with diligence and humility. Indeed, he felt he was fulfilling a higher calling: "Have we lived as we ought to have done? Have our duties all been well done? Have we advanced a station in the march to the temple not

---

[29] John Hope Franklin, *Reconstruction After the Civil War* (Chicago: University of Chicago Press, 1961) 143; Eric Foner, *Reconstruction: America's Unfinished Revolution, 1863–1877* (New York: Harper & Row Publishers, 1988) 206, 365–69, 374–76, 383; Richard A. McLemore, *A History of Mississippi*, 2 vols. (Hattiesburg: University & College Press of Mississippi, 1973) 1:585–86; William C. Harris, *The Day of the Carpetbagger: Republican Reconstruction in Mississippi* (Baton Rouge: Louisiana State University Press, 1979) 291–94, 328, 336; Warren A. Ellem, "The Overthrow of Reconstruction in Mississippi," *Journal of Mississippi History* 54 (May 1992): 191; Jackson (Mississippi) *Daily Clarion*, 7 January 1875.

[30] Eunice Stockwell, ed., *Copies of Newspaper Articles, Marriage and Death Notices from Washington County Times and Greenville Times (1864–1886)*, 2 vols. (n.p., n.d.) 1:4, 2:203, 307, William Alexander Percy Memorial Library, Greenville, Mississippi; Foner, *Reconstruction*, 558–62; Ellem, "The Overthrow of Reconstruction in Mississippi," 177–78; Harris, *Day of the Carpetbagger*, 670–87, 691–96.

made with hands, [but] eternal in the heavens? Or have we too often rested by the wayside when trumpet tongues were calling us to work while the day lasted?" His devotion did not go unnoticed by those who worked with him. On Christmas Day 1895 the officers and teachers of the Sunday school expressed their appreciation to him and presented him with a Bible, inscribed thus: "This copy of the Holy Word, the rule and guide of your noble life and the one text book in the school in which you have superintended with singular fidelity, is presented as a slight token of appreciation by your affectionate co-laborers."[31]

Although busy with his law practice, Nugent continued to attend the annual Methodist conferences in Mississippi where he was appointed to several influential committees. "I always obey such calls," he wrote, "feeling that they come from our great Commander." He also attended the Ecumenical Conference in Washington in 1891.[32]

Nugent also emerged as a leader in the prohibition movement in Mississippi. An enthusiastic prohibitionist, he called for a public meeting in Jackson in the spring of 1881. He addressed the gathering, and was appointed to the committee responsible for calling a state convention. During the conference, he was selected to

---

[31] Alfred P. Hamilton, *Galloway Memorial Methodist Church* (Jackson MS: self published, 1956) 106, 186, 190; James Swan to Col. Nugent, Mr. Stevens, Mr. Hinds, Mr. Greer, Mr. Hemingway and Mr. Galloway, 16 February 1883, Charles B. Galloway Papers, Wilson Library, Millsaps College, Jackson (Mississippi); *Doctrines and Discipline of the Methodist Episcopal Church*, 156; Galloway, *Colonel William L. Nugent*, 27; Bible inscription, 25 December 1895 (photostat), Howorth and Cash Papers.

[32] *Minutes of the Fifty-Eighth Session of the Mississippi Annual Conference, Methodist Episcopal Church South... December 10–15, 1873* (Nashville: Southern Methodist Publishing, 1874) 4, 17–18; *Minutes of the Fifty-Ninth Session of the Mississippi Annual Conference, Methodist Episcopal Church South...December 16–22, 1874* (Jackson: Clarion Steam Printing, 1875) 4, 21–22; *Proceedings of the Mississippi Annual Conference... December 18, 1878* (n.p., n.d) 2–3, 18; *Proceedings of the Mississippi Annual Conference... December 17, 1879* (n.p., n.d) 1–2; *Proceedings of the Mississippi Annual Conference, December 16–24, 1885* (n.p., n.d) 1–2, Wilson Library, Millsaps College, Jackson, Mississippi; Galloway, *Colonel William L. Nugent*, 20.

serve as chairman of the state's executive committee, a position he held for several years.[33]

Nugent as well served his local community faithfully. He played an instrumental role in the establishment of Millsaps College, a school affiliated with the Methodist Church. At the annual session of the Mississippi Conference in 1888, the idea of a Methodist institution of higher learning in the state was proposed. A resolution was passed directing that a six-man committee (three laymen and three ministers) be formed to study the feasibility of such a college. Nugent was selected as one of the three laymen and was largely responsible for the decision to place the college in Jackson. In 1890, he was appointed to the board of trustees of the college, a position he held until his death. Millsaps College opened its doors in 1892. Nugent was on the board of directors of the Jackson High School and the board of trustees of the State Lunatic Asylum. He also served a term as president of the Young Men's Christian Association in Jackson.[34]

Nugent maintained his strong faith after the war. He regularly attended church services, including mid-week prayer meetings; and each morning he made time for a devotional and Bible reading. He also enjoyed debating questions of theology with his pastors. Nugent furthermore remembered the lessons he had learned during the war. Regarding God's purpose for adversity, he remarked: "Trials, troubles, chastisements must come, but they are needed to correct, to purify and ennoble." Following a significant financial loss in 1888, he wrote: "I have always had an abiding confidence that the Lord was

---

[33] T. J. Bailey, *Prohibition in Mississippi or Anti-Liquor Legislation from Territorial Days, with its Results in the Counties* (Jackson: Hederman Brothers Printing, 1917) 54–55; C. B. Galloway, *Handbook of Prohibition* (Jackson: self published, 1886) 11; Galloway, *Colonel William L. Nugent*, 17.

[34] W. B. Murrah, "Origin and Location of Millsaps College," *Publications of the Mississippi Historical Society*, ed. Franklin L. Riley, 4 (1901): 227–28; Board of Trustees Minutes, 10 May 1888; 10 January 1890; 19 February 1891; 29 September 1892; and passim, Board of Trustees' Papers, Wilson Library, Millsaps College, Jackson, Mississippi; William D. McCain, *The Story of Jackson: A History of the Capital of Mississippi, 1821–1951*, 2 vols. (Jackson: J. F. Hyer Publishing Company, 1953) 1:215, 288; Jackson (Mississippi) *Clarion-Ledger*, 18 January 1897.

leading me by a way I knew not, into a fuller realization of his Fatherhood, and to the point where I could say, 'I owe no man anything but to love him.'" About God's faithfulness, he wrote: "My charity teaches me to suffer long and be kind, to bear all things, and to believe all things. Now as this charity will never fail, but will help us all here, go with us through the valley of shadows, and brighten the atmosphere of heaven, it is a safe thing to trust." When death came, it found him ready; he felt no fear, only peace: "To die is a passing pain, 'tis true; but if, when the soul is taking flight from the clay mold that retained it, it sees heaven opening and the angels descending to greet it on the other shore, it appears to me we should rejoice to die when the summons comes." His own summons from this life came in January 1897.[35]

Perhaps the greatest testimony to Nugent's postwar faith and service was what his contemporaries said about him. Charles B. Galloway, Nugent's former pastor, composed a twenty-eight page obituary that described Nugent as one who "had virtues and traits of character that distinguished him among all the men I have ever known." Galloway further remarked that Nugent "accepted unquestioningly the great verities of the Christian religion, and they had been transmuted into the very fiber of his being." Another minister was reported to have said: "'I have met many great Methodist laymen, but I have met only one W. L. Nugent.'"[36]

The three Christian neophytes had markedly different fates. Edward Guerrant became a minister and developed into one of the most successful evangelists ever to serve the Presbyterian Church in the late-nineteenth and early-twentieth centuries. Felix Poché continued his devotion to the Catholic Church as an active layman

---

[35] Galloway, *Colonel William L. Nugent*, 17–22, 25, 28; Jackson (Mississippi) *Clarion-Ledger*, 18 January 1897. Nugent's devotion to God had an influence on his family: his wife and daughter also served in their church, and continued to do so long after his death. See Galloway Methodist Church, Church Register, 1903–1921, 5 February 1911, Mississippi Department of Archives and History, Jackson; and Hamilton, *Galloway Memorial Methodist Church*, 209–10.

[36] Galloway, *Colonel William L. Nugent*, 2, 22; New Orleans *Christian Advocate*, 17 February 1898.

during the postwar era. And Talbert Holt was killed in a skirmish in February 1864.

Edward Owings Guerrant

Like Nugent and Fielder, Edward Guerrant initially believed that God sanctioned the Confederate cause. He maintained, however, that Southerners must conduct themselves piously in order to secure the Lord's blessing. Troubled by what he considered the desecration of the Sabbath day by his fellow officers in early 1862, he wrote: "They...[played] their usual game of 'Boston', at which they spend most of their time.... And I observe again a great partiality for 'something stronger than water.' The prevalence of such vices as these and others is to me the greatest obstacle I observe to the success of Southern arms. God can hardly bless such men."[37]

Guerrant also believed that the Southern people had to trust God, not their own efforts, for victory. Distressing news from the western theater in early 1862 prompted these remarks: "They [Yankees] are pressing the South now on every side—and the continued run of successes seems to be turned against her. We have forgotten to ascribe the cause of our victory to an Omnipotent hand and placed it all in Southern chivalry. He is now teaching us a bitter lesson." Weeks after Fort Donelson was surrendered, Guerrant commented: "Truly, truly, our prospect of success looks gloomy.... 'Whom He *loveth* He *chasteneth*'!" He even attributed the death of Stonewall Jackson to the Lord's chastening hand: "*General Jackson is Dead!*...The Christian Napoleon! A greater than Alexander is dead.... [L]et us bow to the Divine decree and say 'Thy will be done'.... He possessed...the love and confidence of our people. They idolized 'Stonewall' Jackson. God's purposes are wise to have removed him. *'He gave and hath taken away.'*"[38]

---

[37] Edward O. Guerrant diary, 8–9 March 1862, Edward O. Guerrant Papers, Southern Historical Collection, University of North Carolina, Chapel Hill.

[38] Ibid., 16 February, 18 March 1862; 15 May 1863. For more on the meaning Southerners ascribed to Stonewall Jackson's death, see Stowell, "Stonewall Jackson and the Providence of God," 187–90.

Guerrant became increasingly resigned to the will of God during the war. His unwavering belief in divine providence and sovereignty meant that the Lord was responsible for Confederate defeats, for "God cannot be mistaken in the means to an end, or find his purposes changed by unexpected circumstances because perfect knowledge forbids both." Therefore, as a devout Christian, Guerrant accepted military reversals as the plan of an all-wise heavenly father. After the fall of Fort Donelson, he noted: "This is a terrible blow—but 'God reigns'—'His will be done.'" A devastating Union raid on the salt works in southwestern Virginia in December 1864 prompted him to write: "I am drilled in the philosophy that takes every thing as it comes as a dispensation of Providence, and submit to it with a resignation." Guerrant maintained this outlook when he faced other trials as well. Following the death of a fellow officer and close friend in 1864, he wrote: "It is only in our higher faith that 'all is for the best' we can find consolation in our grief at this unexpected stroke from the Hand that 'Doeth all things well.'"[39]

Guerrant returned to Sharpsburg, Kentucky, after the war and plotted his future. His late mother had wanted him to become a minister. His father, a physician, desired that he become a doctor. A medical inclination no doubt coursed through his veins, for in addition to his father, his great-uncle was a doctor and his brother, Richard, intended to become one. But Guerrant felt a stronger calling to the ministry. He resolved the dilemma by combining the two and emulating Luke from the Bible, "the beloved physician." He wrote of his decision, "The *highest* motives for its practice are *not mercenary*. They are found in the exercise of the noblest sentiments of the soul, the relief of suffering, the rescue of the perishing, and the comfort of the dying." After teaching briefly during the summer of 1865, Guerrant headed for Philadelphia, Pennsylvania, where he entered Jefferson Medical College.[40]

---

[39] Guerrant diary, 20 February 1862; 11 May, 27 December 1864; and vol. 19, app.

[40] J. Gray McAllister and Grace Owings Guerrant, *Edward O. Guerrant: Apostle to the Southern Highlanders* (Richmond: Richmond Press, 1950) 55–56; Colossians 4:14; Lisa M. Wilson, "Edward Owings Guerrant: An Appalachian Ministry" (M.Th.

Having concluded his first year of studies, Guerrant returned home in the spring of 1866 and taught school that summer. In the fall, he entered Bellevue Medical College in New York, finishing his work there in the spring of 1867. Following graduation, he opened a medical practice in Mount Sterling, Kentucky, just a few miles from Sharpsburg. In 1868 he married his sweetheart, Mary Jane DeVault, of Leesburg, Tennessee. His practice thriving, Guerrant purchased a large home in 1871 and brought his father and two sisters to live with him in Mount Sterling.[41]

In 1873 Guerrant made a decision that changed the remaining course of his life. Suffering from typhoid fever, the former-soldier-become-physician promised God that if he were spared, he would give up his medical practice and enter the ministry. This was a difficult decision for Guerrant, for he was the sole means of support for his family and would be separated from his loved ones while away at seminary. Nevertheless, Guerrant honored his promise. He entered Union Theological Seminary at Hampton-Sydney, Virginia, in the fall of 1873. In January of the following year, he remarked, "I hope God will not forget the poor sacrifice I make for Him, who sacrificed all for me."[42]

A conscientious pupil, Guerrant made rapid progress in his theological studies. In addition to pursuing his academic preparation for ministry, he often counseled his fellow students and even attended to their medical needs. He participated in the Rhetorical Society and debated the venerable Dr. Robert L. Dabney, a member of the faculty and Stonewall Jackson's former chief of staff. Burdened by the separation from his loved ones, Guerrant—as he had done

---

thesis, Union Theological Seminary, 1993) 7; Guerrant diary, 15 July 1865; and vols. 29 and 31.

[41] McAllister and Guerrant, *Edward O. Guerrant*, 57, 59–60. Guerrant had met DeVault during the war, and the two had corresponded regularly throughout the conflict. See ibid., 50–51. Evidently Guerrant's medical practice occupied much of his time, for he claimed no agricultural productions in the census of 1870. He did, however, own real estate valued at $1,000. See Ninth Census, 1870, Manuscript Returns of Inhabitants, Montgomery County, Kentucky, 284.

[42] McAllister and Guerrant, *Edward O. Guerrant*, 60–62; Guerrant diary, 15 September 1873; 31 January 1874.

during the war—entrusted them to God: "O bless my wife and little children!"[43]

He returned home in the spring of 1874 for his summer break. Determined not to practice medicine but to "prosecute my own studies," he spent the summer preaching, often at far away churches. His preaching began fortuitously. After attending a Baptist service, Guerrant was approached by the pastor and asked to preach at the church in two weeks. Although reluctant, he agreed. Two weeks later, he noted: "Preached my first sermon today...was pale with fear." But he apparently enjoyed the experience; he preached several more times at other local churches, including African-American ones. Even at this early stage in his ministry, Guerrant was an effective preacher. During one lengthy service at a black church, he preached to an overflowing congregation of 300–400, sparking several conversions. In addition to preaching, Guerrant began a Sunday school program at the Springfield Presbyterian Church.[44]

Guerrant returned to seminary in the fall of 1874 for his final year. He completed the course of study in February 1875 and proceeded home. In April, the West Lexington Presbytery examined him thoroughly on "languages, on the Arts and Sciences, on Church History and Government.... Sacraments and Theology." Passing these examinations, he preached a trial sermon, after which the Presbytery licensed him. During his probationary period, he served at Walnut Hill, Union, and Salem churches, which were without pastors. He was examined again in October 1875 for his personal piety, following which the Presbytery ordained him and installed him as pastor of Salem Church. He continued to preach at the three churches until 1876.[45]

---

[43] McAllister and Guerrant, *Edward O. Guerrant*, 69, 71; Guerrant diary, 26 September 1873; 9, 20, 31 January, 14 August 1874; and 9 January 1875.

[44] Guerrant diary, 28 February, 8, 16, 22 March, 5, 12 April, 1, 22, 29 May, 7, 14, 21, 28 June, 5, 9, 12, 19 July 1874.

[45] Ibid., 2 February 1875; 16 May 1876; and passim; McAllister and Guerrant, *Edward O. Guerrant*, 72; West Lexington Presbytery, Minute Book, 1871–1881, 18 April 1874; 17–19 April 1875, Presbyterian Historical Society, Montreat, North Carolina; Presbyterian Church, Salem, Kentucky, Session Minutes, 1, 25 April 1875

In May 1876, the congregation of the Mount Sterling Presbyterian Church issued a call for Guerrant to become their pastor. Although reluctant to leave his three smaller churches, he was delighted with the opportunity to return home. He accepted the call, but continued to preach at his former churches until they found new pastors. Guerrant served as pastor of the Mount Sterling Presbyterian Church from 1876–1878. During this time he became increasingly interested in evangelism and led several protracted meetings at other churches—including those of other denominations.[46]

During the 1870s, the Presbyterian Church in America began to emphasize the importance of missions at home and abroad. It was

---

(microfilm), King Library, University of Kentucky, Lexington. The West Lexington Presbytery was affiliated with the Old School Calvinists and no doubt examined Guerrant on many Calvinistic tenets, including predestination. Predestination, as historically embraced by traditional Calvinistic Presbyterian theology, is the belief that God is utterly sovereign and solely responsible for the salvation of individuals. According to the doctrine, God has graciously preordained the elect to salvation and, by his own mysterious sovereign, righteous, and inscrutable will, destined the non-elect to eternal condemnation. The Presbytery's association with the Old School is made clear in the *Minutes of the General Assembly of the Presbyterian Church in the United States of America, 1866* (Philadelphia: Presbyterian Board of Publishing, 1866) 4. For more on predestination, see *The Constitution of the Presbyterian Church in the United States of America, Containing the Confession of Faith, the Catechisms, and the Directory for the Worship of God...* (Philadelphia: Presbyterian Board of Publication, 1839) 23–27; Randall Balmer and John R. Fitzmier, *The Presbyterians* (Westport CT: Greenwood Press, 1993) 5–7; John W. Kuykendall and Walter L. Lingle, *Presbyterians, Their History and Beliefs* (Atlanta: John Knox Press, 1978) 102–105; and Ernest Trice Thompson, *Presbyterians in the South*, 3 vols. (Richmond: John Knox Press, 1963–73) 1:352–63. Many evangelical denominations during this era prescribed a period of probation for ministerial candidates. Presbyterians examined and licensed a candidate after graduation from college and assigned him to preach at churches that had no pastor. Candidates could not officiate at the sacraments—such as the Lord's Supper or baptism—nor perform weddings until they were ordained. Once ministerial candidates received a call from a church—an invitation to serve as a congregation's pastor—ordination and installation followed. The probationary period was usually short. See Anne C. Loveland, *Southern Evangelicals and the Social Order, 1800–1860* (Baton Rouge: Louisiana State University Press, 1980) 28.

[46] West Lexington Presbytery, Minute Book, 18 May 1876; Guerrant diary, 13, 16, 20, 26 May, 11, 18 June, 16 July, 15 October 1876; 7, 10–11 January, 18 March, 23–30 July, 18 November 1877; 19 May 1878; and passim.

during this time that the Kentucky Synod appointed Guerrant to its Committee of Home Missions. At the 1877 conference, he issued a scathing report on the state of missions in Kentucky. He informed the Synod: "Of the one hundred counties in Kentucky, sixty are entirely unoccupied by our church…. They have jails and gambling hells, but no house for God's worship. And these people are anxious to have God's word preached to them…. [Yet] the church has stood still." Moved by his passion for the lost, the Synod pledged to raise additional funds for home missions.[47]

In 1878, the First Presbyterian Church of Louisville, Kentucky, called Reverend Guerrant as pastor. A large church, First Presbyterian required much of Guerrant's time. Pastoral duties such as visiting the sick and attending meetings of the Session encumbered him and he rarely found time to participate in protracted evangelism meetings. He nevertheless enjoyed much success at the Louisville church: the church doubled its membership during his three years as pastor. Despite this accomplishment, evangelism remained his principal interest.[48]

---

[47] Thompson, *Presbyterians in the South*, 2:272; McAllister and Guerrant, *Edward O. Guerrant*, 78, 80; Edward O. Guerrant, *The Soul Winner* (Lexington KY: John B. Morton & Company, 1896) 122–24. Despite their adherence to the tenet of predestination, Old School Presbyterians believed it was necessary to spread the Gospel in order to spark conversions among the elect. Guerrant, however, may have held a more moderate view of predestination. In his 1884 report to the Kentucky Synod, he appealed to Romans 1:16 in his remarks exhorting the need for evangelism: "The 'gospel is the power of God unto salvation to every one that believeth,' and that it needs only be preached plainly, earnestly and effectionately, and, above all, prayerfully, to accomplish God's pleasure in the salvation of men." Guerrant likely held that the Christian's responsibility was only to preach the Gospel and that God would take care of the results. See *The Constitution of the Presbyterian Church*, 61–64; Guerrant, *Soul Winner*, 94, 138, 171, 183; and Edward O. Guerrant, *The Galax Gatherers: The Gospel Among the Highlanders* (Richmond VA: Onward Press, 1910) 155.

[48] First Presbyterian Church, Louisville, Kentucky, Session Minutes, 1874–1882, 23 October 1878; 30 March 1881; and passim (microfilm), Presbyterian Historical Society, Montreat, North Carolina; Guerrant diary, 25 October 1878; 5, 11 January, 13 May, 15 June, 13 September, 21 December 1879; 10 February, 23 May, 3 October 1880; and 23 November 1881; McAllister and Guerrant, *Edward O. Guerrant*, 83; West Lexington Presbytery, Minute Book, 29 November, 23

As chairman of the Committee on Evangelistic Labor, Guerrant addressed the Kentucky Synod in 1881 and again delivered a blistering report on the state of home missions. He informed members that "many of the citizens of our state are living in absolute ignorance of the gospel, while a still larger proportion…may die without any knowledge of the way of salvation." During this conference, the Synod took decisive action, appointing Guerrant and another pastor as evangelists and dividing Kentucky between them. The First Presbyterian Church of Louisville opposed his selection as Synod Evangelist on "account of the great success of his ministry." When the Presbytery asked his preference, Guerrant remarked, "I believe this is *His will* for me to accept the call of the Synod…. May God direct me in the way of His Commandments, accept my person and services and use me for His glory. If I made a mistake, I pray Him to overrule it to His honor and glory." He accepted the appointment.[49]

Guerrant commenced work immediately and proved to be an indefatigable evangelist. During his first six months he was constantly on the move, conducting 174 services and adding 484 members to the rolls of the Presbyterian Church in Kentucky. Guerrant's preaching even added dozens to the church rolls of other denominations. He organized and reorganized churches, ordained deacons and installed church officers. To achieve the best results, he sent an assistant two or three days ahead of him to announce his visit. Guerrant preached wherever he could gather an audience, often in barrooms or schoolhouses. Occasionally, he ministered to individuals

---

December 1878; *Manual of the First Presbyterian Church* (Louisville: self published, 1909) 24. Guerrant noted in his diary that the Mt. Sterling congregation was "violently opposed to my going to Louisville." See Guerrant diary, 12 November 1878.

[49] *Minutes of the Synod of Kentucky, October 12, 1881…* (Winchester KY: Clark County Democrat Press, 1881) 52, 55. Guerrant had also criticized the state of missions in his 1880 report to the Kentucky Synod. See *Minutes of the Synod of Kentucky, October 13, 1880…* (Paris KY: F. L. & J. R. McChesney Printing, 1880) 12. First Presbyterian's opposition to Guerrant's appointment and his acceptance of the position are recorded in First Presbyterian Church, Louisville, Kentucky, Session Minutes, 13 November 1881; and Guerrant diary, 14 October, 10 November 1881.

in their homes. At a meeting in 1884, Guerrant visited an eighty-three-year old, dirt-poor mountaineer and explained the "way of life to him." He also ministered to the physical needs of the mountain folk. Following a meeting in Hazel Green, Kentucky, he noted: "Crowds of people come to be examined for all sorts of ailments." Guerrant also arranged for other ministers or seminary students to provide follow up ministry where he had preached.[50]

During his stint as Synod Evangelist, Guerrant maintained his ecumenical outlook and frequently preached at churches of other denominations. In 1885, he even preached to a Campbellite congregation—a significant doctrinal challenge to an evangelical Presbyterian minister in that day. About the brethren of other Christian faith traditions, he wrote: "I have had the most cordial support of brethren of the Methodist, Baptist and other churches, because I preached the same great doctrines of grace held by them in common with my own church." Guerrant also extended his ecumenism to revival meetings. In an 1885 report to the Kentucky Synod, he announced that he was working with other ministers to construct a church building in Lewisport, Kentucky, "to be used by *all* denominations."[51]

In 1885, Guerrant issued a report to the Kentucky Synod summarizing his work over the last three years: he had organized twenty-three churches, constructed fifteen new church buildings, added 2,707 new members, and raised over $16,000 for the Presbyterians. Yet he remained humble about his accomplishments and believed that both the "long-neglected children in the Highlands" and the Lord "are worthy of a better advocate." His evangelistic success greatly increased his faith in God, for he saw many miracles in lives that had been transformed by faith.[52]

---

[50] Guerrant diary, 14 April, 7 May, 8 August, 1–9, 17 October 1882; app. in vol. 40; 7 July, 4, 7, 24 August 1884; and passim; Wilson, "Edward Owings Guerrant" 21.

[51] Guerrant diary, 5, 26 February 1882; 11 June 1883; 30 June 1885; Guerrant, *Soul Winner*, 90, 176. Although he possessed an ecumenical spirit, Guerrant did not include Mormons—whom he called "wolves in sheep's clothing"—in that embrace. See Wilson, "Edward Owings Guerrant," 29–30.

[52] Guerrant, *The Galax Gatherers*, v.

Wearied by the unabated pace of ministry and the constant separation from family, Guerrant resigned his position as Synod Evangelist in 1885. He admitted: "I do not know what He has for me to do, or where he means for me to go; nor need I care. I am His servant, and cheerfully, confidently await His orders, with the assurance that the gracious Father who feeds the birds, and clothes the lilies, will not forget even the faithless children of His love." Following his resignation, Guerrant toured the South and preached at such places as Mobile, Alabama, Charleston, South Carolina, and Lynchburg, Virginia. When he returned to Kentucky he became the pastor of two small churches near Lexington. His pastoral success continued and these churches grew rapidly.[53]

Despite his retirement as Synod Evangelist, Guerrant continued to labor in the field of missions. Although he occasionally made an evangelistic tour to the mountains, he mainly facilitated the efforts of other missionaries. In 1896, Guerrant published his first book. Titled *Soul Winner*, it was intended to prepare evangelists. The following year, he organized and became president of the Society of Soul Winners (or the America Inland Mission), whose objective was to carry the Gospel to mountain areas and organize churches. Over the next ten years, the Society conducted over 22,000 services, sparked 6,000 conversions and oversaw the construction of fifty-six churches. The Society also was instrumental in the establishment of three Kentucky colleges: Witherspoon, Highland and Stuart Robinson. Guerrant published two additional books, *The Galax Gatherers* in 1910 and the *Gospel of the Lilies* in 1912. He fervently continued to advance the cause of Christ until his death on 26 April 1916.[54]

Guerrant expressed little interest in postwar politics. Indeed, he cautioned preachers "*not* to preach politics, philosophy, metaphysics, or even your own opinion." Privately, however, he was a Democrat

---

[53] Guerrant diary, 23 October 1885; Guerrant, *Soul Winner*, 173; McAllister and Guerrant, *Edward O. Guerrant*, 102–103.

[54] McAllister and Guerrant, *Edward O. Guerrant*, 103, 107, 138, 142, 150–51, 158; Guerrant, *Soul Winner*, 3; William C. Davis and Meredith L. Swentor, eds., *Bluegrass Confederate: The Headquarters Diary of Edward O. Guerrant* (Baton Rouge: Louisiana State University Press, 1999) 8, 11.

and hoped for his party's success at the polls. In 1876 he supported Samuel Tilden for president and Grover Cleveland in 1884. For Guerrant, however, such temporal matters were of secondary importance. On election day in 1884, he expressed his desire to see Cleveland elected but noted, "in any event 'God Reigns.'"[55]

Felix Pierre Poché

The fall of Port Hudson and rumors of enemy encroachments into Louisiana's Lafourche district prompted Felix Poché to enter Confederate service in July 1863. He considered it his duty to serve, yet he knew that the prospects for a Southern victory were gloomy. Indeed, he often doubted the accuracy of favorable war rumors. Hearing that General Robert E. Lee's forces had captured Washington and that General Joseph E. Johnston had defeated General Ulysses S. Grant in Mississippi, he remarked: "More than likely this glorious news will soon be entirely contradicted and succeeded by some very alarming and distressing rumors." Although there were occasional heartening moments for the Confederacy, Poché remained skeptical that the South would achieve its independence.[56]

Bleak prospects for victory and a prolonged absence from loved ones led Poché to long for peace. These circumstances likely helped him to accept the South's defeat. In February 1865 he wrote: "May God have mercy on us and give us that sweet peace is the fervent prayer from my sad and suffering heart." He hoped that God's intervention to end the war was "not too far distant."[57]

Poché became increasingly resigned to what he perceived was the apparent will of God as the Civil War drew toward its conclusion. He believed God controlled the affairs of men and that military reversals indicated that the Lord's will might well differ from that of

---

[55] Guerrant, *Soul Winner*, 36; Guerrant diary, 7 November 1876; 5 November 1884.

[56] Edwin C. Bearss, ed., *A Louisiana Confederate: Diary of Felix Pierre Poché*, trans. Eugenie Watson Somdal (Natchitoches LA: Louisiana Studies Institute, Northwestern State University, 1972) 3–5, 10, 18, 22, 30, 34–35, 55, 69, 97, 164–65, 174, 202.

[57] Ibid., 211, 214.

Southerners. Learning in July 1864 that a planned expedition to Lafourche would not take place, a disappointed Poché remarked: "How true it is that man proposes and God disposes!" With General Lee's surrender confirmed, Poché wrote in April 1865: "With this state of affairs we cannot hope for a successful end for our poor Confederacy, and we must resign ourselves to return to the domination of the Yankees.... But God, who directs and ordains all for the best, will have pity on us and will see to it that the conquering enemy will be generous toward their victim."[58]

By April 1865, Federal cavalry were conducting an all-out search for Captain Poché and his company of partisan rangers. On 29 April he was ordered by his superiors to cease operations until further notice. When he confirmed that generals Joseph E. Johnston and Richard Taylor had surrendered, Poché led his men to the nearest Federal military post and gave himself up. He was paroled at Bonnet Carré, Louisiana, on 16 May 1865.[59]

Poché returned to his home in St. James Parish and to his wife, Sélima, on 17 May. He immediately resumed his law practice and immersed himself in his legal cases. Working day and night, he reportedly earned an astounding $15,000 his first year. He also served temporarily as the St. James Parish district attorney. Indeed, Poché was so busy that he seldom had time for anything else. According to the 1870 census, his farm was valued at $1,620. Of the 324 acres that comprised the property, he claimed only four improved acres.[60]

---

[58] Ibid., 143, 152, 240–41.

[59] Ibid., 197–200, 229–32, 236, 238, 241, 244; Unfiled Papers and Slips, Belonging to Confederate Compiled Service Records, National Archives, Washington DC; *War of the Rebellion: A Compilation of the Official Records of the Union and Confederate Armies,* 70 vols. in 128 pts. (Washington DC: 1880–1921) 48:167–68.

[60] Bearss, *Louisiana Confederate,* 244; Felix P. Poché diary, 23 June–19 October 1865, (typescript), Eugenie Watson Somdal Papers, Watson Library, Northwestern State University, Natchitoches, Louisiana; *Biographical and Historical Memoirs of Louisiana,* 2 vols. (Chicago: Goodspeed Publishing Company, 1892) 2:315; Ninth Census, 1870, Manuscript Returns of Inhabitants, St. James Parish, Louisiana, 165; Ninth Census, 1870, Manuscript Returns of Productions of Agriculture, St. James

In January 1866 Poché entered politics. He was elected to the state senate and served for two years until the Republicans took control of the government. A staunch Democrat, Poché actively worked to end Republican rule in Louisiana. He regularly attended the Democratic state conventions and presided over the 1879 convention. He also canvassed the state in 1879 for the Democratic ticket. Poché furthermore served as a delegate to the 1879 Constitutional Convention and served on several important committees, including public education, the bill of rights and the judiciary committees. There was a movement within this Democrat-dominated convention to curtail the African-American vote through property or educational qualifications. Poché, however, considered himself a "representative of the people, and did not shrink from declaring he would vote for unlimited suffrage." Others evidently agreed, for the new constitution placed no restrictions on male suffrage. In practice, however, fraud and intimidation served to diminish African-American votes.[61]

Poché was an eminent jurist and exhibited "rare talents, quick apprehension, and great industry." He played an integral role in the creation of the Louisiana Bar Association and served eight years as its

---

Parish, Louisiana, 5. Unfortunately, Poché kept his postwar diary only intermittently and abandoned it altogether in October 1865.

[61] New Orleans *Daily Picayune*, 17 June 1895; *Memoirs of Louisiana*, 2:315; Poché diary, 17 October 1865. Although the early Union occupation of southern Louisiana gave Unionists temporary control of Louisiana's government, ex-Confederates reasserted themselves soon after the war only to lose power again with the onset of radical Reconstruction. See Foner, *Reconstruction*, 48–49, 182–83, 251–307, 316–33; Joe G. Taylor, *Louisiana: A Bicentennial History* (New York: W. W. Norton & Company, 1976) 102–105, 114; Marguerite T. Leach, "The Aftermath of Reconstruction in Louisiana," *Louisiana Historical Quarterly* 32 (July 1949): 630–35. For more on the role Poché played during the 1879 constitutional convention, see New Orleans *Daily Picayune*, 24, 26, 29 April 1879. According to Leach, Democrats had pledged in 1876 to protect African-American rights in exchange for their support in regaining control of the state government. By affixing qualifications to restrict black suffrage, the Democrats would have violated the agreement. Furthermore, rumors were circulating that African Americans planned a mass exodus from the state if the new constitution curtailed their rights. See Leach, "Aftermath of Reconstruction," 667–68, 672–73; and New Orleans *Daily Picayune*, 24 April 1879.

vice-president. In 1880, he was appointed associate justice of the
Louisiana Supreme Court, a position he held for ten years. Resigning
in 1890, he returned to private practice. His death came five years
later, on 16 June 1895.[62]

Little is known about Poché's postwar religious activities. His
reunion with Sélima and the end of the war led to fewer religious
references in his brief postwar diary. He did attend Mass regularly,
occasionally assisting the priest at the altar as he had done during the
war. Poché apparently served in no formal leadership role in his local
church, for unlike the Protestant faiths, the Catholic Church had few
offices in which the laity could serve. His devotion to his faith and
church, however, cannot be doubted. Poché and his family continued
to attend St. Michael's Church; and as had been his custom before
the war, Poché had all of his children baptized very soon after their
births, an indisputable sign of his devoutness.[63]

Hiram Talbert Holt

Like others in this study, Hiram Talbert Holt believed that
human events were directed by a sovereign God. In June 1862 he
wrote: "Gods works and decrees who can prevent?" Holt believed
early on that the Lord sanctioned the Confederate cause. Expecting
an outbreak of hostilities at any moment, he wrote to Carrie on 11
April 1861: "I feel that the God of the just will be with us to shield us

---

[62] New Orleans *Times-Picayune*, 17, 23 June 1895; "The Celebration of the
Centenary of the Supreme Court of Louisiana," *Louisiana Historical Quarterly* 4
(January 1921): 63–65.

[63] Poché diary, 23 June–19 October 1865; *Diocese of Baton Rouge, Catholic Church
Records*, 18 vols. (Baton Rouge: Diocese of Baton Rouge, Department of Archives,
1982–1995) 10:463, 11:428, 12:480, 13:485. The significance of baptism for
Catholics is explained in chapter 1 and in J. Paul Williams, *What Americans Believe
and How They Worship* (New York: Harper & Brothers, Publishers, 1952) 43–44; and
Roderick Strange, *The Catholic Faith* (New York/Oxford: Oxford University Press,
1986) 86–88. In most Catholic churches in the late nineteenth century the role of the
laity was, according to one Catholic historian, solely "to pay, pray, and obey." See
Timothy Walch, *Catholicism in America: A Social History* (Malabar FL: Robert E.
Krieger Publishing, 1989) 45; and Jay P. Dolan, *The American Catholic Experience: A
History from Colonial Times to the Present* (New York: Doubleday Publishing, 1985)
114, 160, 178.

from harm and give us victory." Early military setbacks, however, concerned Holt and may have led him to question whether the Lord supported the South. After Fort Donelson fell in February 1862, he wrote: "I feel so sad lately, probably it is owing to our reverses." Despite his doubt, Holt continued to trust God for deliverance: "Probably by the time this reaches you...another battle the worst the world ever saw will have been fought at Corinth. I tremble for the result.... God save Beauregard and the South. The prayers of the Southern people ought to ascend daily to God to protect them against such odds. All can't fight, but all can pray." Additional defeats prompted similar comments. After the fall of Vicksburg in July 1863, he wrote: "Dark clouds overshadow us now, but let us trust God and praise him for his goodness."[64]

How Holt would have reconciled himself to the South's defeat had he lived may be evident in the way he perceived adversity in general. Depressed over their long separation and the illness of their child, he wrote Carrie in November 1861: "Let us bow to the decrees of our God, whether it be in weal or wo, remember precious metals are often the hardest tried." Two years later, Holt again encouraged Carrie to demonstrate Christian fortitude in the event that their younger child, an infant, was to die: "Welcome it as part of God's providence when it does come. Accustom yourself to take comfort and joy in your Creator's acts, knowing as you do that, He does all for the best, though seeming hard to us." After their infant died in 1864, Holt reminded Carrie: "Whom God loveth he chasteneth. The gold and rubbish are put together in the burning crucible, the gold is melted and separated from the rubbish. So we must also go through many trying ordeals ere we are fitted for those mansions in the skies."[65]

Holt furthermore made clear his willingness to abide by the will of God. When it was rumored that the 38th Alabama would be sent

[64] Talbert Holt to Carrie Holt, 11 April, 29 May 1861; 26 February, 26 April, 23 June 1862; and to Carrie Holt, no date (most likely mid-1863; typescript), all in Robert Partin Papers, Draughon Library, Auburn University, Alabama.
[65] Talbert Holt to Carrie Holt, 9 November 1861; 20 November 1863; 29 January 1864, Partin Papers.

to Virginia in July 1861, he remarked: "Behind a frowning providence there is a smiling face. Let us bear all things with Christian meekness and resignation." When his brother was killed in Virginia, he wrote: "I am resigned to God's will, and would not if I could this day, bring John back to life."[66]

A skirmish near Dalton, Georgia, in February 1864 claimed Talbert Holt's life. The news of his death was a terrible shock to Carrie, but she accepted it as part of God's plan. She was, however, angry about one aspect of her husband's death. By late 1863 she had saved and borrowed enough money to hire a substitute for Talbert. When the substitute arrived at the camp of the 38th Alabama, another soldier in Holt's company bribed him to serve in his place and returned home to Choctaw Corner. He was at home when Holt was killed. Later, the interloping soldier begged Carrie to forgive him as he lay on his deathbed. A testimony to her graciousness, she did.[67]

After Talbert's death, Carrie taught school and lived part of the time with his parents and part of the time with her own. She did not, however, take Talbert's advice to remarry. She died on 11 January 1939.[68]

The two wartime converts who survived the conflict also became the Lord's servants in the postwar years. Giles Cooke fulfilled his wartime pledge and became an Episcopal priest, dedicated to the educational and spiritual needs of Petersburg's freedmen. Ted

---

[66] Talbert Holt to Carrie Holt, 27 July 1861; 13 December 1862; 7 October 1863, ibid.

[67] Robert Partin, "The Sustaining Faith of an Alabama Soldier," *Civil War History* 6 (December 1960): 438; Holt manuscript, 494–95, Partin Papers. Holt mentions the incident in a letter home: "I am sorry that you will be disappointed about me getting a furlough. Stephen Newton never stopped where I was at all, had he done so I would now have been at home." See Talbert Holt to Carrie Holt, 18 December 1863, Partin Papers. The Confederate government abolished the policy of allowing substitutions in December 1863. See James M. McPherson, *Battle Cry of Freedom: The Civil War Era* (New York/Oxford: Oxford University Press, 1988) 603.

[68] Holt manuscript, 495–96, Partin Papers; Ninth Census, 1870, Manuscript Returns of Inhabitants, Clarke County, Alabama, 28. Holt had advised Carrie in July 1861 to remarry in the event of his death. See Talbert Holt to Carrie Holt, 17 July 1861, Partin Papers.

Barclay served as a leader in his home church for forty-six years. Wartime convert Robert Moore was killed at the Battle of Chickamauga in September 1863.

Giles Buckner Cooke

Although he believed that God sanctioned the Confederate cause, Giles Cooke maintained that it was essential to secure God's blessing in order to prevail over the Yankees. As a large Union force approached Corinth, Mississippi, in May 1862, Cooke noted a "sad and gloomy" state of spiritual affairs in the Confederate forces: "Oh, that our soldiers were soldiers of the Cross, then we would not fear any force our enemies might send against us, 'for if the Lord is with us, who can be against us.'" Following Confederate defeats at Gettysburg and Vicksburg, he expressed hope that the Southern people would "[Humble] themselves before the Creator of us and all things...and trust in Him and not thine own strength." When the final defeat of Southern forces was imminent, he concluded that Southerners had not merited God's favor. On Christmas day in 1864 he wrote:

> The saddest day of our national life is upon us.... The times are darker now than they were in the Xmas day in '76.... Let us as a nation humble ourselves before God and invoke His help and all will be well. Let us enter not into gayeties and dissipation—but let us put on sack cloth and ashes, and bow ourselves down...before our Maker.... If we as a people deserve our independence and freedom, it will surely be granted us by the God of battles.

Cooke remained hopeful, however, that the Southern people would make the amends necessary to win God's intervention. In early 1865 he noted: "The times are indeed dark—but my prayer is that our people may so act as to merit the favor of Him, who sits on High. Help us all good Lord to do thy Holy Will."[69]

---

[69] Giles Buckner Cooke diary, 16 May, 3, 6 September 1862; 5 May, 21 August 1863; 25 December 1864; and 1 January 1865, Giles Buckner Cooke Papers, Virginia Historical Society, Richmond.

Cooke's resignation to God's will helped him accept defeat. Hearing a minister's sermon on human suffering and the will of God, he remarked: "Oh! may I be able to realize under any affliction that my Heavenly Father may choose to send upon me—His sustaining grace, and feel that it is to be for the best." Cooke furthermore learned to abide by the Lord's will when it ran contrary to his own. Bad news from home in November 1862 prompted him to pray: "'Thy will—not mine, be done.'" After the fighting near Bermuda Hundred in May 1864, Cooke wrote: "May the God of Mercy soon put an end to the terrible and wicked war, if consistent with His Holy Will."[70]

As the assistant inspector-general on Robert E. Lee's staff, Major Cooke surrendered with the Army of Northern Virginia on 9 April 1865. He remained in Petersburg (where the army had been for ten months) after his parole and worked in an express office handling baggage. In September 1865, he left this menial position and, with Dr. Thomas Hume, opened the Hume and Cooke Classical and Mathematical Institute, a preparatory school for white children. The school continued with much success until 1868, when Cooke departed to become principal of the first African-American public high school in Petersburg.[71]

In 1871 Cooke left the high school and established a private school for freedmen, under the auspices of the Episcopal Church. Although the school received some funds from the Church, it relied primarily on tuition and private contributions. Determined to enter the ministry, Cooke studied theology in his spare time under Dr. Churchill Gibson, the rector of St. Paul's Episcopal Church. During this time he married Martha Southall of Hampton, Virginia.[72]

In addition to preparing for the ministry, Cooke assumed a position of leadership at St. Paul's Church. He served as a teacher

---

[70] Ibid., 9 October, 18 November 1862; 20 May, 5 December 1864.

[71] Compiled Service Records, General and Staff Officers; Autobiographical Sketch, (typescript), 6, Giles B. Cooke folder, Virginia Military Institute; Cooke biography, ch. 7, Cooke Papers.

[72] Cooke diary, 25 September 1871; Cooke questionnaire, 2, and Autobiographical Sketch, 6, both in Cooke folder; Cooke biography, chs. 7 and 8, Cooke Papers.

and superintendent of the congregation's Sunday school. In 1868 he became a lay reader and thereafter routinely conducted services when the rector was absent. In 1871 he was ordained as a deacon and made assistant-minister at St. Paul's. When he was not in the pulpit of his own church, he often preached at others, including the venerable St. Paul's Episcopal Church in Richmond. He also ministered to the poor and spoke to individuals privately when opportunities arose. Approached by a stranger one morning while walking, Cooke seized the chance to share Christ with him: "I humbly trust that I said something that may do him good and strengthen his faith in the blessed saviour."[73]

Cooke's interest in an African-American ministry appears to have developed during the war. He frequently attended church services held for servants and evidently enjoyed them, for he noted in his diary that he was always affected by worshiping "among the colored." As he did with the white services he attended, Cooke listened closely and recorded the text and sermon titles in his diary. After one African-American service in January 1864, he visited with the pastor at length.[74]

While he was Sunday school superintendent at St. Paul's, Cooke organized classes for Petersburg's freedmen. He believed that religious instruction was important for the children. Indeed, during the war he had heard a sermon on the importance of children attending Sunday school and commented that it was necessary "in order that we might... do our respective parts in bringing up our children in the nurture and admonishing of the Lord." These schools also provided educational instruction to the former slaves, an

---

[73] St. Paul's Episcopal Church, Petersburg, Virginia, Vestry Minutes 1720–1986, 7 May 1866; 27 April 1868 (microfilm); Parish Register 1720–1986, 14 June, 12 July 1868; 23–26 February, 30 May, 8 September, 18 October 1869; 1 May, 3 July 1870; 4 June, 22 October 1871, Virginia State Library, Richmond; Autobiographical Sketch, 6, Cooke folder; Cooke diary, 7, 14, 21, 24 January, 4 February, 3 March, 21, 28 April, 8, 19 May 1872; and passim.

[74] Cooke diary, 17, 24 January, 9 October 1864. Although the topic of conversation is unknown, Cooke visited with the white pastors of two African-American churches for five days in January 1864. See ibid., 17, 20–22, 24 January 1864.

important objective of the Episcopal Church in the immediate
postwar period. For openly associating with the freedmen's cause,
however, Cooke was ostracized by the conservative whites in
Petersburg, including many of his friends. When asked long after the
war why he began working with the freedmen, he responded that he
had been inspired by Confederate generals Robert E. Lee and
Stonewall Jackson: Lee had provided religious instruction to his
slaves and Jackson had taught a Sunday school class for slaves before
the war. Cooke insisted that the work must be done and believed that
"no one else would [do it]."[75]

In 1869, Cooke established a Sunday school at St. Stephen's
Episcopal Church, an African-American church in Petersburg. St.
Stephen's, founded in 1867, had received funds from the Freedmen's
Bureau and the Protestant Episcopal Freedman's Commission as well
as from Northern missionaries. The black Episcopalians, supported
by a few white clergy and laymen, acquired an old chapel and
remodeled it for use as a church. Petersburg's conservative whites
grew concerned about this display of self-reliance. On 9 April 1867 a
fire—widely believed to be an act of arson—broke out and destroyed
the chapel. Construction soon began on a new building, which was
completed in 1868. That same year Reverend Joseph S. Atwell

---

[75] *The Bishop Payne Divinity School* (n.p., n.d.) 3, Virginia Historical Society,
Richmond. Robert E. Lee wrote to Cooke in 1866 and commended him for his work
among the freedmen. See Robert E. Lee to Giles B. Cooke, April 1866, in Cooke
Papers. See also Ryan K. Smith, "A Church Fire and Reconstruction: St. Stephen's
Episcopal Church, Petersburg, Virginia" (M.A. thesis, College of William and Mary,
1998) 13–14, 16; Lawrenceville (Virginia) *Southern Missioner*, May 1928; Cooke
diary, 23 November 1862; William W. Manross, *A History of the American Episcopal
Church* (New York: Morehouse-Gorham Company, 1950) 326; Anne M. Boylan,
Sunday School: The Formation of An American Institution, 1790–1880 (New Haven:
Yale University Press, 1988) 29; George F. Bragg, Jr., *The Story of Old St. Stephen's,
Petersburg, Va., and the Origin of the Bishop Payne Divinity School* (n.p., 1917) 125–26,
Virginia Historical Society, Richmond; Cooke biography, ch. 7, Cooke Papers;
Richmond (Virginia) *News Leader*, 5 February 1937; Robert F. Hunter, *Lexington
Presbyterian Church, 1789–1989* (Lexington VA: News-Gazette, 1991) 68.

became the first rector of St. Stephen's and the first African-American priest in the Episcopal Church in Virginia.[76]

In 1873, Reverend Atwell departed St. Stephen's for another parish in Georgia. In May of that year, the congregation called Major Cooke as rector. He immediately accepted and began his duties the following Sunday. Cooke seemed to be a perfect fit for St. Stephen's. The congregation knew him well, for not only had he taught Sunday school there but he had also preached when the rector was absent. In addition to his duties as rector, he taught Sunday school, conducted an adult Bible class, and occasionally preached in other churches, including African-American ones. The following year, Cooke was ordained priest in the Episcopal Church. He served as rector of St. Stephen's until 1885.[77]

When Cooke became rector of St. Stephen's in 1873, he combined his private school with the church school already there. That same year he established a normal department and began training African-American schoolteachers. A Christian education being of paramount importance to him, Cooke implemented a school curriculum that included not only English, mathematics and language, but also courses in truthfulness, honesty and courtesy. He also conducted morning prayers at the school and often prayed with the parents of his pupils. In 1879, he added a theology department, the only African-American divinity school in the Episcopal Church. Cooke traveled to Northern churches soliciting funds for the school. During his tour, he preached at several of the churches he visited. In

---

[76] The Freedman's Commission of the Episcopal church was created in 1865 to support the secular and religious education of the former slaves. See Manross, *American Episcopal Church*, 326. See also *St. Stephen's Episcopal Church, Petersburg, Virginia, Parish Profile* (n.p., 1993) 5–6, St. Stephen's Episcopal Church, Petersburg, Virginia; and Smith, "A Church Fire and Reconstruction," 16, 18, 29–31, 38. Smith believes that the date of the fire is significant: it was the second anniversary of Lee's surrender.

[77] Cooke diary, 24 October 1869; 22 May, 17 June 1870; 26 February, 5, 16, 23, 29 March, 6–7, 13, 19 April, 7–8, 11 May 1873; 22, 29 November 1874; and passim; Autobiographical Sketch, 6, Cooke folder; *St. Stephen's Parish Profile*, 6.

1884, the theology department was renamed the Bishop Payne Divinity School.[78]

In 1885, Cooke departed St. Stephen's to become the rector of a white parish in Charlotte Hall, Maryland. The following year, he returned to an African-American parish, this one in Louisville, Kentucky, and served it until 1889. Afterwards, he was the rector of several other white parishes in Maryland and Virginia until he retired in 1917. He then moved to Mathews, Virginia, where he remained until his death on 4 February 1937. Giles Cooke was nearly ninety-nine years old when he passed away.[79]

Alexander Tedford Barclay

Ted Barclay believed that unrighteous Southerners were responsible for Confederate military setbacks. Following the death of Stonewall Jackson in the Battle of Chancellorsville, Barclay wrote: "He was taken away from us because we made almost an idol of him." Despite such a loss, Barclay remained steadfast in the belief that God would not forsake the Southern cause: "Though we mourn his loss, still we do not feel we are without a leader. God is our leader and protector. He can raise up many a Jackson and will yet deliver us from the power of the enemy."[80]

The Confederate defeat at Gettysburg convinced Barclay that Southerners had failed to secure God's blessing. Advancing down the Shenandoah Valley toward Pennsylvania in June 1863, he wrote confidently: "I fear not the result...through God [we] will be victorious." But the disastrous defeat provoked in Barclay deep reflection about God's role in the conflict. After listening to a sermon in July 1863 titled, "Be ye not deceived, God is not mocked," he

---

[78] Autobiographical Sketch, 6, and Cooke biography, ch. 8, both in Cooke folder; Bragg, *Story of Old St. Stephen's*, 9; Cooke diary, 13, 20, 27 March 1873; 26 April, 11–15 November 1885; and passim; *Bishop Payne Divinity School*, 3–4; George F. Bragg, *History of the Afro-American Group of the Episcopal Church* (1922; reprint, New York: Johnson Reprint Company, 1968) 219–20.

[79] Cooke questionnaire, 2, Cooke folder.

[80] Charles W. Turner, ed., *Ted Barclay, Liberty Hall Volunteers: Letters from the Stonewall Brigade, 1861–1864* (Rockbridge VA: Rockbridge Publishing Company, 1992) 83.

remarked: "Oh, that this army was a bunch of Christian men, then we might indeed expect peace, no longer then would we be punished by the fall of our cities and the repulse of our armies." Barclay believed, however, that God's chastisements always carried great purpose. The death of a close friend in November 1863 prompted this comment: "What a noble fellow was George Chapin, how that family have suffered. But whom God loveth he chasteneth. He intends only their gold to refine, their dross to consume."[81]

Barclay furthermore expressed his willingness to abide by the will of God. Before the Battle of the Wilderness in early May 1864, he wrote: "I would like to survive the conflict, I would like to see our land free from tyrants' grasp and established as one of the stars in the galaxy of nations, but if I am to fall, God help me to say, 'Thy will be done.'"[82]

Following the surrender of Confederate forces, Lieutenant Barclay took an oath of allegiance to the United States at Fort Delaware and was released on 15 June 1865. He returned home to Lexington, Virginia, in July. Although at one time he aspired to be an attorney, Barclay instead took charge of his widowed mother's farm. He primarily grew wheat, but also corn. Barclay owned a few cows and swine as well. The farm was productive and by 1870 it was valued at over $10,000. It was also during this time that Barclay married Virginia Borden Moore of Lexington.[83]

In 1873, his younger brother, Elihu, purchased a newspaper, the *Rockbridge Citizen* (later the *Gazette & Citizen*), and soon thereafter, Ted joined the enterprise as an editor, a position he held for eleven years. A loyal Democrat, Barclay vigorously upheld the party in his columns. He furthermore served as the chairman of the Democratic Executive Committee for Rockbridge in 1888 and supported Grover Cleveland's campaign for the presidency. Although he did not aspire

---

[81] Ibid., 86, 90–97, 117.

[82] Ibid., 144.

[83] Compiled Service Records, 4th Virginia; Lexington (Virginia) *Rockbridge County News*, 2 December 1915; Ninth Census, 1870, Manuscript Returns of Inhabitants, Rockbridge County, Virginia, 506; Ninth Census, 1870, Manuscript Returns of Productions of Agriculture, Rockbridge County, Virginia, 5.

to political office, Barclay was appointed to the county's board of
supervisors in 1870 to complete a member's unfinished term. He
carried out his duties conscientiously and was elected to three more
terms. Supervisor Barclay's efforts proved instrumental in securing a
railroad line to Lexington in the 1880s.[84]

In 1884 Barclay left the *Gazette & Citizen* to become the general
manager of a manufacturing plant in Lexington. In 1889 Rockbridge
County experienced an economic boom when businessmen hastily
established companies to tap into the rich mineral deposits in the
region. One of the first companies created was the Buena Vista
Improvement Company. Its investors unanimously chose Barclay as
president. The company erected a manufacturing town near
Lexington to extract the iron ore in the area. The company proved a
failure, but the town of Buena Vista remains today.[85]

Barclay demonstrated a deep interest in his community and its
institutions. Following in the footsteps of his father and brother, in
1885 he became a trustee of his alma mater, Washington and Lee
University. During his thirty years of service to the institution, he
served on several committees and was known for his "lofty Christian
character." Barclay furthermore served on the executive committee of
the Robert E. Lee Memorial Association, which was responsible for
decorating the grave of the Confederate chieftain. He was also on the
committee charged with erecting a statue of Stonewall Jackson in the
Lexington Presbyterian Church cemetery.[86]

---

[84] Oren F. Morton, *A History of Rockbridge County, Virginia* (Staunton VA: The
McClure Company, 1920) 246; Lexington (Virginia) *Rockbridge County News*, 2
December 1915; Lexington (Virginia) *Gazette & Citizen*, 1 November 1888.

[85] Lexington (Virginia) *Rockbridge County News*, 2 December 1915; Morton,
History of Rockbridge County, 136; Royster Lyle, Jr., "Buena Vista and its Boom,"
Proceedings of the Rockbridge Historical Society 8 (1970–1974) 133–34; *Prospectus of the
Buena Vista Company*, 1, Rockbridge Historical Society Papers, Leyburn Library,
Washington and Lee University, Lexington, Virginia.

[86] *Synopsis of Minutes of Meeting of Board of Trustees of Washington and Lee
University, June 1916*, 11, Trustees' papers, Leyburn Library; Washington and Lee
University, Lexington, Virginia; *Catalogue of the Officers and Alumni of Washington and
Lee University, Lexington, Virginia, 1749–1888* (Baltimore: John Murphy & Co.,
1888) 67, 123; Lexington (Virginia) *Rockbridge County News*, 2 December 1915;
Catalogue of Washington College, Virginia, for the Collegiate Year Ending July 1st, 1870

Barclay returned home from the war a deeply devout Christian. Already a member of the Lexington Presbyterian Church, he became an office bearer after the war. In 1869 he was elected and ordained a deacon. His election to this important church office indicates not only his devotion to God, but also the high regard in which the congregation held him. A deacon's responsibilities included superintending the church's physical buildings, managing finances and distributing charity to the poor. At his first deacons meeting, Barclay was made responsible for collections and appointed to the committee that oversaw the church's physical property. He fulfilled his duties faithfully and once even paid for repairs to the parsonage out of his own pocket. He also served on the committee responsible for dispensing aid to the poor, a task to which he brought compassion. Barclay took his duties seriously and seldom missed the weekly deacons meetings.[87]

In 1882 Barclay was elected to the position of ruling elder. Only the most pious members were chosen as elders and these underwent a rigorous examination before they were ordained and installed. The elders made up the Session, the governing body of the local church. Their responsibilities included examining and admitting new members, maintaining discipline among current members and preparing reports for the Presbytery, the larger regional body of the Presbyterian Church. The Session also selected delegates to attend the meetings of the Presbytery, sending Barclay in 1882.[88]

In addition to his faithful service to the church, Barclay demonstrated a strong personal devotion to Christ. He seldom

---

(Richmond: James E. Goode's Press, 1870) 5; Hunter, *Lexington Presbyterian Church*, 100–101. William N. Pendleton served as the chairman of the executive committee. See "Sketch of the Lee Memorial Association," *Southern Historical Society Papers* 11 (August–September 1883): 390.

[87] Presbyterian Church, Lexington, Virginia, Deacons' Minutes, 1775–1920, 16 December 1869; 25 February 1870; 29 March 1872; 29 January 1873; 12 January, 6 May, 6, 16 October 1874; 27 December 1875; and passim. This description of deacons' duties was gathered from these minutes.

[88] Presbyterian Church, Lexington, Virginia, Session Minutes, 1775-1920, 12, 18 February, 1 April 1882; and 2 January 1916. This description of elders' duties was gathered from these minutes.

missed worship services, even when he was ill. He often prayed before the congregation, moving others with his "deep sense of the solemnity of prayer" and his reverence during worship. He also kept the cause of Christ before him. When his church completed a renovation in 1899, Barclay addressed the congregation: "With the enlargement of our church, let us enlarge our Christian lives…. Let our constant prayer be for the Presence, the indwelling of the Holy Spirit, without whose aid these mere human agencies will be as nothing." In 1900, Barclay spoke to the students of Washington and Lee University about the Liberty Hall Volunteers and their service to the Confederacy. At the conclusion of his speech, he remarked that if he had demonstrated "the value of true Christian character as the only stable and reliable foundation for life-building here and assurance of the life to come, my purpose has been accomplished." Barclay died on 27 November 1915.[89]

Robert Augustus Moore

Lieutenant Robert Augustus Moore was killed at Chickamauga in September 1863. Although he left no clear indication how he might have reconciled his faith with the defeat of the Confederacy had he lived, his earlier comments—even those prior to his conversion—demonstrate how he came to terms with adversity. In June 1861 Moore's cousin, who served in his company, died from fever. After escorting the body back to Holly Springs, a sorrowful Moore remarked: "It seemed hard that one so much beloved by all, one with such a generous heart, should be cut off in the bloom of youth…. But we should be resigned to the will of Almighty God." Undoubtedly, his willingness to abide by the will of God increased after his conversion.[90]

---

[89] Presbyterian Church, Lexington, Virginia, Session Minutes, 2 January 1916; Hunter, *Lexington Presbyterian Church*, 110; Lexington (Virginia) *Rockbridge County News*, 2 December 1915; A. T. Barclay, "The Liberty Hall Volunteers From Lexington to Manassas," *Washington and Lee University, Historical Papers* 6 (1904): 136.

[90] James W. Silver, ed., *A Life for the Confederacy: As Recorded in the Pocket Diaries of Pvt. Robert A. Moore* (Jackson TN: McCowat-Mercer Press, 1959) 24.

Moore believed that God favored the South, a belief he maintained despite military setbacks. Following the Battle of Gettysburg, he wrote: "Times are getting to look dark and gloomy and some are getting feint-hearted. It is indeed a dark hour but we have had as dark before. If our cause be just we will yet triumph." He concluded, however, that the Lord's intervention was necessary in order for Southerners to win their independence. A few days later he wrote: "Today, as usual when our army is at rest, our brigade has assembled more than once, beneath the forest shade, to worship that Being in whom all trust for our deliverance." Moore likely would have accepted the South's defeat as part of God's plan.[91]

Each of the nine soldier-Christians in this study was confident of God's favor when the war began. Early victories were seen as evidence of that favor, and victory over the North appeared certain. By mid-1863, however, decisive military setbacks forced these men to reconsider whether the Lord supported their cause, for did God not control the course of human events? While some believed that God would intervene on behalf of the Confederates at the appropriate time, these men sought an explanation for the defeats. Most concluded that God was chastening Southerners for their unworthiness. These Christian soldiers observed not only iniquity in the military camps, but also faithlessness and idolatry. God, they believed, was purifying them through trying defeats for some greater purpose. Moreover, each believed that if the Lord in his infinite wisdom allowed the defeat of the Confederacy, then such must be accepted as part of God's plan.

The seven men in this study who survived the war returned home with a strong desire to serve the Lord. Three served as clergymen, while three others became lay-leaders in their churches. William Pendleton resumed his position as rector of Grace Episcopal Church, where he faithfully attended to his ministerial duties. He desired to advance the cause of Christ, and thus resumed his college ministry and preached to other congregations when opportunities arose. Edward Guerrant and Giles Cooke entered the ministry and

---

[91] Ibid., 127, 157, 161.

became successful preachers. A Presbyterian evangelist, Guerrant led hundreds to Christ, organized and constructed dozens of churches and raised thousands of dollars for the Presbyterian Church. Cooke tended to the educational and spiritual needs of Petersburg's freedmen despite great social pressure to do otherwise.

Three others faithfully served their churches as laymen. Alfred Fielder resumed his duties as a trustee of Mount Zion Methodist Church and helped charter a new church in Friendship, Tennessee. William Nugent, who held no post in his antebellum church, became an office-bearer in his home church in Greenville. Following a move to Jackson, he became Sunday school superintendent for the First Methodist Church, a position he held for twenty-two years. Ted Barclay, who made a wartime profession of faith, held no position of leadership in his antebellum church, but returned from the war a devout Christian and served as a lay-leader in the Lexington Presbyterian Church for forty-six years.

Although Felix Poché returned from the war a devout Christian and a committed Roman Catholic, it is unlikely that he became a formal leader in the Church, for there were few opportunities for Catholic laymen to serve. He did, however, continue to assist the priest during Mass. Both Talbert Holt and Robert Moore were killed in the war. Whether they would have become church leaders cannot be known. Their ardent devotion to Christ, as well as the postwar service of their Christian comrades, suggest that these men—had they survived the conflict—likely would have also found avenues of service to Christ through the Church.

CONCLUSION

Baptist theologian O. C. S. Wallace once described a Christian's spiritual growth as an upward path: "Whatever heights have been attained there are other heights to be attained. The mountain peaks of God are exceeding many and high.... Attainment is only one step in the progress, preparing the way for other steps in further and more glorious progress." The tribulations of war drove the nine Christian soldiers in this study to new spiritual heights and greater maturity. This is not to suggest that during the war these men attained the highest degree of spirituality—a Christ-like character. Indeed, they continued to exhibit some unbecoming attributes, for they were human. But, by the end of the war, these soldier-Christians exhibited the mature faith described by the Apostle Paul in his letter to Timothy.[1]

During the war, the nine exhibited steadfastness in their religious convictions. Although their fellow soldiers early on showed little interest in spiritual matters, the six who entered the war as Christians maintained their antebellum religious routines as best they could: they attended preaching, prayed regularly, and read their Bibles. Parson Pendleton continued his ministry and faithfully preached to his own men as well as to those in other commands. These six men condemned the vice they saw in camp and resolved to stand firm in their faith. Two of the three wartime converts initially succumbed to temptation in camp, but all three became resolute in their faith after their professions of faith.

The nine's devotion to God also increased. Possessing a sincere desire to worship the Lord, these men conscientiously attended

---

[1] O. C. S. Wallace, *What Baptists Believe* (Nashville: Southern Baptist Convention Sunday School Board, 1913) 109–110.

church and even sought out religious services when they traveled on military business or furlough. They were eager to benefit from the sermons they heard and often recorded the scriptural references and titles, perhaps to study later. And when duties interfered with their church attendance, they noted their disappointment and worshipped privately. Furthermore, prayer took on new meaning for these soldier-Christians as they fervently petitioned God for safekeeping and returned thanks for His faithfulness. And they searched Scripture for solace and understanding concerning the trials they were going through.

The war also served to test and purify their faith or trust in God. The three mature Christians had a strong faith when the war began but saw it strengthened during the conflict. Although older and more experienced, these men had not in the antebellum era endured trials of the magnitude they endured during the war. In addition to experiencing uncertainty about their own lives, they were unable to care for their families. Enemy activity near their homes exacerbated this concern. These three men placed their trust in God and relied on him for their protection as well as that of their families. And as the Lord proved faithful, these men acknowledged it and expressed a willingness to trust him further.

The nascent faith of the three Christian neophytes grew stronger during the conflict as well. Although serving on the periphery of war, these men, like the others, endured significant trials. Like their more mature brethren, they relied on divine protection during the few battles they fought in. But other trials served to test their faith as well. All three demonstrated considerable solicitude about their families back home and realized that, as with their own lives, they exercised little control over what happened to their loved ones. They likewise entrusted their families' welfare to God, and when He proved faithful, their faith in him increased.

The remaining three soldiers were brought up in Christian families and had been regular churchgoers in the antebellum period, yet it was the war that prompted their conversions and strengthened their faith. Young and unmarried, these men seldom expressed concern for loved ones but the possibility of death prompted fervent prayers for divine assistance. And like the others, when God spared them, they acknowledged His faithfulness and their reliance on him grew.

As the nine Christian soldiers drew nearer to God, earthly matters became less important to them. Their references to heaven increased as they found thoughts of an eternal resting place away from hardship and death comforting. A heavenly home also offered the hope of reuniting with loved ones. They furthermore manifested greater concern for the spiritual welfare of their fellow soldiers. These men approved of the religious revivals occurring in the armies and wanted to see the men benefit from the meetings. And all but one grew more ecumenical in outlook, as worship of their heavenly father became far more important than petty denominational differences. Even Alfred Fielder, who had criticized the interdenominational nature of his regiment's Christian Association, later joined it and faithfully attended meetings. Only Felix Poché, a devout Catholic, maintained the belief that his Church was Christ's true Church and never attended religious services of any other denomination.

Furthermore, their nearness to God changed these men. As their own shortcomings became more evident, they expressed a sincere desire to be better Christians. They also grew more conscious of His blessings and His presence.

These nine men went to war convinced that slavery was God-ordained and that Southerners were fighting in self-defense. Therefore, they maintained that the Lord favored their cause. Military setbacks, however, engendered concern, for these men believed that a sovereign God controlled all things. Convinced that God still loved the Southern people, they concluded that He was chastening them, and as His children, they accepted defeat as part of God's plan.

The seven men who survived the war made far fewer references to religion in their postwar writings, for the threat of death and concern for their families were gone. But these veterans neither forsook Christ nor forgot the lessons they learned during the four-year struggle. Indeed, their continued devotion to God is evident in their postwar service. The two older Christians, William Pendleton and Alfred Fielder, resumed their roles in their home churches, while William Nugent, who had held no position in his antebellum church, became an influential layman in the Methodist Church in Mississippi. Both Edward Guerrant and Giles Cooke kept their wartime pledges and entered the ministry; and Ted Barclay served as an office-bearer in his home church for over forty years. Although Felix Poché may not have served his church in a formal sense, he continued to assist at Mass, a clear indication of his devotion to God.

The diary entry of Alfred Fielder cited in the Introduction sums up the thesis of this book: the Civil War did indeed strengthen the faith of these Confederate Christian soldiers. It matured the faith of not only the newly-converted, but also those, like Fielder, who had long professed faith in Christ. These men did not, however, become model Christians in the sense that they had eradicated the sin in their lives. As O. C. S. Wallace points out, when a Christian reaches one point spiritually, there are always new heights to attain. Furthermore, this study demonstrates that war's impact spanned denominations, ages, military ranks, and social classes. Indeed, any of the soldier-Christians included in this study could have genuinely expressed Fielder's sentiments.

Bibliography

Manuscript Collections

Capps Archives and Museum, Delta State University, Cleveland, Mississippi. Lucy Somerville Howorth and William Cash Papers. Lucy Somerville Howorth Papers.

Draughon Library, Auburn University, Alabama. Robert Partin Papers.

Eleanor S. Brockenbrough Library, Museum of the Confederacy, Richmond, Virginia. Pendleton, William Nelson. Letter (G-392).

King Library, University of Kentucky, Lexington. Edward O. Guerrant Family Papers.

Leyburn Library, Washington and Lee University, Lexington, Virginia. Rockbridge Historical Society Papers. Trustees' Papers. Washington and Lee Miscellaneous Collection.

National Archives, Washington DC. Compiled Service Records. General and Staff Officers. Compiled Service Records, Unfiled Papers and Slips.

University of North Carolina, Chapel Hill. Southern Historical Collection. Battle Family Papers. Edward O. Guerrant Papers. William Nelson Pendleton Papers.

US Bureau of the Census. Manuscript Returns of Free Inhabitants, Alabama, Kentucky, Louisiana, Mississippi, and Virginia. Eighth Census, 1860. Washington DC.

———. Manuscript Returns of Productions of Agriculture, Alabama, Louisiana, Mississippi, Tennessee, and Virginia. Eighth Census, 1860. Washington DC.

———. Manuscript Returns of Slaves, Alabama, Kentucky, Louisiana, Tennessee, and Virginia. Eighth Census, 1860. Washington DC.

———. Manuscript Returns of Inhabitants, Alabama, Kentucky, Louisiana, Mississippi, Tennessee, and Virginia. Ninth Census, 1870. Washington DC.

————. Manuscript Returns of Productions of Agriculture, Louisiana, Mississippi, Tennessee, and Virginia. Ninth Census, 1870. Washington DC.

————. Manuscript Returns of Free Inhabitants, Alabama, Kentucky, Mississippi, and Virginia. Seventh Census, 1850. Washington DC.

————. Manuscript Returns of Productions of Agriculture, Alabama, Mississippi, and Tennessee. Seventh Census, 1850. Washington DC.

————. Manuscript Returns of Slaves, Alabama, Kentucky, Mississippi, Tennessee, and Virginia. Seventh Census, 1850. Washington DC.

Virginia Historical Society, Richmond. Giles Buckner Cooke Papers.

Virginia Military Institute, Lexington. Giles Buckner Cooke Folder.

Watson Library, Northwestern State University, Natchitoches, Louisiana, Eugenie Watson Somdal Papers.

William Alexander Percy Memorial Library, Greenville, Mississippi. Susie Trigg Papers.

Wilson Library, Millsaps College, Jackson, Mississippi. Millsaps Board of Trustee Minutes. Charles B. Galloway Papers.

CHURCH RECORDS

First Methodist Church, Greenville, Mississippi. Greenville District Quarterly Conference Minutes, 1867-1881.

King Library, University of Kentucky, Lexington. Presbyterian Church, Salem, Kentucky, Records, 1811-1955.

McIver's Grant Public Library, Dyersburg, Tennessee. Dyersburg District Conference Journal, 1884-1898.

Mississippi Department of Archives and History, Jackson. Galloway Methodist Church, Jackson, Mississippi, Records, 1903-1921. Wesley Chapel Methodist Church, Holly Springs, Mississippi, Records, 1837-1936.

Presbyterian Church, Lexington, Virginia. Lexington Presbyterian Church Records, 1775-1920.

Presbyterian Historical Society, Montreat, North Carolina. First Presbyterian Church, Louisville, Kentucky, Session Minutes, 1874-1882. Presbyterian Church, Sharpsburg, Kentucky, Records, 1848-1930. Second Presbyterian Church, Danville, Kentucky, Session Minutes, 1852-1969. West Lexington Presbytery Minute Book, 1871-1881.

Robert E. Lee Memorial Church, Lexington, Virginia. Grace Episcopal
     Church Vestry Minutes, 1840-1913.
Virginia State Library, Richmond. St. Paul's Episcopal Church, Petersburg,
     Virginia, Vestry Minutes, 1720-1986.

NEWSPAPERS
Greenville (Mississippi) *Times*
Grove Hill (Alabama) *Clarke County Journal*
Jackson (Mississippi) *Clarion-Ledger*
Jackson (Mississippi) *Daily Clarion*
Lawrenceville (Virginia) *Southern Missioner*
Lexington (Virginia) *Gazette*
Lexington (Virginia) *Gazette & Citizen*
Lexington (Virginia) *Rockbridge County News*
Nashville *Republican Banner*
New Orleans *Christian Advocate*
New Orleans *Daily Picayune*
New Orleans *Times Picayune*
Richmond (Virginia) *News Leader*
Thibodaux (Louisiana) *Sentinel*

COUNTY GOVERNMENT RECORDS
Clarke County Courthouse, Grove Hill, Alabama. Probate Office. Record
     Books L, 1861–1865 and M, 1864–1866.
Dyersburg County Courthouse, Dyersburg, Tennessee. Register of Deeds
     Office. Deed Book L, 1858–1859.

PRIMARY SOURCES
Barclay, A. T. "The Liberty Hall Volunteers From Lexington to Manassas."
     Washington and Lee University, Historical Papers 6 (1904): 123–36.
Bearss, Edwin C., editor. *A Louisiana Confederate: Diary of Felix Pierre Poché.*
     Translated by Eugenie Watson Somdal. Natchitoches: Louisiana
     Studies Institute, Northwestern State University, 1972.
Bridges, Katherine. "A Louisiana Schoolboy in Kentucky: Felix Pierre
     Poché's Diary, 1854." *Louisiana Studies* 10 (Fall 1971): 187–92.
Cash, William M., and Lucy Somerville Howorth, editors. *My Dear Nellie:
     The Civil War Letters of William L. Nugent to Eleanor Smith Nugent.*
     Jackson: University Press of Mississippi, 1977.

Catalog of Washington College, Virginia, for the Collegiate Year Ending July 1st, 1870. Richmond: MacFarlane & Fergusson, 1870.

Catalog of Washington College, Virginia, for the Collegiate Year Ending June, 1860. Richmond: MacFarlane & Fergusson, 1860.

Catalog of the Officers and Alumni of Washington and Lee University, Lexington, Virginia, 1749–1888. Baltimore: John Murphy & Company, 1888.

Constitution, By-Laws and Catalogue of Christian Association of The Stonewall Brigade. Richmond VA: William H. Clemmitt Printing, 1864. In *Confederate Imprints,* edited by Richard Harwell and Marjorie Lyle. New Haven CT: Research Publications, 1974.

The Constitution of the Presbyterian Church in the United States of America, Containing the Confession of Faith, the Catechisms, and the Directory for the Worship of God. Philadelphia: Presbyterian Board of Publication, 1839.

Crist, Lynda L., Kenneth H. Williams, and Peggy L. Dillard, editors. *The Papers of Jefferson Davis.* Volume 10. Baton Rouge: Louisiana State University Press, 1999.

Davis, William C., and Meredith L. Swentor, editors. *Bluegrass Confederate: The Headquarters Diary of Edward O. Guerrant.* Baton Rouge: Louisiana State University Press, 1999.

Diocese of Baton Rouge. *Diocese of Baton Rouge Catholic Church Records.* 18 volumes. Baton Rouge: Catholic Diocese of Baton Rouge, 1978–1995.

The Doctrines and Discipline of the Methodist Episcopal Church. New York: Nelson & Phillips Publishing, 1876.

Franklin, Ann York, editor. *The Civil War Diaries of Capt. Alfred Tyler Fielder, 12th Tennessee Regiment Infantry, Company B, 1861–1865.* Louisville KY: Privately printed, 1996.

Galloway, Charles B. D. D. *Colonel William L. Nugent.* N.p., n.d. Mississippi Department of Archives and History, Jackson.

———. *Handbook of Prohibition.* Jackson: Privately printed, 1886.

Guerrant, Edward O. *The Galax Gatherers: The Gospel Among the Highlanders.* Richmond VA: Onward Press, 1910.

———. *The Soul Winner.* Lexington KY: John B. Morton & Company, 1896.

Hewett, Janet B., Noah Andre Trudeau, and Bryce A. Suderow, editors. *Supplement to the Official Records of the Union and Confederate Armies: Record of Events.* 80 volumes. Wilmington NC: Broadfoot Publishing, 1994–98.

Historical Records Survey, Tennessee. *Minutes of the County Court of Dyer County, 1848–1852*. Nashville: N.p., 1942.

History of Tennessee from the Earliest Time to the Present; Together With an Historical and a Biographical Sketch of Gibson, Obion, Dyer, Weakley and Lake Counties. Nashville: Goodspeed Publishing Company, 1887.

Lee, Susan P. *Memoirs of William Nelson Pendleton, D. D.* Philadelphia: J. B. Lippincott Company, 1893.

Minutes of the Fifty-Eighth Session of the Mississippi Annual Conference, Methodist Episcopal Church South…December 10–15, 1873. Nashville: Southern Methodist Publishing, 1874.

Minutes of the Fifty-Fourth Session of the Mississippi Annual Conference, Methodist Episcopal Church South…December 8–15, 1869. Jackson: Clarion Steam Printing, 1870.

Minutes of the Fifty-Ninth Session of the Mississippi Annual Conference, Methodist Episcopal Church South…December 16–22, 1874. Jackson: Clarion Steam Printing, 1875.

Minutes of the General Assembly of the Presbyterian Church in the United States of America, 1866. Philadelphia: Presbyterian Board of Publishing, 1866.

Minutes of the Synod of Kentucky, October 13, 1880. Paris KY: F. L. & J. R. McChesney Printing, 1880.

Minutes of the Synod of Kentucky, October 12, 1881. Winchester KY: Clark County Democrat Press, 1881.

Minutes of the Twenty-Eighth Annual Meeting of the Bethel Baptist Association, South Alabama…in Clarke County, 1848. Tuscaloosa: Privately printed, 1848.

Proceedings of the Mississippi Annual Conference…December 18, 1878. N.p., n.d. Wilson Library, Millsaps College, Jackson, Mississippi.

Proceedings of the Mississippi Annual Conference…December 17, 1879. N.p., n.d. Wilson Library, Millsaps College, Jackson, Mississippi.

Proceedings of the Mississippi Annual Conference, December 16–24, 1885. N.p., n.d. Wilson Library, Millsaps College, Jackson, Mississippi.

Ryrie, Charles Caldwell. *The Ryrie Study Bible*. Chicago: Moody Press, 1978.

Silver, James W., editor. *A Life for the Confederacy: As Recorded in the Pocket Diaries of Pvt. Robert A. Moore*. Jackson TN: McCowat-Mercer Press, 1959.

Stockwell, Eunice, editor. *Copies of Newspaper Articles, Marriage and Death Notices from Washington County Times and Greenville Times (1864–1886)*.

2 volumes. N.p., n.d. William Alexander Percy Memorial Library, Greenville, Mississippi.

Turner, Charles W., editor. "General David Hunter's Sack of Lexington, Virginia, June 10–14, 1864: An Account by Rose Page Pendleton." *Virginia Magazine of History and Biography* 83 (April 1975): 173–83.

———., editor. *Ted Barclay, Liberty Hall Volunteers: Letters From the Stonewall Brigade (1861– 1864).* Natural Bridge Station VA: Rockbridge Publishing Company, 1992.

United States War Department. *The War of the Rebellion: A Compilation of the Official Records of the Union and Confederate Armies.* 70 volumes in 128 parts. Washington DC: 1880–1901.

SECONDARY SOURCES

Addison, James Thayer. *The Episcopal Church in the United States, 1789–1931.* New York: Scribner's, 1951.

Akens, David S. "Clarke County to 1860." M.A. thesis, University of Alabama, 1956.

Akens, Helen M. "Clarke County, 1860–1865." M.A. thesis, University of Alabama, 1956.

Ash, Stephen V. *A Year in the South: Four Lives in 1865.* New York: Palgrave Macmillan, 2002.

———. *Middle Tennessee Society Transformed, 1860–1870: War and Peace in the Upper South.* Baton Rouge: Louisiana State University Press, 1988.

———. *When the Yankees Came: Conflict and Chaos in the Occupied South, 1861–1865.* Chapel Hill: University of North Carolina Press, 1995.

Bailey, T. J. *Prohibition in Mississippi.* Jackson: Hederman Brothers Printing, 1955.

Ball, T. H. *A Glance into the Great South-East, or, Clarke County, Alabama and its Surroundings, From 1540–1877.* 1879. Reprint, Tuscaloosa: Willo Publishing Company, 1962.

Balmer, Randall, and John R. Fitzmier. *The Presbyterians.* Westport CT: Greenwood Press, 1993.

Bartlett, Napier. *Military Record of Louisiana.* Baton Rouge: Louisiana State University Press, 1964.

Barton, Michael. *Goodmen: The Character of Civil War Soldiers.* University Park: Pennsylvania State University Press, 1981.

Bean, W. G. *The Liberty Hall Volunteers: Stonewall's College Boys.* Charlottesville: University Press of Virginia, 1964.

———. *Stonewall's Man: Sandie Pendleton.* Chapel Hill: University of North Carolina Press, 1959.

Beringer, Richard, E., Herman Hattaway, Archer Jones, and William N. Still, Jr. *Why the South Lost the Civil War.* Athens: University of Georgia Press, 1986.

Biographical and Historical Memoirs of Louisiana. 2 volumes. Chicago: Goodspeed Publishing Company, 1892.

Biographical and Historical Memoirs of Mississippi. 2 volumes. Chicago: Goodspeed Publishing Company, 1891.

The Bishop Payne Divinity School. N.p., n.d. Virginia Historical Society, Richmond.

Boylan, Anne M. *Sunday School: The Formation of An American Institution, 1790–1880.* New Haven: Yale University Press, 1988.

Bragg, George F., Jr. *History of the Afro-American Group of the Episcopal Church.* 1922 Reprint, New York: Johnson Reprint Company, 1968.

———. *The Story of Old St. Stephen's, Petersburg, Va., and the Origin of the Bishop Payne Divinity School.* N.p., 1917. Virginia Historical Society, Richmond.

Brinsfield, John W., William C. Davis, Benedict Maryniak, and James I. Robertson, Jr., editors. *Faith in the Fight: Civil War Chaplains.* Mechanicsburg PA: Stackpole Books, 2003.

Brooke, George M., Jr. *General Lee's Church.* Lexington VA: News-Gazette, 1984.

Bruce, Dickson D. *And They All Sang Hallelujah: Plain-Folk Camp-Meeting Religion, 1800–1845.* Knoxville: University of Tennessee Press, 1974.

Butler, Diana H. *Standing Against the Whirlwind: Evangelical Episcopalians in Nineteenth-Century America.* New York/Oxford: Oxford University Press, 1995.

"The Celebration of the Centenary of the Supreme Court of Louisiana." *Louisiana Historical Quarterly* 4 (January 1921): 5–124.

Chorley, E. Clowes. *Men and Movements in the American Episcopal Church.* New York: Charles Scribner's Sons, 1946.

Coulter, E. Merton. *The Civil War and Readjustment in Kentucky.* 1926. Reprint, Gloucester MA: Peter Smith, 1966.

Daniel, Larry. *Soldiering in the Army of Tennessee.* Chapel Hill: University of North Carolina Press, 1991.

Deupree, J. G. "The Capture of Holly Springs, Mississippi, Dec. 20, 1862."
    Publications of the Mississippi Historical Society. Edited by Franklin L.
    Riley, 4 (1901): 49–61.

Dolan, Jay P. *The American Catholic Experience: A History from Colonial Times
    to the Present.* New York: Doubleday Publishing, 1985.

Driver, Robert J., Jr. *Lexington and Rockbridge County in the Civil War.*
    Lynchburg VA: H. E. Howard Publishing, 1989.

Dunagon, Pearl, Elizabeth Kirby, and Virginia Kirby. *The History of
    Friendship Methodist Church.* N.p., n.d. Friendship Methodist Church,
    Friendship, Tennessee.

Ellem, Warren A. "The Overthrow of Reconstruction in Mississippi."
    Journal of Mississippi History 54 (May 1992): 175–201.

Faust, Drew Gilpin. "Christian Soldiers: The Meaning of Revivalism in the
    Confederate Army." *Journal of Southern History* 53 (February 1987):
    63–90.

———. "The Civil War Soldier and the Art of Dying." *Journal of Southern
    History* 67 (February 2001): 3–38.

Faust, Patricia L., editor. *Historical Times Illustrated Encyclopedia of the Civil
    War.* New York: Harper & Row, Publishers, 1986.

Flynt, Wayne. *Alabama Baptists: Southern Baptists in the Heart of Dixie.*
    Tuscaloosa: University of Alabama Press, 1998.

Folmsbee, Stanley J., Robert E. Corlew, and Enoch L. Mitchell. *History of
    Tennessee.* 2 volumes. New York: Lewis Historical Publishing
    Company, 1960.

Foner, Eric. *Reconstruction: America's Unfinished Revolution, 1863–1877.* New
    York: Harper & Row Publishers, 1988.

Franklin, John Hope. *Reconstruction After the Civil War.* Chicago: University
    of Chicago Press, 1961.

Freeman, Douglas Southall. *Lee's Lieutenants: A Study in Command.* 3
    volumes. New York: Charles Scribner's Sons, 1942–44.

Genovese, Eugene D. *A Consuming Fire: The Fall of the Confederacy in the
    Mind of the White Christian South.* Athens: University of Georgia Press,
    1998.

Graham, John S. *History of Clarke County.* Greenville SC: Southern
    Historical Press, 1994.

Hamilton, Alfred P. *Galloway Memorial Methodist Church, 1836–1956.*
    Jackson MS: Privately printed, 1956.

Hardon, John A. *The Catholic Catechism*. New York: Doubleday & Company, 1975.

Harris, William C. *The Day of the Carpetbagger: Republican Reconstruction in Mississippi*. Baton Rouge: Louisiana State University Press, 1979.

Hess, Earl J. *The Union Soldier in Battle: Enduring the Ordeal of Combat*. Lawrence: University Press of Kansas, 1997.

Heyrman, Christine Leigh. *Southern Cross: The Beginnings of the Bible Belt*. New York: Alfred A. Knopf, 1997.

Hill, Samuel S., Jr. *Religion and the Solid South*. New York: Abingdon Press, 1972.

————, editor. *Religion in the Southern States: A Historical Study*. Macon GA: Mercer University Press, 1983.

————. *The South and the North in American Religion*. Athens: University of Georgia Press, 1980.

————. *Southern Churches in Crisis*. New York: Holt, Rinehart and Winston, 1966.

————, editor. *Varieties of Southern Religious Experience*. Baton Rouge: Louisiana State University Press, 1988.

The History of the Mt. Zion Methodist Church. N.p., n.d. In private possession of Ms. Mary Alice Badget, Friendship, Tennessee.

History of Tennessee from the Earliest Time to the Present; Together With an Historical and a Biographical Sketch of Gibson, Obion, Dyer, Weakley and Lake Counties. Nashville: Goodspeed Publishing Company, 1887.

History of Tennessee from the Earliest Time to the Present; Together With an Historical and a Biographical Sketch of Lauderdale, Tipton, Haywood and Crockett Counties. Nashville: Goodspeed Publishing Company, 1887.

Holifield, E. Brooks. *Gentlemen Theologians: American Theology in Southern Culture, 1795–1860*. Durham: Duke University Press, 1978.

Hunter, Robert F. *Lexington Presbyterian Church, 1789–1989*. Lexington VA: News-Gazette, 1991.

Keating, Bern. *A History of Washington County, Mississippi*. Greenville MS: Privately printed, 1976.

Kirby, James E., Russell E. Richey, and Kenneth E. Rowe. *The Methodists*. Westport CT: Greenwood Press, 1996.

Kuykendall, John W., and Walter L. Lingle. *Presbyterians, Their History and Beliefs*. Atlanta: John Knox Press, 1978.

Langford, Thomas, A. *Methodist Theology*. Peterborough UK: Epworth Press, 1998.

Leach, Marguerite, T. "The Aftermath of Reconstruction in Louisiana." *Louisiana Historical Quarterly* 32 (July 1949): 631–717.

Losson, Christopher. *Tennessee's Forgotten Warriors.* Knoxville: University of Tennessee Press, 1989.

Loveland, Anne C. *Southern Evangelicals and the Social Order, 1800–1860.* Baton Rouge: Louisiana State University Press, 1980.

Lyle, Royster, Jr. "Buena Vista and its Boom, 1889–1891." *Proceedings of the Rockbridge Historical Society* 8 (1970–1974): 131–44.

McAllister, J. Gray, and Grace Owings Guerrant. *Edward O. Guerrant: Apostle to the Southern Highlanders.* Richmond VA: Richmond Press, 1950.

McBride, Robert M., and Dan M. Robison. *Biographical Directory of the Tennessee General Assembly.* 2 volumes. Nashville: Tennessee State Library and Archives and the Tennessee Historical Commission, 1979.

McCain, William D. *The Story of Jackson: A History of the Capital of Mississippi, 1821–1951.* 2 volumes. Jackson: J. F. Hyer Publishing Company, 1953.

McLemore, Richard A. *A History of Mississippi.* 2 volumes. Hattiesburg: University & College Press of Mississippi, 1973.

McPherson, James M. *Battle Cry of Freedom: The Civil War Era.* New York/Oxford: Oxford University Press, 1988.

———. *For Cause and Comrades: Why Men Fought in the Civil War.* New York/Oxford: Oxford University Press, 1997.

———. *What They Fought For, 1861–1865.* Baton Rouge: Louisiana State University Press, 1994.

Manross, William W. *A History of the American Episcopal Church.* New York: Morehouse-Gorham Company, 1950.

Manual of the First Presbyterian Church. Louisville KY: Privately printed, 1909.

Mathews, Donald G. *Religion in the Old South.* Chicago: University of Chicago Press, 1977.

Miller, Randall M., and Jon L. Wakelyn, editors. *Catholics in the Old South: Essays on Church and Culture.* Macon GA: Mercer University Press, 1983.

———, Harry S. Stout, and Charles Reagan Wilson, editors. *Religion and the American Civil War.* New York/Oxford: Oxford University Press, 1998.

Mitchell, Reid. *Civil War Soldiers.* New York: Viking Penguin, 1988.

Morton, Oren F. *A History of Rockbridge County, Virginia*. Staunton VA: The McClure Company, 1920.

Murrah, W. B. "Origin and Location of Millsaps College." Edited by Franklin L. Riley. *Publications of the Mississippi Historical Society* 4 (1901): 227–31.

Nelson, William H. *A Burning Torch and a Flaming Fire: The Story of Centenary College of Louisiana*. Nashville: Methodist Publishing House, 1931.

Norton, Herman. *Rebel Religion: The Story of Confederate Chaplains*. St. Louis: Bethany Press, 1961.

Partin, Robert. "A Confederate Sergeant's Report to His Wife During the Campaign from Tullahoma to Dalton." *Tennessee Historical Quarterly* 12 (December 1953): 291–308.

———. "'The Money Matters' of a Confederate Soldier." *Alabama Historical Quarterly* 25 (Spring and Summer 1963): 49–69.

———. "The Sustaining Faith of an Alabama Soldier." *Civil War History* 6 (December 1960): 425–38.

Pena, Christopher G. *Touched by War: Battles Fought in the Lafourche District*. Thibodaux LA: C. G. P. Press, 1998.

Pittenger, W. Norman. *The Episcopalian Way of Life*. Englewood Cliffs NJ: Prentice-Hall, 1957.

Posey, Walter B. *Religious Strife on the Southern Frontier*. Baton Rouge: Louisiana State University Press, 1965.

Prichard, Robert W. *The Nature of Salvation: Theological Consensus in the Episcopal Church, 1801–73*. Urbana: University of Illinois Press, 1997.

Prim, G. Clinton. "Revivals in the Armies of Mississippi During the Civil War." *Journal of Mississippi History* 44 (August 1982): 227–35.

———. "Southern Methodism in the Confederacy." *Methodist History* 23 (July 1985): 240–49.

Rahner, Karl. *The Church and the Sacraments*. Translated by W. J. O'Hara. New York: Herder and Herder, 1963.

Rice, Edwin W. *The Sunday-School Movement (1780–1917) and the American Sunday-School Union (1817–1917)*. 1917. Reprint, New York: Arno Press & the New York Times, 1971.

Robertson, James I. *Soldiers Blue and Gray*. Columbia: University of South Carolina Press, 1988.

———. *The Stonewall Brigade*. Baton Rouge: Louisiana State University Press, 1963.

Rowland, Dunbar. *Courts, Judges, and Lawyers of Mississippi, 1798–1935*. Jackson: Hederman Brothers Printing, 1935.

St. Stephen's Episcopal Church, Petersburg, Virginia, Parish Profile. N.p., 1993. Saint Stephen's Episcopal Church, Petersburg, Virginia.

Saum, Lewis O. *The Popular Mood of Pre-Civil War America*. Westport CT: Greenwood Press, 1980.

Shattuck, Gardiner H., Jr. *A Shield and Hiding Place: The Religious Life of the Civil War Armies*. Macon GA: Mercer University Press, 1987.

Shaw, Arthur Marvin, Jr. "Rampant Individualism in an Ante-Bellum Southern College." *Louisiana Historical Quarterly* 31 (October 1948): 877–96.

Sifakis, Stewart. *Compendium of the Confederate Armies: Alabama*. New York: Facts On File, 1992.

———. *Compendium of the Confederate Armies: Mississippi*. New York: Facts On File, 1995.

Silver, James W. *Confederate Morale and Church Propaganda*. New York: W. W. Norton and Company, 1967.

"Sketch of the Lee Memorial Association." *Southern Historical Society Papers* (August–September 1883): 388–417.

Smith, Ryan K. "A Church Fire and Reconstruction: St. Stephen's Episcopal Church, Petersburg, Virginia." M.A. thesis, College of William and Mary, 1998.

Stanbery, George W. "The Tennessee Constitutional Convention of 1870." M.A. thesis, University of Tennessee, 1940.

Stowell, Daniel W. *Rebuilding Zion: The Religious Reconstruction of the South, 1863–1877*. New York/Oxford: Oxford University Press, 1998.

Strange, Roderick. *The Catholic Faith*. New York/Oxford: Oxford University Press, 1986.

Sumner, David E. *The Episcopal Church's History: 1945–1985*. Wilton CT: Morehouse-Barlow, 1987.

Sutherland, Daniel E. "Guerrilla Warfare, Democracy, and the Fate of the Confederacy." *Journal of Southern History* 68 (May 2002): 259–92.

Taylor, Joe G. *Louisiana: A Bicentennial History*. New York: W. W. Norton & Company, 1976.

Thomas, Nell. *This Is Our Story…This Is Our Song: First United Methodist Church, Greenville, Mississippi, 1844–1994*. Greenville MS: Burford Brothers Printing, 1994.

Thompson, Ernest Trice. *Presbyterians in the South*. 3 volumes. Richmond: John Knox Press, 1963–73.

Walch, Timothy. *Catholicism in America: A Social History*. Malabar FL: Robert E. Krieger Publishing, 1989.

Wallace, Nancy C., editor. *History of Friendship, Tennessee 1824–1986*. N.p., n.d. Tennessee State Library and Archives, Nashville.

Wallace, O. C. S. *What Baptists Believe*. Nashville: Southern Baptist Convention Sunday School Board, 1913.

Warner, Ezra J. *Generals in Gray: Lives of the Confederate Commanders*. Baton Rouge: Louisiana State University Press, 1959.

Watkins, Ruth. "Reconstruction in Marshall County." Edited by Franklin L. Riley. *Publications of the Mississippi Historical Society* 12 (1912): 155–213.

Watson, Samuel J. "Religion and Combat Motivation in the Confederate Armies." *Journal of Military History* 58 (January 1994): 29–55.

Wiley, Bell I. *The Life of Johnny Reb: The Common Soldier of the Confederacy*. Baton Rouge: Louisiana State University Press, 1943.

Williams, Paul. *What Americans Believe and How They Worship*. New York: Harper & Brothers, Publishers, 1952.

Wilson, Lisa Marie. "Edward Owings Guerrant: An Appalachian Ministry." M.Th. thesis, Union Theological Seminary, 1993.

Wilson, Charles Reagan, editor. *Religion in the South*. Jackson: University Press of Mississippi, 1985.

Winters, John D. *The Civil War in Louisiana*. Baton Rouge: Louisiana State University Press, 1963.

Woodworth, Steven E. *While God Is Marching On: The Religious World of Civil War Soldiers*. Lawrence: University Press of Kansas, 2001.

INDEX